RED BLOOD, YELLOW SKIN

A Young Girl's Survival in War-Torn Vietnam

LINDA L.T. BAER

(Formerly) Nguyen Thi Loan

RIVER GROVE
BOOKS

Published by River Grove Books
Austin, TX
www.rivergrovebooks.com

Distributed by River Grove Books

For ordering information or special discounts for bulk purchases, please contact River Grove Books at PO Box 91869, Austin, TX 78709, 512.891.6100.

Design and composition by Greenleaf Book Group
Cover design by Greenleaf Book Group
Cover images:
©iStockphoto.com/pressdigital

Publisher's Cataloging Publication Data is available.

ISBN: 978-1-63299-027-3

First Edition

Other Edition(s):
eBook ISBN: 978-1-63299-028-0

Advance Praise

"*Red Blood, Yellow Skin* is a story of courage, compassion, and faith. It is a fascinating account of the Vietnamese people's love of family, strength of character, and will to survive unbelievable hardships. Linda B. is a remarkable and successful woman and proud to be an American."

—GENERAL AND MRS. WILLIAM C. WESTMORELAND

"Reading gives opportunity to live (although temporarily) a life of experiences in places, and with people, previously unknown and even unimagined. *Red Blood, Yellow Skin* offers the opportunity to join the life of a young girl, as she experiences many difficult obstacles in her struggles to get through childhood and teen years in a beautiful but harsh land that is increasingly torn by the havoc of war. One experiences the joys of extended family closeness and loyalty; the confusion of interruption of family serenity by death and intrusion of others; the uncertainty, difficulty, and fears of frequent moves from place to place; the periods of near-starvation and poverty; and many other experiences generally unknown to middle-class Americans. The road to survival, and ultimately into the arms of true love and security, keeps the reader on the edge along with the main character as she deals with the disappointments, encouragements, struggles, victories, weakness, and tenacity so skillfully presented in *Red Blood, Yellow Skin*."

—JOHN R. BRAUN, ED.D, Emeritus professor of chemistry,
The Citadel, Charleston, SC

CONTENTS

FOREWORD

IN APRIL 1968, I was assigned to Tan Son Nhut Air Force Base, near Saigon. I spent one year there as a casualty officer in the US Air Force. After going back to America and retiring in 1969, I returned to Vietnam, where I worked on US Army Government contracts for a period of four years. Having spent a total of five years in Vietnam during the war, I am personally familiar with the horror and violence that Vietnam experienced.

It wasn't until I read Linda Baer's *Red Blood, Yellow Skin*, however, that I realized how brutally affected the Vietnamese people were by that terrible war. Linda tells the story of how she and her family survived so many narrow escapes with death, while many of her family members were not so lucky. In her heartwarming innocence, we witness the resilience, strength, and courage that she and so many of the Vietnamese people demonstrated, so often overlooked when history describes that war. Linda's will and determination to survive are beyond my imagination, resulting in a fascinating reflection of how a human being can endure during trying times. This struggle is frequently softened by her unending love and sense of humor, which she is somehow able to maintain in the midst of countless disappointments and suffering.

I know that her story is true, because in 1968, I met and fell in love with Linda. She was the reason I returned to Vietnam in 1969. Through her, I was introduced to Vietnam, not as I witnessed it from behind the walls of an air force base, but as it truly was—with all the death and destruction that brutal war forced upon its gentle and courageous people. And through her and her precious family, I was also introduced to a peaceful civilization that dated back thousands of years, with culture and traditions that I could never have imagined. I learned the value of close family relationships that went far beyond any that I had ever known. I witnessed the depth of sorrow that her family and so many others felt when a loved one was lost to age, illness, or the insanity of war.

I was welcomed into Linda's family, even with my blue eyes, auburn hair, and strange-sounding language. They accepted and loved me as though I were a blood relative. And today, nearly fifty years later, her family still treats me with the respect and consideration they extended when we first met. They are a loving, warm group, who overlook my many faults and always hold their arms out to me. Their laughter and joy continue to teach me that happiness does not come from outside influences, but from love and empathy within the soul. I am happy and proud to be a part of their family unit.

In *Red Blood, Yellow Skin,* Linda tells the truth, though sometimes brutal, about her experiences, from losing her father to the terrors of her family moving to a new land with nothing more than the clothes they wore on their backs. She looks the corruption of that era straight in the eye and relates the struggles she experienced while trying to survive. However, she never overlooks the beauty of Vietnam or the family that she loved so dearly. She always lets us know that even though none of us are perfect, she can still see the light of beauty and love in everyone. And she manages, somehow, to present this very moving and serious story with guile and enough humor to evoke laughter—indeed, it will make you laugh and cry.

Though I may sound partial, the fact is Linda is an intelligent, loving woman with an explosive sense of humor. She is an incredible author, who has managed to bring to us her experiences during a dreadful war, but at the same time shows us the depth of love and joy that the Vietnamese have mustered in spite of that. This book will leave you with a newfound respect for a culture few of us in America have ever imagined, an understanding of the horrors and insanity of war, and amazement at how Linda and her homeland have survived.

K. DONALD BAER
Captain, US Air Force, Retired

ACKNOWLEDGMENTS

THANKS TO MY mother, who taught me by her example, through the most difficult of times, the values and qualities of life that I hold so dear; to General and Mrs. Westmoreland, for their wonderful review of my story; and to all of my friends and clients, who read my story, gave me powerful comments, and encouraged me to publish my book.

A special thanks to my husband, for his research and creative historical input, for the numerous hours helping me edit my book, and for standing by me through thick and thin. By loving me, he gave me the freedom and encouragement to be the best that I can be. Without Don's help, this book would not exist.

Thanks to my children and grandchildren, who love and share their life with me. And to my brothers and sister, and my nieces and nephews, whose love and respect for me is endless.

May God bless them all!

INTRODUCTION

THE NIGHT THE Viet Minh attacked our village, they found my father hiding in the church steeple. They shot him in the neck and pushed him through a window. He landed on a mound of broken glass. One attacker heard him moan and ran over to finish him off. With a machete, he chopped my father's face into four pieces—the sign of the cross. My father fell silent. I saw his bloody face soon after he died. I was four years old. The Viet Minh occupied our village and destroyed my peaceful existence.

The French and Viet Minh battles forced my mother and me to flee from place to place. My mother sought escape from impoverishment by marrying a rich and dominating widower, another victim of the war. While my stepfather and mother got to know each other in another village, I was left behind to fend for myself, with little help from my relatives.

We escaped from communist persecution by moving to South Vietnam in 1954. We settled in a primitive refugee camp in the middle of a forest near Tay Ninh Province, where tiger attacks were common. I was lucky to escape one of them. We sought only peace and security; we found neither.

I broke away from the cruelty of my stepfather by running away to Saigon when I was thirteen, where I worked at various menial jobs. When I was seventeen, I was introduced to bars, nightclubs, and Saigon tea, and was raped by an American serviceman, whom I thought was a friend.

In this story, I expose the corruption that jailed innocent people, including me, who were unable or unwilling to pay the bribes demanded. I reveal the dark humor associated with the American experience in our land and how at the age of eighteen, I fell in love and moved in with a young American airman. Two months after our baby was born, the airman returned to America, and I never heard from him again. I was left to raise my son by myself, against my parent's demands. Time healed my heart and allowed me to love again, this time to an American air force officer.

This is a story about romance, humor, culture, customs, traditions, and family life. It describes the pain, struggle, despair, and violence as I lived it. The story is mine, but it is also an account of Vietnam, not as seen by foreigners on televised images of war and tragedy, but by those of us who were uprooted, displaced, brutalized, and left homeless. This is a story about our struggle for survival. My Vietnam was frightening but tender, it was tragic but humorous, it was chaotic but beautiful—it was ultimately a contradiction. Vietnam was my home—the home that I love and for which I have wept endless tears.

I now live in America, and although I have grown to love my adopted county, I still carry a deep sorrow for my homeland. My memories of Vietnam are just as vivid as they were when I experienced them.

General William C. Westmoreland and his wife Katherine, after reading my manuscript, wrote, "[this] is a story of courage, compassion, and faith. It is a fascinating account of the Vietnamese peoples' love of family, strength of character, and will to survive unbelievable hardships. Linda B. is now a remarkable and successful woman, and proud to be an American."

The large number of people who read my story strongly urged me to publish it for others to read. It is my hope that you will enjoy reading this story as much as I enjoyed writing it. I am now working on my second book, *Journey on Edge*.

Thank you for reading my book, and may God bless you.

LINDA L. T. BAER
(Formerly) NGUYEN THI LOAN

Chapter 1

MOUNTAIN OF BROKEN GLASS

HOLDING A BROKEN clay pot full of wiggling leeches, I sat on the branch of a fig tree, overhanging the fishpond. I dangled my feet in the water, moving them back and forth, waiting for more leeches to attach themselves to me. Counting each as I pulled them off my feet, "six, seven, eight," I heard, "Loan Oi!" Mother was calling me.

It was 1951, the year of the cat, and I was almost four years old. We lived in the small, rural village of Tao Xa near Thai Binh, some sixty miles southeast of Hanoi City in North Vietnam. There were no more than a few hundred homes in the area, all made from clay, bamboo sticks, and rice straw, and all without running water or electricity. Rice fields and swamps surrounded the village. Small dirt roads and walking paths bound our village together.

In the center stood a magnificent red brick and grey stucco Catholic church, with a steeple that seemed to climb straight to heaven. It was beautiful!

Surrounding the church was a red-tiled courtyard. Two small buildings stood nearby—one for storing church equipment, the other the priest's quarters. Several rundown and deserted brick buildings were scattered throughout the village, left there by the French occupation several years earlier.

Our house sat at the edge of the village, near several small fishponds, hidden from view by beautiful fruit trees and wildflowers. It had a small dirt courtyard in front, with a tea and vegetable garden in back.

The house had two rooms. The larger served as a living room and was where my father slept. It was furnished with a small bed, a table, and two benches, all made of bamboo. My mother and I shared a bed in a smaller adjoining room at the right side of the house. A large bamboo bin, in which we stored rice, stood in the corner. It took up almost half of our room. We had no closets or cabinets. Instead, we used a long rope stretched between two walls, on which we hung most of our clothes. The rest were hung on a few bamboo sticks protruding from the wall that were inserted when the house was built. Our bed was larger than Father's and was set over a huge, deep hole. We used the hole as a shelter from bombs and severe weather, such as typhoons and storms that often struck our village.

My home in Tao Xa, as it appeared in 1996 when we visited. Although the surrounding area has changed, my home is very much the same as it was. The main house is on the right; the separate kitchen is on the left.

A small clay hut, separate from the main house, was our kitchen. Inside the hut was a pile of rice stalks, stacked high in a corner, used for cooking fuel. Our food and leftovers were stored on a homemade bamboo rack in another corner. In the middle of the room were two clay cooking stoves, and behind them, a tall pile of ashes, left over from cooking. We used the ashes as fertilizer for our garden and for outhouse purposes. We also hung our cooking pots on the protruding bamboo sticks. Mother made all of her cooking stoves, pots, lanterns, and water barrels from clay. They broke easily, so Mother had to continually remake them. I used the broken ones for toys. All of the villagers used a similar method for cooking their food in the same kind of kitchen.

I had no brothers or sisters, and I had no friends. The only clothes I had were two pairs of pajamas. They consisted of loose, brown cotton tops that hung down to my thigh, with large sleeves, over long, black, baggy pants. One pair was old and torn, and I wore it almost every day. When the old pair was soiled, my mother washed it in the pond, to get rid of dirt and mud. While my clothes dried, I often went naked. The other newer pair of pajamas was reserved for church or special occasions. My clothes were similar to those worn by my mother.

Close-up of our kitchen, outside of the main house. Bricks were added in recent years.

My parents worked either in the rice fields or for others, and we had just enough to keep us alive from day to day. Although I was quite young, my parents had to leave me home alone. They went to work before sunrise and came home after sunset every day. In the mornings, they ate breakfast and took food with them for lunch. They always left some behind for me. When I woke, I ate and then played by myself. My toys were birds, frogs, insects, worms, and leeches. I caught leeches by sticking my feet in the pond and letting them attach themselves to me. It didn't take long to fill up an empty, broken clay pot with them. When I grew bored, I turned the leeches inside out with a bamboo stick, threw them back into the water, and watched them sink to the bottom.

Catching chicken choker worms was also among my favorite pastimes. I pushed young bamboo leaves into the wormholes and waited for the leaf to move. When it did, I knew there was a worm on the other end. I pulled the leaf up, and the worm hung on to it. I played with them for a while and then fed them to my pet birds.

When I was tired, I fell asleep wherever I felt comfortable, most often under a tree or along the pond where I had been playing. I seldom saw my parents during weekdays. When I woke up, they were already gone, and when they returned, I was asleep. If they didn't see me inside or in bed, they looked for me outside, and when they found me, they carried me back inside.

I loved Sundays. That was the one day I could be with my parents all day long. We woke early, washed in the pond, put on our best clothes, and walked to church.

My parents used our walk to church to teach me valuable lessons. I remember them well. One particular day, for example, Mother said, "When you grow up you should not lie, cheat, or steal, because God will not love you if you do."

"Besides," Father added, "for everything you steal, you must pay back tenfold." Each walk brought new lessons and words of wisdom. In church Mother taught me how to pray, and together we prayed for peace, for love, and for enough food to survive.

After church, we went home, cooked, ate, and did chores around the house. Sometimes, we visited my aunt and uncle and cousins. Father worked in the garden on Sunday afternoons. Mother and I went to the pond to catch something to eat. Rolling her black pants above her knees, she waded into the water. Using a bamboo basket, she scooped under the grass overhanging the edge of the pond for fish, shrimp, little crabs, water bugs, and anything else that was edible. She placed whatever she caught into a covered basket, which she tied to her waist.

I followed Mother along on the bank, playing with the leeches that she threw to me. She knew I liked to play with them. I was happy being with her, and I laughed at everything she did. Knowing that, she would go to extra lengths to amuse me, such as putting mud above her upper lip to make it look like she had a mustache.

Once she caught enough to eat, she carried the covered basket to the dirt yard in front of our house, where she separated the catch. I liked to play with the critters, but now and then, the crabs or bugs pinched me, and I let out a scream. Mother and I both laughed. She discarded the leeches and anything else that we couldn't eat. Then, she took what was left to the small bamboo bridge built above the pond and washed everything. She took her day's catch into the kitchen, dumped everything into a clay cooking pot, and added a lot of salt. She cooked this over one fire and had a pot of white rice going on the other. Within a few minutes, the fish, shrimp, crabs, and water bugs turned chalky white because of all the salt. We ate them with rice. In our house, we never had a meal without rice. And the critters were not the only thing that turned white. After our meal, our lips also turned white and felt numb from all the salt. I liked everything, but the water bugs were my favorite treat.

One time, I complained to Mother and asked her why she put so much salt in our food. She gave me a stern look and said, "We are lucky to have what we have. Our food is scarce and precious. Remember, we don't live to eat; we eat to be alive. Be thankful that you have a few creatures to add some spice to your rice; it's better than eating salt and rice alone." I never mentioned the matter again.

The roof of our house, made from rice straw, often leaked, and more so during the monsoon season when rain poured like waterfalls from heaven. Sometimes a whole portion of the roof caved in from the weight of the water-soaked straw. Then we had to move everything to a drier part of the house, until my father found time to repair it.

My parents spent six months of the year in the rice fields, performing the backbreaking labor of planting and caring for each stalk of rice. When it was ready, they cut the rice stalk and brought it home. They separated the grain from the straw by beating the stalk against logs or by rolling a heavy stone wheel over them.

The grain dried in the sun and was stored in a rice bin. The straw was saved for cooking fuel, roofing material, and food for the water buffalo. My parents rented a water buffalo during the planting season, paying for it with their labor.

They spent the other six months at home, growing fresh vegetables in our garden or working for others. Mother collected tea leaves from the garden and walked many miles to sell them in the market. With what little money she made, she bought the materials she used to make our clothes. During this time, she also cut our hair. She cut my father's hair like Saint Francis, with circles above the ears, and cut mine above the shoulder, with bangs straight across my forehead. I always ran to the pond to look at my reflection in the water after each haircut. We didn't have a mirror or even know that mirrors existed.

In the dry season, my parents and our neighbors gathered to empty their ponds and catch the fish. Using special buckets designed for this process, two people stood on a small bank between two ponds and gripped opposite ends of a strong rope. At the center of the rope was a bucket. Like graceful ballerinas, synchronized to perfection, they dropped the bucket into one pond, filled it with water, and flung it over the narrow bank into the next pond. They repeated this hundreds, if not thousands of times, until there was no water left in the pond. Then they walked down into the slippery mud and collected every living creature in it, except for the leeches that were thrown into a separate container

A water buffalo and her calf having lunch on a rice stalk,
between our kitchen and the main house.

and destroyed. They repeated this process with each pond, until they were done. Then each empty pond was refilled. The days of strenuous labor were rewarded with bountiful food. The villagers separated the shrimp and fish by size. They threw snails, water bugs, and the many other edible delicacies into one big bucket. Some large fish were thrown back into the pond for breeding. The rest were divided among the people—those who owned the pond and those who worked so hard to harvest it.

During this period, my parents shared their fish with relatives and the elders who lived nearby. They gave the largest fish to the town's Catholic priest. He was a man of God and was treated with deep love and respect.

Sometimes a few fish were kept alive for a while in a large, clay barrel. I loved to watch them swim around in it. When I thought no one was watching, I tried to catch the fish. I'd reach in, my face and hair touching the water. The fish were hard to hold on to, and somehow,

Mother always saw me and told me to quit playing with them. Disappointed, I'd walk away, drying my face with my shirttail.

Most of the smaller fish were salted. Mother kept part of them in a clay barrel and let them ferment. The fermented fish were made into a fish sauce that we used for cooking and spicing our rice. The rest were dried out under the sun, and we ate them later, during the rice-growing season. Even though I enjoyed eating the big fish, the water bugs and snails were still my favorites.

My parents were good people. They lived at peace among their friends and neighbors and were devout, practicing Catholics. The village was small, and people cared for each other. They gave special attention to the elders, who could no longer work or had no one to take care of them. I loved my peaceful little village.

That peace was shattered when the Viet Minh decided to take over our village, causing my life to forever change.

Led by Ho Chi Minh, the Viet Minh was a band of stubborn guerrillas, fighting to unify Vietnam and prevent the French from reoccupying the country. After the Second World War, the French, supported by Britain and America, controlled southern Vietnam and many large coastal cities in the North. The Viet Minh had few successes against the French, until aid came to them from Communist China in 1949. In the early 1950s, the Viet Minh intensified their efforts to control the countryside of North Vietnam, and the peaceful village of Tao Xa became one of their targets.

Soon the townspeople learned of the Viet Minh plans to attack, and they prepared for the fight. My father and many other young men from our village decided to organize a defense. We did not want the French or the Viet Minh to control us. There were few guns and little ammunition in our village, and not many of the townspeople knew how to use them.

The anticipated day arrived, and the Viet Minh attacked our ill-prepared village with full force. Our men and boys fought long and hard, until they grew weaker and had to retreat. Mother and I remained at home, hiding and praying. The noise of gunfire and the sounds of bullets flying overhead terrified us all through the night.

Some of the men, including my father, ran to the Catholic church, where they filled empty bottles with water, climbed the church's steeple, and threw the bottles to the courtyard below. The noise of breaking bottles sounded like gunshots, which they hoped would fool the Viet Minh into believing they still had ammunition. The ruse did not work for long and proved to be the last futile attempt of our villagers to protect their homes. The enemy realized our village was helpless, so they entered and found their way to the church.

My eleven-year-old cousin, Tuan, was with the men in the church, and he hid behind the bell-tower wall. He watched in helpless horror as the Viet Minh entered the church and shot everyone in sight. Tuan saw them shoot my father in the neck and then push him through an open window, high in the bell tower, to the glass-covered courtyard below.

My father suffered a slow and agonizing death. He lay on top of a mound of broken glass, crying out in pain. A Viet Minh soldier noticed him lying there, unable to defend himself, and proceeded to finish the job. Using a machete, he chopped my father's face into four pieces, making a symbolic sign of the cross. Father twisted and turned for a few moments, and then he fell silent.

The massacre ended, along with our peaceful existence. A handful of invaders stayed behind to control and govern the village. The rest disappeared before dawn, leaving behind a trail of dead and broken bodies in their wake.

When it was safe, Tuan left his hiding place and raced down from the steeple to my father's body. Once he realized his uncle was dead, he ran like lightning to our house and banged on the door. Mother had been awake all night, worrying about Father. When she heard the banging on our door, she jumped to answer it. I heard Tuan sputter through his tears, "He's dead! He's dead!"

The church and the broken window (below clock tower) from which my father was thrown; as of 1996, it had not been repaired, from lack of funds.

In a trembling voice, Mother asked, "What did you say?"

"Uncle Thap is dead!" Tuan said. "They killed him!"

A strange and mournful wail filled the air. Mother screamed and cried, as she grabbed my arm and raced toward the church. I could see Tuan running ahead of us in the early morning haze.

"What is happening?" I asked, crying and confused by Mother's behavior.

"Your father is dead!" Mother wailed. "Your father is dead!"

I didn't understand what was going on. Dead? What did she mean that my father was dead? I knew she was upset and frantic, but I didn't know why, and it scared me. We approached the church courtyard, and I saw my father lying on top of a mountain of broken glass with his face cut to pieces. Blood was everywhere.

Tuan reached him before we did and laid his head on my father's chest. "Uncle, please don't die and leave me like this!" he pleaded through his tears. "I love you, Uncle! Oh, Uncle, please don't leave me!"

As soon as Mother saw my father, she left me behind and ran through the broken glass in her bare feet. She cradled my father's bloodied and mutilated head to her chest, and cried, "Oh my God! What happened to you? Why are you like this? What did you do to deserve this? Oh, God! Oh, my loving God!"

I watched as my mother and cousin bent over my father, their tears soaking his bloodstained shirt. In their anguish, they had forgotten about me standing in the distance, watching them. It seemed like a long time before Mother was able to collect herself enough to stand. She wiped her tears and asked Tuan to help carry my father to the smooth grass nearby. I ran over and looked at his face. At first, I didn't recognize him. I stretched my arm and touched his face with my finger. His skin was cold, and when I touched his hand, his fingers were stiff. I could not understand what had happened to my father or why his face was that way. I cried because Mother and Tuan were crying.

Mother turned to Tuan, as tears streaked down her cheeks, and said, "Run to our relatives and let them know what happened to your uncle."

Before long, about half a dozen people arrived. They brought fresh banana leaves and grass mats to cover my father's body. They cried as they approached him. Some touched him, others held his hand, and some began picking the broken glass from his body. They wrapped him in a grass mat and carried him to Aunt Ba's house, which was near the church. His body lay there, while the coffin was made. Mother sat with my father's body and cried all morning. She ate and drank nothing and didn't even get up to relieve herself.

As word spread about my father's death, more relatives showed up. By afternoon, Aunt Ba's house was full of people. Their mournful cries mingled with the sound of hammering, as the coffin was prepared from rough pinewood. By late afternoon, when it was finished, they laid my father's body inside, closed it, and secured it with rope. The next morning, they carried his coffin back to the church. Some coffins were already there, as were several bodies, wrapped only in grass mats. Those without coffins were from families who could not afford wood.

During the service, the priest sprinkled the bodies with holy water and prayed for their souls. Then they carried the dead to the cemetery. Mother and I followed behind my father's coffin, which my cousin Tuan helped carry, accompanied by all of my relatives.

Mother held onto a corner of Father's coffin as we walked. "Why are you leaving us?" she cried. "We will never see you again. How can we live without you?"

Those following the dead were crying or praying. I still did not understand what had happened or what was going on. Mother talked to my father as if he were sleeping in the coffin. I imitated her sorrow and talked to him as she had. "Please take me with you!" I cried. "How can I live without you!"

We walked from the church, through town, and to the cemetery at the edge of the village, not far from our house. Some graves were ready, while others were still being dug. They placed my father's coffin next to one of the holes and waited for the priest to give the last rites. The holy man went from coffin to coffin, and from grave to grave, saying his prayers and sprinkling holy water on each of the dead men. He sprinkled holy water on my father's coffin and then walked to the next one. A few men stood around, waiting for the priest to leave; then they lowered my father's coffin into the ground and shoveled dirt on top of it.

It was then that I realized what was happening. They were burying my father! I ran to them and tried to stop them, but someone kept holding me back. I kicked and pushed those who were holding me, but I couldn't get loose. I screamed and cried at the top of my lungs. I begged those who were burying my father to stop throwing dirt on him. But in the end, I was forced to stand like a cross, with two people holding my arms outstretched at my side. I cried as I watched people continue to shovel dirt on top of him. I yelled at my mother to help him, but she was too busy trying to throw herself into my father's grave. Several people had to restrain her as well.

When the grave was filled, they kept shoveling dirt on it, until it became a big mound. People began leaving soon after. I was turned loose and left alone with my mother. I ran to the mound of dirt, began digging with my hands, while Mother threw herself across the grave and wailed. As I removed the dirt, I pleaded for my father to get out of there and go home with us.

Mother looked at me and said through her tears, "You can't dig him out, he is dead. Your father is dead. He has gone to heaven to be with God. He has left us forever. From now on, we will be all by ourselves." At first, she tried to fill the hole I dug, but I moved and dug another one. I kept digging, and she tried to fill the holes. She grew tired and gave up. I watched as she rested her head back on the dirt mound and continued to cry.

I screamed at her, "He is not dead, and he is not leaving us! He was just buried, and that is why I have to dig him out. I can't leave him in there."

Again Mother tried to explain his death and how he could never live or be with us again. I wouldn't listen to her and kept shoveling dirt with my hands. The hole I had been digging was getting bigger, when Mother turned to me and said, "Let's go home. My feet hurt, and they are still bleeding from stepping on the glass. I think some of the glass slivers are still in my feet. I need to go home and pull them out."

I was concerned, because I didn't want to see Mother in pain, but I tried to ignore her and kept digging. My hands were red and began to bleed. Even though I made a big hole in my father's grave, I couldn't reach his coffin.

"I don't want to go without Father," I cried. "You go ahead, and I'll stay here with him."

Mother knew I wouldn't leave on my own. She struggled with me and tried to shove me aside and fill the holes I dug. I pushed her away and continued my digging, but in the end, she was stronger than I was. She managed to get hold of my wrist and dragged me all the way home, with my bottom bouncing on the ground.

Mother held me while she changed her clothes and tried to make me understand. I listened to her and was quiet for a moment. She left me to go clean her wounds. I took advantage of her brief absence and bolted out of the yard, running for my father's grave. I couldn't believe what happened or why everyone was so mean, including my mother, for burying my father and then leaving him there alone. Mother heard me running and ran after me. She caught up with me and grabbed me with her arm around my waist. She dragged me back to the house. I was kicking and screaming all the way. Mother kept a close eye on me, and each time I attempted to escape, she grabbed me and brought me back. I got tired of struggling with her, went to a corner of the house, and cried myself to sleep.

Chapter 2

WATER BUGS

DURING THE YEARS following my father's death, Mother worked twice as hard to provide enough food for both of us. While she labored in the flooded rice fields, I walked along the banks looking for crickets, grasshoppers, crabs, shrimp, and little fish. When I caught a cricket or a grasshopper, I pinched their necks until they died, so they wouldn't jump out of my bamboo basket. Whatever I caught, we took home for dinner. Mother and I cleaned the crickets and grasshoppers by pulling off their heads, which also removed their guts. We stuffed them with salt and a hot pepper, then roasted them along with other critters in a clay pot over an open fire. We ate them with rice.

It was sad without Father, but somehow we managed to survive. Mother told me he was in heaven, watching over us. It made me feel better to know he was always with us in that way. When I wanted to be near him, I made the short walk to the cemetery for a visit. Mother and I kept his grave free of weeds, and always brought him fresh wildflowers.

He was such a gentle man; he helped anyone who needed him. He had been very active in the community and often helped the priest in the church. He was a very devout Catholic. I thought his Saint Francis haircut looked funny, because it was different from everybody else, but I never asked him about it. To me he was perfect. He did not deserve to die as he did.

The Viet Minh controlled our village with an iron hand, demanding taxes from everyone. Though Mother just made enough to keep us alive, she still had to pay these taxes. Conditions in our village became intolerable for us, so Mother decided we should try to escape the oppression by moving to the neighboring town of Cao Moc. The people there were strong. They had repulsed the Viet Minh and remained independent.

The fighting in North Vietnam between the Viet Minh and the French was explosive. With continued help from China, the Viet Minh were becoming more daring and challenged the French and local civil authority at every opportunity. North Vietnam was turning into one huge battlefield and the innocent civilians suffered most.

We began our trek early in the morning. There was no transportation available in the countryside, so we had to walk to our new home. Mother took only those things we needed for our trip. She packed our clothes, some rice, and dried fish in two large bamboo baskets. Mother hung the baskets on each end of a bamboo yoke and balanced the yoke on her shoulders.

Street vendors carrying yokes with produce, similar to the yokes my mother carried me in.

When it was time for lunch, we stopped under a large banyan tree to rest. We ate what Mother had prepared, then we went down to a small pool of water in a rice field. Mother tapped on the water's surface to scare away the water bugs, and using our hands, we scooped up water to drink. My hands were too small, so most of the water spilled out before I had a chance to slurp it. Mother saw me struggling, scooped water into her hands, and let me drink until I filled my stomach. Afterward, we rested for a few minutes before continuing on our journey.

Suddenly, we heard gunfire and the sound of bullets whizzing overhead. We dropped our belongings on the road and jumped into the rice field. We crouched down, crossed ourselves, and prayed until Mother thought it was safe for us to leave. This time, instead of walking, we ran. The fighting would spring up again without warning. Whenever it did, we ran and ducked until I became so tired that I could run no further. Mother had to remove everything from one basket, stuff it into the other, and then put me in the empty basket. She hoisted the baskets with the yoke, balancing them on her shoulders, and began running for her life. It took us almost all day to travel the few miles to Cao Moc.

We arrived late that afternoon and visited a family that my parents had known for years. The house looked similar to ours but was much larger. We walked into the yard and saw that it was full of people of all ages. Mother put the baskets down, I stepped out, and we walked around the crowded yard. Mother recognized some of the people there and greeted them with a warm smile.

"Who are these people?" I asked.

"Some of them are from our village." she replied.

She told me to go back to where we left our belongings to keep an eye on them.

She needed to look for the property owners, to ask if we could stay there. I went back and stood like a statue, guarding our yoke. Mother stopped a woman. I couldn't hear what she was saying, but I guessed Mother was asking her for the owner. She followed the lady's pointed finger and disappeared into the crowd.

By then I was so tired that I couldn't stand up any longer, so I squatted on the ground and waited for Mother. She returned, and with a smile, told me the owner, a kindhearted widow, would let us stay as long as we wanted. We just had to provide our own food. We walked around the yard until we found an empty spot, and we moved in. Mother straightened out our belongings and spread out the grass mat. She told me the owner opened her home for those who needed a place to stay. Since the house was already filled with refugees by the time we arrived, we had to stay out in the open yard, along with the other latecomers. Thank God it was the dry season, and we didn't have to worry about rain for another six months or so. Mother stacked our things in order and told me to step into our little nest. I jumped in with both feet and sat down for a few moments. I started to say something, but I was so tired I couldn't remember what I was going to say. So, I lay down on the mat and fell asleep.

Weeks passed, and we just about ran out of the food that Mother brought with us. During the day, she picked tea leaves to exchange for food, and she helped others with their babies as well as their cooking and sewing. We lived in the yard without cover. Each night I lay on my back and counted stars until their twinkling lured me to sleep. I awoke one day, itching like crazy, and Mother helped me scratch my back. She examined me and discovered I was covered with lice. She told me to sit still while she picked the lice from my head. She squeezed them between her thumbnails to kill them. That didn't help my itching, though. She told me to take off my clothes, so she could have a closer look. She turned my clothes inside out and found body lice in them. She began picking out the lice, and I stood there naked, scratching my head and watching her pick the tiny tormentors from my clothes. I saw many others doing the same as Mother. Some of the people became so frustrated they took off their clothes and chewed along the seams, where the lice were hiding, trying to kill the bugs and destroy their eggs.

In desperation, Mother talked to several other people who had the same problem. They decided to go to a distant creek and carry back bucket after bucket of water. They dumped the water into a big metal drum, gathered wood and straw to make a fire, and boiled the water. Those infested took turns throwing their clothes into the boiling water. When they thought the lice were dead, they took the clothes out, wrung them, and then hung them on lines, fences, poles, trees, and sticks, or whatever they could find. From a distance, it looked as if a swarm of giant butterflies with torn wings had invaded the yard. Boiling the clothes relieved the lice problem for a while, but soon we had to repeat the process.

Because of the hot, dry season, we had little water for bathing. Our clothes began to smell, and our bodies turned sour. The enclosure was overcrowded, and the stench of unwashed bodies was overwhelming. Mother decided it was time for us to find another place to live. She searched and found an older couple who let us move in with them in exchange for helping them with household chores and their garden. They were poor, and we worked only for food and a roof over our head. There was not always enough to eat, and some nights we went to sleep hungry, but we didn't complain. Mother said, "We are luckier and better off than most of the refugees."

The older couple we lived with was rather strange. Neither of them spoke to us, and they seldom smiled, which made it hard to tell if they liked us or not.

Part of Mother's job was picking tea leaves from the garden and taking them to market to sell. I helped her fill a bamboo basket with green leaves, and she lifted it to her head. Mother told me before she left for the market, "Stay home, be careful, and don't go anywhere."

"Yes, Mother," I said, and followed her for a short distance, until she told me to go back. I stopped walking and watched her balance the basket on her head, wishing I were with her.

I saw a large black dog lying in front of a neighbor's house, and I went closer to investigate. The dog lunged at me, knocked me to the ground, and bit me. I yelled for help, and an old woman came out. She commanded the dog to stop and pointed her finger for the dog to get back to the house.

She then turned to me and yelled, "Get out of here and don't tease my dog again!" She walked away in a huff while I sat there, crying in pain. I was most upset about the way she reacted toward me. I glared at the old woman until she disappeared. Then I stood up and examined myself. The dog's bite and scratches drew blood from my right side. I went home to the pond and washed the blood off.

When Mother came back, I ran to her, showed her my wounds, and told her about the dog. "From now on," she said, as she put ointment on my wound, which was still bleeding a little, "when you see a big dog, don't go near it, because you never know what it might do."

She took my hand and led me to a basket of food. We sat on the doorstep and ate sticky, sweet rice with roasted sesame seeds, mixed with salt. Mother told me she heard news at the market that conditions in our village had improved, and she had decided to take me home. I was so excited. The next morning, we gathered our belongings and packed them into our baskets and said goodbye to our hosts. Mother balanced the baskets with the yoke over her shoulders, and we started the long trek back to our home in Tao Xa. When we approached our house, we could see that parts of the walls were crumbling and a section of the roof had caved in while we were away.

Mother walked into the yard, put the yoke down, and paused. She sighed and said, "After moving around like this for most of my life, you'd think I would get used to it by now. When I was younger, the French were here. They were very brutal. If people didn't pay their taxes, they were beaten and even beheaded. That's why we often left home. Now the French are gone, but I don't know why we still have to run." With tears in her eyes, Mother looked into the distance. "My God, when will all this fighting stop?" I felt sorry for her—how sad it must have been, with the house falling apart and Father not there to help her rebuild.

As we unpacked, Mother continued, "When the French went away, they left behind their dirty guns, their empty buildings, and their bad reputation. But at least we had some peace for a while."

Then, after a long silence, she glanced up at the roof and said, "I'll have to get some old rice stalks from the backyard and fix it tomorrow."

The French were again making a concentrated effort to take back the village. After coming home, we could no longer use our bed, and had to sleep on the floor next to the bunker, to avoid stray bullets. We settled into a routine of finding food during the day and hiding from the fighting at night.

When I turned five, I was old enough to go into the pond to help Mother. This is when she taught me how to catch fish with a bamboo basket. We often talked, laughed, and cried together while working. She also liked to tell me the stories about her and my father. "When I was younger," she said with a smile, "many young men were interested in me. I was interested in some of them, but as a girl, I was supposed to do what my parents told me to do when it came to marriage. That's why I couldn't choose my own husband. My parents had already arranged for me to marry your father. He was not very handsome, but he was a good man. After our marriage, I learned to love him, and I loved him very much."

I enjoyed listening to her stories, and she enjoyed telling them. Many of her recollections were more than just reflections of her past—they were also lessons about our culture and the traditions of our people.

After my father's death, several men showed an interest in Mother. At thirty-five, she was still a very beautiful and charming woman, but she wanted to remain a widow and raise me, instead of marrying again.

While we were in the pond, covered with mud, two strange men, dressed in formal, black Ao Dai, white pants and traditional head turbans, walked toward us.

One said, "We are looking for Mrs. Nhuan."

Mother looked up and replied, "That is my name. How can I help you?"

The taller man walked closer and said, "I have come looking for you, because I want to marry you."

Mother's beautiful eyes opened wide as she responded, "I don't even know you. Who are you?" She thought they were just joking with her, because they knew she was a widow.

The man smiled and introduced himself. "I am Doctor Thuy." He pointed to the shorter man and said, "and this is my friend. I am from Luong Dong. I heard that you are very beautiful and that you are a hard worker. That's why I've come to ask you to marry me. I was married before and had four children," he added, "but a French bomb killed my wife, my father, and my youngest son."

He talked for a while without stopping, while his friend just stood there, smiling. Mother and I were silent while the man told his story. When he finished, Mother said, "I'm very sorry you suffered such a loss, but if you want to discuss the matter further, please come back later, when I'm more prepared."

The two men seemed disappointed, but they said goodbye and left. Mother and I looked at each other and laughed, and then we continued catching our food.

My stepfather in formal dress, forty-eight years old, in 1954.

After our meal that afternoon, we washed dishes in the pond and then jumped in to take a bath. We swam and dove around for a few minutes, then climbed back onto the bamboo platform to avoid the leeches and scrub off the dirt. Then we jumped back into the pond to rinse off.

After we went back inside and changed into clean clothes, the two men who spoke to us at the pond earlier returned. Mother invited them into the house and told me to go play outside. I asked her why I couldn't stay, and she told me I was too young to listen to their grown-up conversation. So, I went outside, against my will.

I climbed up a guava tree and sat on a limb. I ate fruit and wondered what they were talking about. Soon, the two men left. I waved goodbye and ran inside, looking for my mother.

"What's going on?" I asked.

"One of the men wants to marry me," she replied, "and I have to think about it. He is a doctor of Chinese medicine, and he's very rich. If I marry him, you and I will have servants and maids, and we will never have to work hard again."

"That sounds all right," I responded, "but I don't want to see you get married again. I don't want to share you with anyone else. Besides, Father wouldn't like it."

Mother didn't like the way the discussion was going, and in her usual way of avoiding conflict, she changed the subject. "It's getting late," she said, "and we should start our prayers now." She dropped to her knees and glanced at me, waiting for me to do the same. I was disappointed at being cut off, but I dropped to my knees and began to pray. We went to bed, but I couldn't sleep. I lay awake, thinking about what had happened earlier and what might happen in the future. It took me a long time to fall asleep that night.

Weeks passed, and I didn't see those men return. But there was something different about Mother. She acted strange, as if she were meeting them in secrecy. I noticed she didn't work as much as she used to. She spent a lot of money and time making new clothes for herself and running around to see my relatives more often than she had before. I had no idea what was going on, but neither of us raised the subject of her marriage again.

One day, Mother decided to make new cooking pots. We filled a bamboo basket with wet clay from the edge of the pond and took it back to the courtyard. We separated the clay into small piles of various sizes. The size of the clay pile depended on what Mother intended to make. We kneaded each pile of clay and molded it into a pot. Mine always looked crooked and lopsided, but Mother humored me and used mine as well. After we made the pots, she usually laid them out in the sun to dry. When they were dry, Mother baked them in rice stalks until they turned red. Then, she put out the fire and let the pots cool. Later, she soaked them in the pond for a few more days to harden. After that, they were then ready to use.

While we were working hard with the clay, the taller man came back. He walked straight to her, stopped in front of her, smiled, and said, "You are still very pretty, even with mud on your face." This time Mother acted friendlier and smiled back at him, as if they had known each other for some time. I was jealous, and I didn't like the way they were looking at each other.

"Are you going to marry my mother?" I asked with a frown.

"Yes," he replied with a smile, "and I am going to take care of you, too."

"I don't need to be taken care of," I said. "We are doing just fine by ourselves."

The man frowned, and Mother gave me a disapproving look. The atmosphere grew tense. I sensed that I wasn't welcome, so I went to the pond to wash my hands, then played in the garden, and left them to talk to each other. When I returned, the man was gone.

Chapter 3

BITTER GUAVA

TWO MONTHS AFTER the men first came to visit, I woke up one morning to an empty house. Mother was gone. I called and looked for her but couldn't find her. I assumed she had gone to the market or to visit neighbors, and I was used to staying home by myself, so I soon forgot about her absence and began my usual day.

That afternoon, while I was in my favorite guava tree, I saw Mother's older sister, Aunt Ba, come toward our house. I called out to her from where I was perched, and she walked toward me. She smiled and said, "Get down from the tree, gather your clothes, and come with me."

"Why?" I questioned, puzzled by her unusual order.

"Because you are going to live with me for a while," she answered.

"Where is my mother?" I asked, as fear began mounting in my heart.

"She's gone to Luong Dong to get married. She'll come back for you later," she replied.

I couldn't believe my ears. With my mouth still full of sweet guava, I started to cry. "Why didn't she tell me or take me with her?" I asked.

"You're too young to understand," she replied, as she helped me down from the tree.

The sweet guava turned bitter in my mouth, and I spit it out. With tears flowing down my cheeks, I went inside to get my clothes. I looked up at the clothesline and noticed that all of Mother's clothes were gone. I grabbed my pajamas and went with my aunt. She didn't say a word. She just held my hand. I cried all the way to her house. When we arrived, she told me to stop crying and put my clothes away.

"Are you hungry?" she asked.

"No, the guava filled me," I replied.

She left me there alone and went about her business. I threw my clothes on a bench, went to a corner, and cried myself to sleep.

I awoke the following morning and realized it wasn't a bad dream. It was real; my mother was gone! My stomach growled, reminding me that I needed food, but I didn't feel like eating anything. I got up and dragged myself to the pond outside. Aunt Ba's house, like most of the homes in the village, had its own pond. Some were larger than others, and Aunt Ba's pond was larger than ours. I slumped under a tree and watched a small school of red, baby mudfish jumping up and down on the surface. I could see their big mother swimming beneath them. I thought of my mother and tears poured from my eyes.

"Where is she? How could she just leave me like this? How could she just desert me?" I cried.

Weeks passed, but there was no sign of my mother. No one mentioned her except me. Anytime I asked about her, there was only silence. Everyone acted as if they didn't know where she was.

My aunt's family was as poor as mine. Except for an adolescent son, all of her children were grown and had moved away. I didn't like her son, because he was mean to me. He often tricked me into giving him my food, and he took away my toys.

Their house was similar to ours, but was somewhat larger and had more furniture. They had three beds and a few tables and benches, all made of bamboo. A simple shelf on the wall was full of pictures and religious figurines.

My aunt and her husband worked in the rice fields every day, just like my parents. Nobody paid much attention to me. I was free to go wherever I wanted, eat whatever I could find, and sleep whenever I felt like it. There was little to do, but sit under the big fig tree, thinking about my mother. I wondered where she was and what she was doing.

During Mother's absence, I thought of all the hardships and trouble we had gone through, but even those days were happy times, because we were together. She was gone, and I didn't know when I'd see her again. I missed her so much; it hurt to think of her.

Besides Aunt Ba, I had two uncles, Uncle Tu and Uncle Ky. All of them were older than my mother. Uncle Tu lived on the opposite side of the pond from my aunt. He had four children, two of whom were grown and married. Two daughters were still at home. They were older than I was, but we became very close friends anyway.

Poor Uncle Tu was an alcoholic. When he drank, he was mean and would do and say things to hurt people. He often chased us and beat us for no reason. Once, while in a drunken rage, he chased me with a stick, but he couldn't catch me, and yelled from a distance, "Your mother left you for a rich man, and she is going to have a new baby. She won't love you or want you anymore." His body swayed with the wind, and he laughed out loud. His words cut through me like a knife. I just stood there like a statue, and let my tears flow. I wondered if his words were true.

Uncle Tu's house is the on the left and Aunt Ba's house is on the right. The two stacks of rice stalks between them were used for cooking fuel, roof repair, and water buffalo food.

Uncle Ky, on the other hand, was just the opposite. He was very considerate and always had interesting stories to tell. I loved him and his family very much. His two sons, cousins Tuan and Bao, were like brothers to me. Tuan was about eleven or twelve. He was with my father when he was killed. Bao was my age or maybe a little younger. They lived some distance from my aunt, and I was unable to see them very often. I couldn't live with Uncle Ky, because he was very poor and couldn't even feed his own family. Instead, I could only visit him now and then.

While on my way to his house one afternoon, I passed by one of the old, deserted French buildings, which had once been used for tax administration. I heard the French had committed terrible atrocities there—villagers who couldn't pay their taxes were tortured and even beheaded. Many believed the ghosts of those murdered haunted the building, so no one went there at night. An open door aroused my interest, however, and I went inside.

It was dark and dingy, with many rooms and long, empty hallways. Part of the red-tiled roof had caved in and threads of light seeped through. Wildflowers and weeds were growing through cracks in the tile floor, and musty mold left a pungent odor in the air. I climbed on an open ceiling beam to play and found a sparrow's nest with four babies in it. I took the nest and cradled it in one hand, while holding on to the beam with the other. The bird's parents were angry with me for stealing their nest and flew back and forth over my head, pecking at me as I climbed down to the floor. I sat with the nest until the parents gave up and flew away. After they were gone, I began playing with the baby birds. I fed them insects and petted each one before putting them back in the nest. I placed the nest aside, sat down, and leaned back against the wall to rest. Within moments, I was fast asleep.

I opened my eyes to a pitch-black, unfamiliar space. I tried to figure out where I was and remembered the baby birds. I felt around for them, picked up the nest, and held it close to my chest, as I rose to my feet and looked for a way out. I kept running into walls or corridors that led nowhere. I was scared and cried for help, but nobody came. Besides, if anyone heard me, I'm sure they would have thought that I was one of the ghosts that roamed the empty building at night. I grew tired of running around and sat back down. Covering my face with one hand and holding on to my bird's nest with the other, I closed my eyes to avoid looking into the darkness, hoping daylight would come soon.

I shivered in the damp, cold night and remembered a story Uncle Ky told my two cousins and me about the old building. "When the French occupied the building," he said, "I worked as a guard for them. One cold, rainy night, I was sitting in one of the dark rooms by myself, watching the rain and lightning outside through an open door. All of a sudden, I heard something fall from the ceiling. I turned to look and saw a bloody head rolling on the floor. Its short hair stood straight up, and it had a pale, chalky face. Its white, shining eyes were wide open."

When we heard the story, my cousins and I grew frightened, and we huddled closer to each other. From the corner of my eyes, I could see a satisfied smile on Uncle Ky's face. I knew he often exaggerated or made up stories just to scare us, but knowing that didn't stop our fear; we couldn't help ourselves.

He continued his story. "I was too scared to move and just stared at the head. Seconds later, I heard two more loud plops, as two bloody legs fell. They moved with a kicking motion, back and forth. Soon, two arms fell, one after another. They were twitching and turning around like lizards' tails that had just been cut off. I stared in petrified silence and heard a louder PLOP!"

All three of us let out a scream and moved even closer together, as Uncle Ky continued.

"A bloody torso fell from thin air. Like magic, the arms and legs wiggled around, moved close to the torso, and attached themselves to it. The headless body stood up, walked toward the head, picked it up, and placed the gruesome head on its bloody neck. Then it turned to glare at me. Its white, chalky eyes turned blood red, and it disappeared. After that day, I never went back to the building again!"

My cousins and I felt relieved when the story ended. I tried to convince myself again and again that Uncle Ky made up the story just to scare us, and he did a good job of it.

As I stood there in the dark thinking of my uncle's story, I was terrified. I opened my eyes, and my imagination ran away with me. I saw what looked like a tall, white figure, walking toward me, with bright, bloody eyes shining in the darkness.

I jumped up and started running. After bumping into a half dozen obstacles, I found an exit and ran outside. I ran down the dark winding road and didn't slow down until I reached Uncle Ky's house. It was late, and everyone was already asleep, so I found myself a comfortable place on the front porch, put my bird's nest aside, and dozed off.

Uncle Ky woke me with a smile when he opened the door and asked, "Why did you sleep here? Why didn't you come inside? The door is never locked."

"It was too late," I said, "I didn't want to disturb you."

I followed him to the kitchen building, outside. While he cooked rice for breakfast, I asked, "Can I stay with you, Uncle?"

"That would be fine with me," he said with a sweet smile, "but you would have to be prepared to go hungry."

"I don't mind," I told him.

The next day, when we went to church, I stopped at my aunt's house to let her know I was going to live with Uncle Ky. She just looked at me, smiled, and nodded her head but said nothing. I guessed that it was fine with her. Even though there was never enough food to eat at Uncle Ky's, I was happy. I didn't feel hungry, because the good times I had and the love my uncle's family gave me outweighed any hunger I felt.

Since Cousin Tuan was older, he took us fishing and taught us how to make fishing gear. We used wire to make hooks, thread for line, bamboo sticks for rods, and worms for bait. Besides fishing, Cousin Tuan showed me how to pick edible weeds for meals. The simple gear, and the lessons he taught me, kept me from starving.

Now and then, I took a break to visit my father's grave. The cemetery was overgrown with weeds, and it took me a while to find his grave the first time. I pulled up the weeds and often gathered wildflowers to place on top of his grave, as Mother and I used to do. When finished, I sat and talked to him as if he were still alive; in my mind and heart, he always would be.

"Father, do you know where Mother has gone?" I asked him one day. "Well, I don't know where she is either, but I do miss her, and I miss you, too. I wish you and Mother were still with me. Uncle Ky told me that one day I'd see you again in heaven. I hope it will be soon. And I hope I'll see Mother again, too, just like Uncle Ky said." I sat beside his grave for a long time before standing up. I wiped my tears, looked around for a moment, and decided to visit my old home. It had been a while since I last visited. I was afraid of the sadness I would feel without either of my parents with me, and that's why I had not returned since I began staying with Aunt Ba.

I followed the small, winding dirt road to my house. I stood like a statue, staring at the deserted home. The roof had caved in, and the fruit trees were dried out and dying from lack of care. The only things that grew were weeds. I started to remember the good times there, and tears began to run down my cheek, making me wish my parents were still with me.

From behind me, I heard a small voice call my name, "Loan Oi." I turned around and thought I was seeing a ghost. A pale, thin, old woman, about my height or a little taller, was standing in the path, with a big, toothless smile on her face. She stretched out her hands and walked toward me. I recognized her and returned the smile—she was my mother's old friend, Ba Cu. I walked to her and grabbed her cold and bony hand—it was like holding hands with Death. Her hands felt even colder when she cradled my face.

"Every time I pass your house, I always stop to look at it," she said. "I've been hoping that you and your mother would move back here again. After your father died, I moved away and lived with my daugh-ter and her husband for a few years. When I came back, you and your mother were gone, and I didn't know what happened to either of you. I am so happy to see you. You have grown a lot." Even though she put on a happy face, I could hear the sadness in her voice. She asked how I had been and where I lived. I told her about Mother being gone and about me living with my uncle and my aunt.

"Can you come to my house for a while?" she asked.

"Sure, I would like that," I replied, and walked away with her. Using her cane for support, she led me around several ponds and through a tea garden.

"My son was killed in the fight at the same time your father was killed, and I went to live with my only daughter," she said. "I didn't like her husband, so I decided to move back home and live by myself."

"If I had known you were here, I would have come to see you sooner," I said.

We stopped in front of a house that looked no better than mine—the roof was caving in, and the walls were crumbling. I helped her climb the steps to the clay porch.

I stood at the door and glanced inside. There was an old, broken bamboo bed, with a rolled-up grass mat on top. In a nearby corner were a few chipped cooking pots made from clay. One of the larger pots had water in it. Next to the pots were a small bag of uncooked rice and a bowl of rock salt. Three pieces of curved clay brick, standing on their sides, served as her stove. White ashes and some half-burnt tea stems surrounded the bricks. Next to the stove were a couple of empty bottles, an old rusted kerosene lantern, and a small bundle of dried tea sticks, used as cooking fuel. She asked me to come into the part of the house that was still standing.

"Each time my daughter comes to visit, she always brings me food, but it has been a while since I've seen her," she said. "I hope my daughter is doing fine and hope her husband hasn't killed her." She continued, "My neighbors who used to care for me moved away, and now I have to go around and beg for food."

She looked at me with her toothless smile again. Quietly, she took a grass mat from the bed and spread it out on the floor, next to her stove, told me to sit with her, and then began asking about my family again.

I told her everything that had happened to us, up to my mother disappearing one day. We talked until late afternoon.

When I realized it was growing late, I stood up and said, "I have to leave now."

"Since you're already here, you should stay and eat with me," she said.

I looked at her and saw the loneliness in her tired eyes; I didn't have the heart to leave, so I accepted her invitation and helped her prepare the food.

I stacked a handful of tea sticks between the bricks and started a fire with an old cigarette lighter. We cooked a small pot of rice, and she said, "I'm sorry I don't have good food to offer you. Except for rice and salt, I have nothing else to eat."

"That's just fine," I replied. "That's what I eat almost every day."

After the rice was done, we scooped it into an old chipped bowl, added salt, and then used chopsticks to eat. Soon after, the sky turned black, and thunder exploded. The rain came down as if heaven opened its door. Now and then, a piece of the straw roof followed the rain and fell in front of us.

We finished eating and moved to a drier corner, to avoid the rain. We sat, watching the water come through the roof, and talked. The lightning lit up the sky, and the thunder sounded like bombs exploding. The heavy rain and strong wind turned violent, and I thought, "I can't go home now, even if I wanted to. I just hope her house holds up."

We covered ourselves with a thin grass mat to keep warm. She reached for my hand and said, "I am so glad you are here with me." I looked at her and grinned. The warmth of her body comforted me, and I fell into a deep sleep.

When I woke up the next morning, she had already warmed the leftover rice.

"It's time for breakfast," she said, with a big smile on her face.

After we ate, I helped her tidy up the house and remove the rotten rice straw that fell from the roof the night before. "Do you need any help with your food or anything else?" I asked. "If you do, I will ask my aunt or my uncles to help you."

"No," she answered, "I have enough rice and salt to last for several more months."

There was not much more to do, so I said, "I am going to leave now, but I promise I'll be back to see you soon."

She looked sad, left the pile of tea sticks she was trying to stack up, and walked toward me. She held my hand and said, "I don't want you to leave, but I know you have to, because your aunt and uncle will worry about you."

I didn't think that was the case. No one knew where I was and no one worried enough to look for me, but I didn't say anything to her.

"I'll come back to see you in a day or two," I assured her. I let go of her hand and walked to the door. We waved goodbye to each other as I left.

As I promised, I went back to visit her often and sometimes brought my cousins and even spent the night there. She became like a second mother to me. I spent time helping her gather sticks and twigs for cooking fuel, and I brought her little fish and shrimp from my aunt's or uncles' homes. I enjoyed being with her and helping her when I could. I felt very fortunate that she was willing to spend her time with me as well.

I noticed that she was not looking well the last few times I was there. She sounded like she was catching a bad cold, as she coughed a lot and looked paler than usual. Once when I came to visit, she was sitting on a grass mat on the floor next to her broken bamboo bed with her back against the wall, staring at the sky through the holes in the roof. She smiled when I walked in, but it was a weak one. I could tell that she was not herself. She asked me to come and sit beside her.

She stroked my hair and said, "Promise me that if I die, you'll not cry or be sad."

"I don't want you to talk like that," I said. "You'll be all right."

I held her hand and watched her, wishing there were something more I could do for her. She was sick and didn't even have a decent bed to lie on. My cousin Tuan and I fixed her broken bed often, but it would never stay together. I asked her many times to move in with my uncle or my aunt, but she always refused, saying she would be all right by herself and didn't want to burden anybody.

"Besides," she said, "my daughter will be coming home to see me soon."

"I sure hope so," I replied. I asked her again that day to come with me to Uncle Ky's house, but she refused. I squeezed her hand, and tears flowed down my cheek.

"Are you hungry?" I asked, to change the subject.

"No," she answered, as she attempted a weak smile. She looked very tired, so I helped her lie down on the grass mat and stayed with her until late afternoon.

"I have to go now," I told her, "but I will be back tomorrow. I'll bring you more food and a grass mat to keep you warm." We looked at each other for a few seconds, and I patted her shoulder and walked out, fully intending to return the following day.

Instead, I went with my Uncle Ky and his two sons to help net fish at the church pond, near Aunt Ba's and Uncle Tu's homes. Uncle Ky used a triangle net to scoop fish from around the pond. He dumped each catch on the ground, and we picked out edible creatures like shrimp, fish, and water bugs, just like Mother and I used to do. The midday sun baked my head, and I was tired of picking up jumping and crawling things from the hot dirt, so I asked my uncle to let me visit Uncle Tu's daughters. He looked up and nodded his head. I let his two sons help him and ran to Uncle Tu's house, just a few yards away.

I found my two girl cousins. We climbed trees, ate fruit, and had a good time all afternoon. While we were playing, I told them about my old friend being sick, and they both felt bad for her.

"Thong, Teo!" We heard a loud and angry call from Uncle Tu.

"Oh, my God!" I said. "Your father is calling you, and from the sound of his voice, he's going to kill you." In a panic, I climbed down from the tree and took off running.

I went back to the pond where Uncle Ky was about ready to stop his netting. Worried about my cousins, I told him that Uncle Tu was going to beat up his daughters and asked Uncle Ky to help them. Uncle Ky said, "Oh, your uncle is drunk, and everything will be fine tomorrow. He is my older brother, and I don't have authority to tell him what to do or how to treat his kids. If I get involved, he will beat me up again, like he did before."

There was nothing I could do to help my cousins, so I turned to help pick up the basket full of creatures. Cousin Tuan picked up one side, and I picked up the other. We walked behind Cousin Bao in single file, following Uncle Ky, with his fish net on his shoulder on the way home. With his wife's help, we separated the water bugs, shrimp, and fish into small piles. My aunt cooked almost everything, saving some for her fermented fish sauce.

Uncle Ky's wife was a very sweet woman, but she seldom talked or smiled. It was as if she were there just to fulfill her duties as mother and wife. She seemed to have no opinion of her own. She didn't mind if I came or went, and seldom talked to me. I didn't know whether she liked me or not, but I loved her, because she was my uncle's wife.

After we ate dinner, it was too late to go to see my old friend. I planned to see her the next day, but instead, I ran some errands with my uncle.

The third day, I got up early, wrapped some cooked shrimp and fish in a banana leaf, and with a small grass mat under my arm, I ran all the way to her house.

"Ba Oi, I'm here!" I called, as I climbed the steps. "I've brought you some gifts."

As I tiptoed inside, I noticed she was lying in the same spot I had left her, only she had turned away and was now facing the wall. At first, I didn't want to disturb her and placed the food near her on the mat. I sat next to her for a moment and then called to her. "Wake up Ba Oi. I've come to see you."

She didn't answer, so I touched her hand. Her skin was cold and stiff.

Cautiously, I looked at her face—it was purple, and her mouth and eyes were half open. She did not seem to be breathing. Something was very wrong. I panicked and called to her even louder. I begged her to wake up, but she didn't move. I tried to turn her over, but she was stiff and too heavy. I ran outside to get help, but I didn't want to leave her, so I went back inside. I ran back and forth, crying my eyes out, not knowing what to do.

Then I thought of my uncle. I dashed to his house, but he was not home. Frantically, I ran around looking for him and found him at a neighbor's, sitting on a grass mat on the floor with his friends, drinking rice whiskey and eating dog meat. He was about to put a bite of meat into his mouth with his chopsticks, when I stopped him and yelled, "Help me Uncle! Something is wrong with Ba Cu! I think she is dead! Please hurry, Uncle!"

He threw down his chopsticks and ran with me. Uncle Ky and I crossed ourselves and prayed for her soul as we ran. When we arrived at her house, Uncle Ky knelt down and touched her. He turned to me and said, "I'm sorry, but she's dead. She's been dead for some time now."

I knelt beside her. "Ba Oi! Please don't be dead!" I cried, and shook her shoulder. "Wake up! Don't leave me!"

Uncle Ky moved me away from her, stroked my head, and said, "She's gone to see God and your father in heaven. You will see them again. She may have left you in body, but she will always be with you in spirit."

His gentle words comforted me and gave me hope. He covered her body with the grass mat I brought and said, "I have to go for help." I sat with my friend, crying, as I waited for my uncle to return. He came back with a couple of friends, a machete, a shovel, and some ropes. Carefully, they wrapped her body in the mat, tied it with the ropes, and carried her to the field. As they dug her grave, I sat crying beside her. When the hole was deep enough, they lowered her body into it and filled it with dirt. We gathered around the grave and said a last prayer for her. Uncle Ky cut a limb from a tree, made it into a cross, and placed it on her grave.

I thanked him and asked, "May I stay for a while?"

He looked at me with a soft smile, nodded his head, and walked away with his friends. I gathered wildflowers and placed them on the grave next to the food I had brought earlier.

Kneeling on the edge of the mound of dirt, with tears streaming down my face, I asked "Why did you have to leave me? I wish you didn't have to die." I stayed with her until darkness approached. "I have to go now," I said. "But I'll be back to see you soon. I love you, and I know you will always be with me in spirit, just like Uncle Ky said."

I stood up, dusted off my clothes, and dragged my heavy feet along, feeling like a body without a soul, to Uncle Ky's house. The oil lamp was lit, and my two cousins were inside, cooking crickets and grasshoppers in the lamp's flame. I sat next to them and, with a broken heart, told them what happened. They looked sympathetic for a few moments, then invited me to eat roasted insects with them.

It might have been a year since Mother left, but it seemed like an eternity to me, and I still hadn't heard a word from her. My pajamas had turned to rags, so I had to wear my Aunt Ba's clothes. They were so big that they made me look like a scarecrow. Soon, they too turned to rags, but I was lucky to have rags to wear.

One day, I went to Uncle Tu's house to look for his two daughters, to see if they wanted to go swimming with me. I saw Uncle Tu instead. He was in front of his house, and I could tell that he was already drunk. He walked as if one leg was shorter than the other, and he was mumbling to himself.

"Where are my two cousins?" I asked.

"They aren't home," he grumbled.

I decided not to disturb him any further and went swimming by myself. I took off my oversized clothes, hung them on a tree, and jumped into the pond. I dove under and then floated on my back. I'd swim fast and then slow. I was having a good time, when I felt a sharp pain on my chest. I looked down and saw a huge buffalo leech, the size of a small banana, hanging from one side of my chest to the other. I liked to play with leeches, but this kind was not a toy. With all my strength, I tried to pull the leech off, but it wouldn't move. I panicked and swam to shore. I thought it would be easier to get the leech off once my feet were on solid ground.

I struggled to remove the leech, but it was strong and didn't want to let go. It was then that my drunken uncle saw me and decided to chase me. I took off running naked, with the leech still hanging from my chest. I slowed down when I felt he was farther behind. I looked back and saw him staggering.

He waved a stick and yelled, "I'm going to kill you, if I catch you!"

I believed him. I had heard a rumor that he killed his first wife by accident, in one of his drunken rages.

I continued to run to the other side of the pond, trying to get far enough away from him, so I could pull the leech off my chest. Finally, I was able to remove it, but it left a bloody gash. I covered the wound with my finger to stop the bleeding and watched the huge leech squirm back into the pond. Vowing to never swim in that pond again, I waited until my uncle went back to his house before I returned to the tree where I left my clothes. I used them to wipe the blood off my chest before putting them back on. I went to my aunt's house, climbed up to the mantel, retrieved a small kerosene lamp, and poured kerosene on my wound, to kill germs and stop the bleeding, as Mother had taught me.

After the excitement was over, I found a bamboo basket in Aunt Ba's kitchen and took it to the rice fields. I was hoping to catch something for dinner. I scooped several little white fish and shrimp from a small pool of water. I stared at my catch jumping up and down in the basket, and wondered what they would taste like raw. I gathered all my nerve and tried one. "It tastes good!" I thought, and before long, I had eaten all of them. When I finally had my fill, I caught a few more and wrapped them in elephant leaves, intending to take them back to Aunt Ba's house. Hard-drying mud covered me from head to toe. I tried to peel it off my face as I walked. I looked like a mud statue, carrying a muddy basket, with muddied balls of shrimp.

In the courtyard, I saw a well-dressed woman talking to my aunt. I was curious and walked closer. To my surprise, the strange lady was my mother! Our eyes met, and she smiled when she saw me. I was so happy to see her. My heart was pounding, and I wanted to run to her, but instead I walked toward the pond without a word. She stopped talking to my aunt and called to me, "Loan Oi," and followed me to the pond. I ignored her, stripped off my clothes, and left them on the dock. I jumped into the water and began scrubbing the mud off. She came to the dock and said something, but with water in my ears, I couldn't hear her, nor did I want to. I felt resentment and anger toward her for leaving me behind for so long. I dove under the water and swam like I was mad, but I also swam like I was happy. But mainly I swam, because I was hurt and confused.

Mother disappeared for a few minutes. When she came back, I noticed she was holding something yellow in her hand. She waved for me to come to her. I climbed to the bamboo dock and looked at her. She looked different. She had gained a lot of weight, and her stomach was much bigger. I said nothing to her, as I walked closer to investigate the yellow thing in her hand. At the same time, she saw the wound in my chest left there by the leech.

"Come here and let me see what happened to you," she said. I looked down and saw blood still oozing from the leech bites. I was huffing and puffing in the water, causing the wounds to open up again.

"What is that, and why is it still bleeding?" she asked.

"A water buffalo leech did that to me today." I answered grumpily.

She took a closer look at the injuries. "Let me clean it with kerosene," she said.

"I already did," I replied.

"Then why is it still bleeding?" she asked, with concern.

"I don't know." I said. "Perhaps I was swimming too hard."

She knew I was angry at her, and she tried to make peace by offering me a pair of new yellow pajamas.

"These are for you," she said.

"I don't want them," I replied in a muffled voice, as I reached for my dirty old rags.

"If you wear these, I'll take you with me," she said.

I stared at them for a moment, grabbed them from her hands, and tried them on. They fit! I looked at the clothes and at my mother. For a moment I couldn't hide my excitement, I forgot the hurt, and smiled at her. I took Mother's outstretched hand, and we walked to the kitchen to help my aunt fix dinner. They cooked my catch, along with vegetables, and brought them to the table, where my aunt, her husband, her son, my mother, and I all shared the meal.

I remained silent while we ate, but listened with intense interest to Mother's conversation. I discovered she was married to a rich man, was six months pregnant, and her husband was very dominating. He had four live-in maids, two rice field hands, and one gardener. Listening to Mother, I wondered why she had taken so long to come for me if she was so rich. I couldn't help but let my mind wander back to what Uncle Tu said. After dinner, we drank fresh green tea and had bananas for dessert.

The following day was Sunday, and I was so anxious to go to church to show off my new clothes. "No children in our village have clothes as pretty as mine," I thought. That night, I twisted and turned, but I couldn't go to sleep until early morning.

When I woke up, the house was empty. I ran outside just in time to see Mother and aunt Ba coming home. I realized I had overslept and missed church. I was very upset, because I knew I'd missed my chance to show off my clothes.

I ran to my aunt and asked, "Why didn't you wake me?"

My aunt smiled and said, "You were sound asleep, and I didn't want to bother you."

Mother saw my sadness and tried to cheer me up. "I'm going to take you with me to your new home," she said. "But you must be happy before I do that." Smiling, she rubbed my head.

I looked at her and my aunt with little enthusiasm and asked, "When?"

"In a couple of days," Mother said.

I replied with a halfhearted smile. She seemed to act differently now. I didn't feel the love and warmth from her that I had always felt before. I thought again about what Uncle Tu said. Maybe he was right. She is having a new baby, and perhaps she doesn't love me anymore. That thought caused silent tears to begin rolling down my cheeks, but I wiped them off before anyone saw me crying.

For the next two days, Mother was busy visiting relatives, and we didn't say much to each other, but we did exchange a few weak smiles. I think she still felt some guilt, and I some resentment.

On the third day, after breakfast at my aunt's house, Mother and I sat for the first time and talked with each other. "How has everything been?" she asked.

"Everything is fine," I replied. "I just missed you," I added and then told her all about my experiences while she was gone, including the death of her old friend. She grew silent, and tears streamed down her face.

She dried her tears and said, "I'm so sorry that I left you as I did. Your stepfather made me agree to leave you behind while he and I got to know each other better. I wanted to come for you sooner, but he wouldn't let me. I also thought that you and I would have a better life there, and it would be worth sacrificing our present time together. Besides, I believed that all of our relatives here would take good care of you."

"Why didn't you tell me this before you left?" I asked.

"It was so painful that I couldn't bring myself to tell you," she replied. "That's why I walked out as I did." Feeling sorry for her, I let my guard down.

Because we planned to leave the following day, Mother decided that we should say goodbye to our relatives and thank them for taking care of me. We first went to see Uncle Tu, because he lived closest.

"Did you stay with your Uncle Tu?" she asked.

"Not often," I said. "I only stayed with him when he was sober. But when he was drunk, he hit me and his two daughters for no reason. Sometimes, my cousins had to hide at Aunt Ba's or a neighbor's house until he sobered up."

Uncle Tu was a very decent person when he was sober. He caught fish and shrimp to feed us, or he'd sell them to buy extra food, like pork and chicken. When he had money, he also bought ingredients for his homemade moonshine. Then he drank for days, until it was gone or until he passed out.

We arrived at his house and stepped up on the porch. We went to the open door and saw him sitting on a grass mat on the floor in the middle of the room. Some dishes of food were in front of him, and he was as drunk as a jellyfish. The moment he saw us, he picked up a dish and threw it at us. We jumped out of its way.

Mother smiled at him and said, "We just came to say goodbye and wish you good luck until we see you again."

"Luck!" he yelled. "I don't need any luck! Take your luck and don't forget to take your ornery daughter with you and get out of my house! And don't you dare come back!" After cursing us, he went back to his drinking.

We both felt sorry for him, but there was nothing we could do. Mother attempted to say something to him, but he didn't respond. We just stood there watching him drink in silence. We thought it was best to leave him alone, so we wiped our tears and walked away.

Before leaving Uncle Tu's yard, I asked Mother to wait for me while I looked for my two cousins to say goodbye, but she decided to go with me. We found them playing in a neighbor's fig tree. The tree was so big that we often hid in it from Uncle Tu when he was drinking and couldn't climb. Besides, there was enough fruit in the tree to keep us alive for days. I called to them as soon as I saw them and said, "I have to leave now and go with my mother." Mother looked up and smiled at them.

They climbed down from the tree, and Teo came close to me. She reached out to hold my hand and said, "I don't want you to leave."

"Don't worry, I'll be back," I told her.

Mother rubbed both of their heads and gave them some money from her bag. "You two be good and look after your father," she said. "We will come back to see you as soon as we can."

They nodded their heads and followed us for a short distance, before they stopped and watched us walk away. Tears rolled down my cheek, and I could hear them crying behind me.

Saying goodbye to Uncle Ky's family was just as hard. His two sons kept telling me to come back soon, as Uncle Ky rubbed my head.

He whispered, "Be a good girl and take good care of your mother." I looked up at him and saw tears swell in his eyes. Saying goodbye to all of my cousins was hard for me, but it was so much harder to say goodbye to Uncle Ky. I knew he would miss me, and I would miss him even more. I didn't know if I would see any of them ever again. Mother took a stack of money from her bag, handed some to Uncle Ky, and some to Tuan and Bao. Tears streamed down our faces as we walked away, and they told me to hurry back.

We went to my father's grave for a brief and final visit. We returned to my aunt's house with red, swollen eyes and began packing for the next day's trip. When Mother saw me folding my old clothes, she said, "Throw those rags away. You'll never have to wear them again."

I looked at the pile of torn clothes, which I had grown attached to, and thought, "I'm going to miss them, too."

Mother made rice balls for the trip, wrapping them in banana leaves. Then she roasted sesame seeds, ground them up, and added salt. She also cooked salt and pepper shrimp to take with us. Mother told me it would be a long walk, and we must make sure to bring enough food. The thought of our journey excited me so much that I slept little that night. Mother woke me very early in the morning. We had a quick breakfast with my aunt and her husband. I saw Mother give Aunt Ba a roll of money, just as she gave to Uncle Ky. After a tearful goodbye with my aunt, we gathered our belongings and left.

We walked until the sun was overhead, before stopping to sit under the shade of a huge tree to eat our lunch. Mother took me to a nearby pond, where she fashioned a drinking cup from a water lily. She disturbed the surface of the water to clear out the debris and scare the water bugs away. Then, she scooped the water for me to drink first, before having her fill. We resumed our trip through the rice fields and on small dirt roads. Because of Mother's condition and my short legs, we couldn't walk very fast.

Darkness fell, and we were both exhausted. I had been walking barefoot all day, and my feet were blistered. The shoes Mother brought for me were too small, so I had to carry them. We stopped and spent the night at the home of an acquaintance. We awoke in the morning, had breakfast, and continued our walk. By that afternoon, we arrived at Luong Dong, the town I would be calling my new home.

Chapter 4

TARNISHED SILK

THE VILLAGE OF Luong Dong was much larger than Tao Xa. It had more homes and wider clay roads. Some of the homes were similar to ours, while others were larger and made of brick, with red-tiled roofs. From a distance, Mother pointed to one of those larger houses that was visible above the tree line and said, "That is your new home. It is the largest house in the area."

We walked around a pond, entered through the back gate, and walked into a huge courtyard. I stopped and looked around in awe. I'd never seen such a magnificent place. "Are you sure this is where you live?" I asked Mother. Without waiting for an answer, I walked away to take a closer look at everything.

The main house had two wings at either end, with a courtyard in the middle, giving the building a U-shaped appearance. Beyond the courtyard, stood a long line of fruit trees, and beyond them was a beautiful fishpond. There were more ponds behind the house and to the side as well.

Many people were going in and out of the house, and when they saw Mother, they each bowed to show their respect. They all seemed happy to see her. After bowing to her, they smiled and waved at me. From their dress and their actions, I could tell they were the maids that Mother told me about. I stood and stared in wonderment at the sight before me.

Mother jolted me from my amazement by saying, "Loan Oi, come with me, I want you to say hello to your father." As I followed her, she instructed, "You must remember to call him Father." I was a little confused, for I thought my father was dead, but said nothing.

We entered the middle of a room in the main house. I was amazed by the room and surprised by the man—the same man who had visited my mother before. He sat on a beautiful hand-carved, wooden bench, wearing a casual white outfit, drinking rice whiskey and eating snacks from several brass and silver plates.

The room, a combination dining and living area, was full of elegant ironwood furniture. In one corner sat a large wooden divan, and in the center of the room stood an enormous rectangular table and several ornate chairs. Artful flowers and animals, hand-carved into the wood, adorned the furniture. The house and its priceless furnishings had been left to my stepfather by prior generations of his family.

The man looked at me with half a smile. I forgot what I was supposed to do until Mother reminded me. Then quickly, I bowed and said, "Hello, Father." He pointed to a divan and signaled for us to sit. Mother sat down like a puppy and pulled me beside her.

"How was the trip?" he asked.

Mother told him about my relatives and my hometown, and he nodded his head as if he understood. When she finished, she asked to be excused. He nodded again, like a king granting his royal permission, and we left the room.

"We are going to see your grandmother now," Mother said as she led the way. I had to follow.

In the next room, I saw an old lady rolling a green leaf with a bit of lime in it. "This must be my grandmother," I thought.

Placed in front of her was a tray of betel nuts, a stack of the green leaves, a container full of white lime, and a bowl filled with rolled leaves. I remembered how my aunt and uncle often chewed the same kind of green leaves. Once, my aunt gave me one to chew, and within a minute, my mouth turned blood red from the contents of the lime, betel nut, and leaf. I became dizzy from the mild narcotic effect and declared, "I'll never do that again."

Mother bowed to her and said, "Hello, Mother. I just got home and brought your granddaughter to see you."

I stared at her, without blinking my eyes. Mother pinched me to remind me to bow, and I bowed so deep my hair almost brushed the floor.

"Hello, Grandmother," I said. We stood in silence, while she placed the rolled leaf, containing a piece of betel nut, in her mouth and began chewing it.

She looked at us for a moment and, with obvious irritation, motioned for us to move to one side. We were blocking her sunlight from the door. Satisfied that her demand was met, she looked back down and started rolling more of her little leaves and nuts. As many as she rolled, she must chew the leaves all day and all night, I thought. My poor aunt and uncle only chewed them after each meal. They couldn't afford to chew more.

My step-grandmother, as she appeared in 1974,
shortly before her death at 102 years old.

From the way my grandmother acted, I got the impression she didn't think much of my mother and thought even less of me. We looked at each other, and after a few moments of awkward silence, we asked to be excused. My step grandmother nodded, without looking up, and we backed out of the room.

Mother held my hand and led me from the main house to a room in one of the wings. She smiled and said, "I'm taking you to a room that's been fixed up just for you."

The room was furnished with a bamboo bed, a table, and a wooden wardrobe. I asked, "Are you sure this is mine? It's much too big for me. Are you going to sleep with me?" Mother smiled and said nothing.

A middle-aged woman walked in and bowed. She looked straight at me and announced, "The Master wants to see you."

We followed the woman to the courtyard where several people were lined up, as if for an inspection. As we entered, my stepfather motioned for me to come to him. I looked to Mother for reassurance, and she signaled for me to obey him. I tentatively walked closer to him, and he waved his hand for me to hurry up. So I scurried over to where he stood, and he started introducing these strange people.

"This is Cay," he said, pointing to the first woman in line. She was about thirty years old. "From now on you are under her supervision, and you must do as she says. She is your guardian and will take care of you," my stepfather ordered.

"Yes, Father," I said.

He then presented the rest of them. Nhan, the cook, Hong, who took care of the water buffaloes, Ba Do, the gardener and cook's helper, Ba Gioi, responsible for picking tea leaves, selling them to the market, and making sure tea was always available, and Anh Thu and Phan, who worked together in the rice fields. After the introductions, he instructed them to go back to their chores. Mother just stood in the background, watching us.

She waited for everyone to leave, then grabbed my arm, and showed me the rest of the place. The main house was only one story, but it looked much taller because of the high cathedral ceilings and the foundation that had been raised to avoid the floodwater. It had red tiles on the roof and four massive columns that supported the front porch.

I never dreamed I would live in such a place. The main house consisted of three separate sections. Family and social gatherings took place in the center portion, where we ate. Patients were treated and medicine was stored in the left wing of the house, while rice and food were stored in the right wing.

The wings were not as grand as the main building. They were longer and had massive roofs made from rice straw. The right wing contained the servants' quarters, an animal shelter, and the kitchen. The left wing consisted of four rooms. My parents' room was on one end, which overlooked the fishpond, and was near mine. The next two rooms were used for raising silk worms and spinning silk.

While showing me around, Mother tried to teach me a few quick lessons. "You are not to swim in the pond or climb trees," she warned. "When you walk in front of elders, like your grandmother and your father, for example, you must always bow," she continued. "This is a new life, and you must learn new manners."

I heard her, but my eyes were fixed on every detail of the house. I said, "Yes, Mother," now and then, but paid little attention to what she was saying. I had a feeling it was not going to be easy to follow her instructions.

Changing the subject, I asked if I could look the place over by myself. She nodded her head and cautioned, "Go ahead, but be careful."

"Yes, Mother," I said, as I walked away. I wandered around for a while and went to the front gate, where a large, yellow dog appeared from nowhere. It growled, ran straight at me, and bit me on the chest. Blood poured from the wound as I screamed for help. The maids ran to me, pulled the dog away, and carried me to the courtyard.

My mother and stepfather heard the commotion and ran to the scene. My stepfather examined the dog bite and told a maid to take me to his office. He cleaned the wound, and Mother helped him apply medicine to stop the bleeding. They left the room and told me to lie still for a few minutes. I lay there, crying from pain, and made up my mind to teach that dog a lesson and show him who was boss someday.

From my stepfather's office, I heard the maids preparing to serve dinner. Mother called me to come to the table, and when I saw all the different kinds of food that had been prepared, I couldn't believe my eyes. Before I had a chance to sit, an older boy, about eleven or twelve, ambled in and gave me an unwelcome look as he sat.

Maids and servants hurried back and forth, making sure the table was perfect. When everything was ready, my stepfather sat at the end, my step-grandmother sat to his right, Mother sat to his left. Mother told me to sit next to her, opposite the boy on the other side of the table.

She pointed to the boy and whispered, "That is Den, your older brother. You must address him as Anh Den. You have another older brother, Hen, who is away at college, and a sister, Ka, who is married and lives in another town." From the way Den looked at me, I didn't think he liked me.

This was all so new to me, I watched those around me to see what to do next. Before anyone picked up their chopsticks, my stepfather said a prayer. After the prayer, my step-grandmother reached for her chopsticks, and I immediately grabbed mine. I couldn't wait to taste all the delectable food and dug into the different dishes, gulping the food down as fast as I could.

I noticed the table was very quiet, and I looked up. Everyone was frowning at me as they ate. Feeling very uncomfortable with all those disapproving glares, I finished the bowl of rice, laid my chopsticks aside, excused myself, and went outside.

In the courtyard was a strange looking, two-wheeled machine, standing by itself. As I examined this strange object, Den came out, didn't say a word, climbed on the machine, and almost knocked me over as he rode away.

"What is that thing?" I asked Mother, as she walked toward me.

"That's a bicycle," she replied and told me to follow her.

Mother led me toward the pond. "Stay where you are," she ordered, "I'm going back to the house for a change of clothes and some soap."

When she returned, I was in the pond, naked and swimming around like a fish.

"Get out of there!" she yelled in a panic. "That is where your father raises his golden carp! You can't swim in there."

I climbed the brick steps, and Mother told me to sit. Again, she reminded me about the rules and tried to teach me some manners, as she bathed me using water from the pond. At the dinner table," Mother said, "the oldest is supposed to start eating first and the youngest last. Since you are the youngest, you must always wait."

"How long?" I asked.

"Until they've all taken their first bite," she replied. I knew then why everyone had frowned at me during the meal.

"Look," she said, changing the subject and pointing to a repaired section of the red-tile roof. "A bomb hit and killed three people there."

My eyes opened wide as they followed her pointing finger to the large round spot where the roof's tile had a different color. "Where are they buried?" I asked.

"I don't know, I guess somewhere in a cemetery," she replied. From that day on, I got cold chills whenever I passed that section of the house.

Mother dried me, and after she dressed me in another new outfit, I sat on the top stair, watching her wash herself and watching maids carry towels and a pot of water to the dining room.

"Why are they doing that?" I asked Mother.

"Those are for your father and grandmother to wash their mouth and hands after they eat," she replied.

"Why don't they go to the pond and wash their hands instead?"

"Because your grandmother and father are rich," Mother replied, "and they don't have to."

I had been silent about this for too long. "She is not my grandmother, and he is not my father!" I blurted. "My grandmother and my father are dead!"

Mother gave me a sharp look and scolded, "You will address them as Father and Grandmother. I don't want to hear you ever speak with disrespect like that again," she warned. "Do you understand me?"

"Yes, Mother," I replied, and walked away.

I wandered into the kitchen and saw four of the maids sitting around a serving tray on the floor, talking and laughing while they ate. I could tell they were eating leftovers from our table. When they saw me, they all smiled.

I noticed some of them were missing and asked, "Where are the other three?"

"They don't stay here," Cay said. "When they finish their work, they go home to their families."

Cay smiled and invited me to join them. Although I had already eaten, I was still hungry and accepted her invitation. Cay gave me a bowl of rice and a pair of chopsticks, and I dug in. The food tasted better in the kitchen than it did in the dining room. I felt more comfortable there and didn't worry about silly table manners.

My stepfather walked by and saw me eating with the maids. He came into the kitchen, grabbed my arm, and pulled me outside.

"From now on, you are to stay away from the kitchen, and you are not to eat there! Do you understand?" he demanded. I was scared and confused by my stepfather's sudden reaction.

Cay came to my rescue and said, "It's all my fault, sir. I asked her to eat with us. Please don't blame her." He gave Cay a harsh look and walked away. I looked at Cay with gratitude as she put her arm around me.

"From now on I will try to take better care of you," she said with a smile. "I'll do my best to keep you out of trouble."

It was only my first day in the house, but because of all I had experienced, it felt like I had been there for weeks. During the next two months, I learned much more about rules and manners. Some of my old habits were hard to break though, like climbing trees and swimming in ponds, when no one was around to watch me. I just couldn't resist the temptation.

One morning, thinking it was safe, I jumped into the pond fully clothed. As I was swimming around, I heard voices and realized that someone was approaching. To my surprise, my stepfather had come home early, and he was not alone. My stepfather wanted to show the rare fish to his friend.

"Get out of the pond this minute!" he demanded when he saw me. "And change your clothes. I'll talk to you later."

I scrambled out of the pond and ran as fast as I could up to my room. After his friend left, my stepfather came to my room while I was changing clothes and told me to come out.

"Go to the backyard and find me a big stick," he ordered.

"Why, Father?" I asked.

"Just do it," he growled, "and don't you dare question me again!"

I didn't know what he wanted the stick for, but I obeyed him anyway. I found a stick and brought it to him. He grabbed the stick and me at the same time and hit me with it until I was black and blue.

Cay heard me screaming and ran to the scene. "Please stop hitting her," she begged, as she jumped between the stick and me. Trying to wrench the stick from his hand, she received a few whacks herself. "It was all my fault for not keeping an eye on her," she pleaded. "I promise I will watch her better from now on."

When he finally let go, he said, "Don't forget this lesson!" and stalked away.

Cay comforted me as best she could, and rubbed menthol cream on my welts. "I'm sorry," she said, "This is all my fault."

"I've never been hit like this before," I sobbed.

When Mother came home, I showed her my welts and bruises, hoping for some sympathy. Instead, she frowned at me and warned, "I hope that will teach you a lesson. You'd better not go swimming in the pond again."

I couldn't believe my ears! I looked at her in complete dismay and walked to my room to be with my pets. Her lack of concern hurt me, and I told my baby birds about the incident. Whenever I felt sad, I sought comfort with my collection of creatures—my birds, frogs, and insects that I captured in the storage wings of our home. Talking to them always made me feel better. I separated the insects and frogs into jars and left the birds in their original nests. I fed the birds with insects I didn't like. When they were big enough to fly, I let the birds go. Sometimes, I tied their legs to keep them longer, until I was ready to let them go. Even when they were free to go, the birds often lingered around for a while, demanding food. I kept feeding them, until they were ready to leave for good. For the most part, my animals kept me occupied and out of trouble.

I always tried to keep my door closed to keep out my stepfather's big, yellow cat. If given the chance, I knew he would eat my pets. Even with all of my precautions, one day I caught the cat chewing on one of my birds. I got so upset that I took him up a ladder to the roof of our house and threw him to the courtyard below. He wasn't even hurt! He landed on all four feet and ran away. I was still angry, so I caught him again. This time, I climbed a tree that overhung the fishpond and hurled the cat into the water. I assumed he would swim away and thought no more about him. When I got back to my room to check on my pets, I found that he had eaten all three of my baby birds and destroyed their nest.

A few days later, a maid found the cat floating in the pond, its swollen body tangled in water lilies and vegetation. The cat's death upset my stepfather very much. I felt bad because I didn't mean to kill him, but I wasn't about to tell anyone what I had done.

One day, not long after the cat had been found in the pond, one of my stepfather's friends came to the house. When he heard about the dead cat, he patted my stepfather on the back and said, "Don't feel bad. I have a litter of kittens, and I'll be happy to give you some."

A few days later, he brought over three fat kittens that looked just like the one that died. "What a mess," I thought. "Now I have three cats to deal with instead of one." I learned to tolerate and even love them, just as I did Vang, the dog that bit me. Eventually, he and I became the best of friends.

One boring afternoon, I sneaked into the kitchen, and while no one was looking, I grabbed a handful of rock salt. I climbed an Asian apple tree that overhung the pond and began picking its sour fruit. Suddenly, the limb I was standing on broke, and down I tumbled. I fell right on top of the water lilies, right where I had thrown the cat before. I tried to swim but got tangled in the water vegetation and vines. Luckily, Cay saw me struggling, jumped in, and pulled me to the surface. We swam to the steps and climbed out, hoping to get out of the pond before my stepfather came home.

Exhausted, Cay rested on the step, while I choked and coughed and tried to spit the water out. I thought about the poor cat, and how he must have felt before he died. Cay shook her head and said, "You better hurry up and change your clothes before your father gets home."

To my dismay, the door to my mother's room, where my clothes were kept, was locked, so I had no choice but to dry myself in the sun. The water was cold, and I sat shaking like a leaf. Before my clothes had a chance to dry, my parents came home and saw me sitting in the hot sun with wet clothes.

"What happened to you?" Mother asked. Father stood by, listening to my answer.

For a moment, I forgot I was not supposed to climb trees and told her the truth. "I was climbing a tree and fell into the pond, and I almost drowned." Mother was not at all sympathetic. In fact, she looked quite angry. "Go back to the tree you fell from and kneel under it," she demanded.

However, that was not enough punishment to suit my stepfather. He grabbed a nearby stick and hit me several times. Then he told Cay to bring him rope, and he tied me to the tree.

"You have been told many times not to climb trees," he growled, "but you never listen! This will teach you a lesson!"

I screamed and begged my mother to help me, but she just stood there, watching, and did nothing.

"Please let me go, Father," I begged. "I'm kneeling right over an ant hill and they are biting me, Father."

He ignored my pleas and after checking the rope to make sure it was tight, he walked away. Mother felt sorry for me and tried to untie me, but my stepfather came back, grabbed her arm, and pulled her away. "Leave her alone," he said. "She will learn."

Before walking away, Mother signaled for Cay to release me, and thankfully, she did. If I had stayed there much longer, I'm sure I would have died from the ant bites.

My stepfather kept dozens of bamboo sticks hidden in various places around the house. He wanted them to be handy so he could use them on me to teach me lessons. I didn't like my stepfather's lessons, and I hated those sticks. I often looked for them, and when I found them, I threw them away.

Months passed, and when Mother finally went into labor, it was like a circus erupted in our house. Nhan, one of the maids, went for the midwife, but the rest of the help didn't know what to do. Everyone just scurried around, including Vang, the yellow dog.

I didn't know what was going on either, but I was caught up in the excitement, and I complicated the situation by running back and forth—I was having a great time. Amidst the confusion, I bumped into Ba Do, the oldest maid, and we fell.

When we got to our feet, I asked, "What is going on?"

"Your mother is having a baby," she replied.

"Where has Father gone?" I asked.

She looked around and said, "He was here earlier, but he disappeared."

About that time, Nhan came rushing in with the midwife. As they ran past me, I followed right behind. They reached Mother's bedroom, but before the midwife went in, she asked Nhan to boil a large pot of water. Nhan went to the kitchen while I stood at the door and watched. The midwife examined my mother's stomach, saw me, and motioned for me to go away. I left the door and moved to the window, where I could continue watching. The midwife was too busy to notice I was still there.

Carefully, she removed Mother's pajama bottoms, and as she continued to check her, she yelled for someone to hurry up with the hot water. Mother was moaning in pain, letting out a low scream now and then as she pushed. A few minutes later, I watched the midwife pull a bloody baby boy out of my mother's stomach. She laid the baby on top of her, and then, to my horror, the midwife cut off part of the baby's intestines with a sharp piece of bamboo and tied it in a knot! The baby screamed and cried at the top of his lungs.

After delivering the water, Nhan came out of the room. Horrified, I asked, "Why are the baby's intestines hanging out, and why did the lady cut it off? Is he going to die?"

Nhan laughed as she replied, "He is fine. Those aren't his intestines; that's just his umbilical cord."

I didn't understand what she was talking about, so I decided not to ask any more questions and turned back to continue watching. The baby was crying so loudly, I knew he must have been in a lot of pain. "If my intestines were hanging out and had been cut off like that poor baby, I'd be crying too," I thought.

My parents later named him Kinh. When he was two or three months old, Mother felt confident enough to let me keep an eye on him while she took a bath. The maids heated water and filled a large brass pot, which they placed in an adjoining room, for Mother to use to clean herself.

"Loan Oi," Mother called. "Do you want to watch the baby for me, while I bathe myself?" she asked.

"Yes, Mother!" I answered. He was such a sweet baby, and I was very excited to be able to watch him and help my mother.

As I sat with Kinh, he began chewing his fist, which I took to mean that he was hungry, so I decided to feed him. I ran outside, climbed an Asian apple tree, and since there weren't any apples ripe enough, I picked a handful of little green ones. I put them in my mouth, chewed them up, and spit the whole thing into Kinh's mouth—I'd often seen other mothers feeding their infants this way, so I tried to do the same. To my horror, instead of swallowing it, he choked.

Mother heard him and ran into the room. When she saw him choking on a mouthful of green fruit, she lifted him up and tried to remove the fruit bits from his mouth with her fingers. His face turned blue as he gasped for air. It looked like he was going to die. I watched as Mother tried to help him, feeling guilty and scared. Finally, Mother was able to clear his throat, and he started breathing again.

Just then, my stepfather walked in, and after watching the situation for a few minutes, he realized what I had done. Right then his full attention was on Kinh, but when he calmed down, my stepfather turned to me and slapped me several times on the face, then dragged me outside by the ear. He grabbed one of his bamboo sticks, and whacked me until his hand grew tired. I screamed and begged for him to stop.

He yelled, "From now on, you are not allowed to go near the baby. Do you understand?"

"Yes, Father," I answered through my tears. I walked to the pond and slumped under a tree. I understood my stepfather was trying to teach me lessons and manners, but I wished his lessons were not so painful. For a long time, I couldn't go near Kinh, unless Father was away, or someone held him. Otherwise, I could only watch him from a distance.

It had been about a year since I moved to Luong Dong. The Viet Minh who occupied the town were not as brutal as the group who took over my old home village—they even opened a school for children and for adults who had never been to school. My parents heard of the school's opening, and thought it would be good for me to attend.

During the extended French occupation of Vietnam, thousands of Vietnamese schools were closed. The French believed that if they could keep the Vietnamese from being educated, they would be easier to control. Before the French takeover in 1883, most Vietnamese could read and write, but by the end of World War II, 80 percent were illiterate.

Being that I was almost seven years old and had never attended school, I was very much looking forward to my first day. And when that day came, Cay dressed me in my finest clothes—the light yellow outfit. Most of my clothes were of different shades of yellow because they were made from silk that had not been dyed. Cay took me to a large brick building that the Viet Minh had converted to a schoolhouse. She stayed at the door and told me to go in. Tentatively, I entered and saw many students of both sexes and all ages—some were as old as my parents. A young man, about thirty, and dressed in a khaki uniform, saw me come in. As he approached, he smiled and took me to an empty bench that reminded me of a church pew and told me to sit there. Forty or fifty students sat at several long benches, behind narrow, chest-high tables.

The man in khakis introduced himself. "My name is Do Tri," he said with a smile. "I will be your friend and teacher."

Everyone bowed, and said, "Chao Thay," which means, "Hello, Teacher."

"I'm a nephew of Uncle Ho Chi Minh," he proclaimed. "Just like everyone here and everyone that lives in this country. I will teach you to read, to write, and to be better citizens." He preached to us for some time about Uncle Ho and his accomplishments, told us what we would need for class, and then let us go home early.

Within weeks, I learned several communist songs and dances and was told that if I loved Uncle Ho and my country, I would have to do my part and support the party. I didn't understand what he meant about supporting a party, but I did have a lot of fun in school.

My stepfather had to feed a large group of communist soldiers each week, because his younger brother was a local leader. While the group was in our home, they sang and danced before and after their meal. Most of them were men, and all wore black pajamas. It was just like a party, and I enjoyed the excitement.

Because of my stepfather's wealth, the Viet Minh labeled him a capitalist and they watched his every move. They even ordered him to report whenever he butchered an animal, big or small. My stepfather was infuriated, but he could do nothing but grumble about it to us. He vowed to my mother that he was going to get out of his economic shackles.

Chapter 5

DRAGON FEATHERS

BY MID-1953, the French had grown tired of what they called the "Dirty War." Even with massive economic and military aid from America, they continued to suffer heavy losses at the hands of the Viet Minh. The French had set up a puppet government under King Bao Dai in the South and proposed a separate state be established there as a French colony. The Viet Minh were against such an arrangement but did agree to negotiate an end to the conflict.

The United States, Russia, Great Britain, and China agreed to participate in the negotiations, and they scheduled talks in Geneva, Switzerland during the spring of 1954. Meanwhile, the fighting intensified as each side tried to strengthen their negotiating position.

The French bombed our village, usually at night, and we were in and out of the bunker so much, we often chose to sleep in it. As the fighting worsened, my parents let most of the maids go home at night, because we didn't have enough bomb shelters for them.

There were two bunkers in the house—the larger one was in my parents' bedroom, and the other was in the kitchen near the maid's quarters. The bunker in my parents' room had a clay step, which helped us get in and out, and an escape tunnel connecting it to the fishpond outside, in case the house caught fire. When it rained, water from the pond backed up, and filled the bunker. We still had to use it, even when it was full. Because I was so short, the water sometimes came up to my neck, and I had to sleep standing up.

We had to share the bunker with visitors from the pond—fish, snakes, frogs, and leeches. It was not too bad, as long as the visitors behaved themselves, but that was not always so. Snakes often tried to get out by crawling up on our necks and shoulders, and the leeches attached themselves to us. We pulled them off and threw them on the floor above, but they soon crawled right back into the bunker with us. Mother solved the problem by placing a bucket of urine next to the bunker. We would put the leeches in the bucket to kill them, and it worked!

My baby brother didn't like staying in the bunker. Sometimes, he screamed and cried all night long. Mother tried to comfort him by forcing her breast in his mouth, but it seldom did much good. One night in frustration, Mother breathed a heavy sigh and exclaimed, "I don't know which is worse, freezing to death in this hole or dying from the bombing outside."

My stepfather, joking with her, said, "At least if we die here, no one will have to bury us. We would already be in our graves." We were scared but still laughed at his remarks.

Finally, my brother calmed down, and I dozed off in an uneasy sleep. Pain under my arm and on my stomach woke me. "Help me, Mother!" I yelled, "Leeches are all over me!" She tried to help, but it was too dark for her to see. Somehow, I managed to remove them and put them in the urine bucket by myself.

When I calmed down, Mother said to me, "Those leeches remind me of when you were a year old and had the measles. You had a high fever, and I had to take you to an herb doctor in another town. We walked right under a mortar attack and had to jump in a ditch full of water. When the explosions stopped, we climbed back to dry ground and found leeches covering us. By the time I got rid of them, your fever was gone, so we returned home."

Just as Mother finished her story, we heard a loud explosion from above. The force of the blast caused part of the bunker to cave in, and my brother started screaming louder than ever. My stepfather listened for a moment and said, "That bomb hit our house again, I just don't know where." We crossed ourselves and prayed for everyone's safety. My step grandmother and my stepbrother, Den, were away, but two maids were in the other bunker in the kitchen.

My stepfather waited for a while and climbed out. A few moments later, he returned and said, "No one was hurt, but the bomb damaged the house, and I think some of our animals were killed. I'll have to wait until daylight to see more." He sighed as he lowered himself into the bunker.

Before morning broke, I got out of the bunker after my stepfather and ran to the scene. The bomb flattened one corner of the big house where they stored food and vegetables and part of the wing where the animals were kept. Fruits, vegetables, and dead animals, mixed with fallen red bricks were scattered all over the courtyard. The bomb killed many of our chickens, pigs, and one of my stepfather's favorite water buffaloes, who was gentle, hardworking, and very timid. He had been more than just a work animal; he was also my stepfather's pet.

Upon hearing the news of the bombing, relatives and neighbors came to help. My job was to help stack the broken bricks into one big pile while the others cleaned and swept. The dead animals were cleaned, dressed, and cooked, so that when the work was done, we had a feast. The leftovers were shared with those who had helped. Within weeks, we had restored the house to near normal, with only a few patches and scars remaining.

Not long after the bomb struck our home, school went on summer break, and unfortunately, my stepbrother Den and I were home together. It was like putting a dog and a cat in the same pen. Since Den was older and had more authority, I was at a disadvantage, and it was no use telling my parents about any mistreatment.

Den thought of himself as quite the bird hunter. He made a powerful slingshot from a hardwood limb and a strip of bicycle inner tube. It was my job to provide the ammunition—dried clay balls. He showed me how to make them. First, I had to go to the pond and collect moist clay, then I rolled the clay into marble-sized balls and dried them in the sun. When they were dry, I took them to the kitchen and cooked them with rice straw until they turned pale red and hardened. Den knew my step-father had forbidden me from going into the kitchen, and he always made sure no one was around before he ordered me to make another batch. If they were not the right size, he made me redo them.

He was not as good with the slingshot as he thought, and he always blamed me when he came home from a hunt empty-handed, saying that I had not made the pellets right. He would punish me by making me stand in the courtyard and using me for target practice. I didn't dare cry or complain, and I was too scared of him to tell my parents—he threatened that if I told anyone about him, and what he had done to me, he would punish me harder.

One afternoon, I was in a jackfruit tree, singing songs I had learned in school, when I felt something hit me. Looking down, I saw Den with his slingshot and knew he was responsible. Another pellet hit my face, and I cried as I scrambled down the tree. Just then, Mother came home.

She saw my tears and noticed the welts on my face. "What happened to you?" she asked. But I was afraid to tell her the truth, because Den was nearby listening, and I was frightened of what he might do to me if I did.

"While I was in the tree, ants bit me," I replied.

"You are not supposed to be climbing trees," Mother scolded. "You got what you deserved." From the corner of my eye, I could see Den, sitting across the courtyard with a satisfied grin on his face.

Not long after that, I was alone sitting on the steps watching the fish, and I thought about how much fun it would be to catch them. I went to Den's room and borrowed his bamboo rod, with the line and hook attached. I walked out onto the porch where there were several decorated, brass pots of various sizes. They were used to clean vegetables, wash clothes and dishes, and the largest were used for bathing. I dragged the largest pot near the pond and filled it with water. Using flies and grasshoppers for bait, I caught a pot full of fish. When I was done fishing, I looked in the pot and noticed that some were dying and could only swim sideways; some were dead and floated upside down. I couldn't wait for Mother to come home, so that I could show her all the fish I had caught for dinner.

Unfortunately for me, my stepfather came home first. When he saw the fish, his face turned blue with anger. "Do you want to fish?" he shouted. "I'll teach you how to fish!"

He grabbed the rod from my hand with a fish still hanging from the line, and beat me with it until it broke. He threw the rod aside, picked me up, and threw me into the pond. Still angry, he picked up the huge pot full of fish and dumped it on top of me. He threw the pot aside, and was huffing and puffing as he stormed away.

Mother came home and saw the tail end of the fracas. "Please help me," I sobbed. "I was just trying to catch dinner, but Father is so mad. Please, Mother, ask Father to forgive me."

Before she had a chance to respond, my stepfather returned and told her what I had done. She glared at the dead fish and at me, and then ordered, "Get out of the pond right now!"

With tears streaming down my face, I climbed out. Mother grabbed the back of my collar and dragged me to the courtyard. She made me lay face down while she looked for a stick.

There was no stick to be found, and Mother glared at me. "Where are the sticks?" she asked.

"They are all gone," I told her between sobs. "I didn't like them and threw them away."

This made her even angrier. "For every stick you threw away, you're going to get one on your behind," she yelled.

"She should get one for every fish she killed, too," my stepfather added.

Mother found a stick and gave me several good whacks. "Go wash your face and change your clothes," she said. "If I ever catch you fishing or throwing sticks away again, I'll hit you one hundred times as hard." I said nothing as I sobbed all the way to my room. I changed clothes, went to the pond, and washed my face. I looked at all of the dead fish floating in the pond and wondered why Mother didn't cook them as she used to.

The day after I got in trouble over the fish, Mother woke me before dawn and told me to go to church with her. Being a devout Catholic, she went to church almost every morning, waiting until the bombing quieted down before she left the house.

"After being so bad yesterday, you need to go to church and ask God for forgiveness," she admonished. We climbed out of the bunker and changed clothes.

Mother wore a pale yellow ao dai, and I wore a white one. Our ao dais looked like the top of our pajamas, except they had two longer flaps, which hung long, close to our ankles. This was considered our formal attire, and people from the village often wore them over daily clothes, for church, and other functions.

It was so early that it was still dark when we left the house. I was scared of the darkness, so I walked behind Mother, holding onto her dress with one hand and covering one eye with the other. As we came near a large banyan tree, I hesitated. "I don't want to walk near the haunted tree," I said. "Why don't we go the way we always do?"

"Come on and hurry up," she responded, "or we'll be late for Mass. If you get scared, cross yourself, and start praying. God will protect you."

Still afraid, I kept one of my eyes covered and looked up into the dark branches with the other. My overactive imagination started playing tricks on me, and I saw a horrible face looking straight at me. "There's something in the tree!" I whimpered. "It looks like someone's face."

"Don't be silly," Mother chided. "I've passed here often in the dark, and I've seen nothing. Keep walking and stop looking up there."

I listened to Mother, closed both of my eyes, and let her guide me.

After we passed the tree, Mother confided, "One dark morning I did see what looked like a young man, hanging by a rope from the tree. His eyes were rolled up, his tongue was sticking out, and his clothes were ghostly white."

Before she told her story, I was scared, but after she finished her story, I was terrified. I jumped up and, like a magnet, wrapped both of my arms around her waist and both of my legs around her legs so tight that she couldn't walk. I was crying from fright, and she was laughing so hard she couldn't move. She tried to pull me away, but she couldn't loosen my grip.

She struggled with me for a while but grew concerned that we'd be late for church, so she lifted me to her back and carried me the rest of the way.

I held on to her neck with my eyes closed, and she told me the history of the haunted tree. "A long time ago, two young people were very much in love," she said. "The girl's family was very rich, but the boy's family was poor. He worked as a gardener for her father. They fell in love and wanted to get married, but the girl's father wouldn't allow it. He told the boy he must bring expensive engagement gifts, like gold, silver, tea, and liqueur. In addition, before the wedding day, he must come up with cows, water buffaloes, pigs, and chickens, and he must prepare for an extravagant wedding party for hundreds of guests. The boy didn't have enough to eat, much less the means to provide what her father demanded."

"One quiet night, while everyone was asleep, the two lovers were so desperate to be together they took ropes to the tree and hung themselves. The following morning, when they were found, their faces had turned blue, their eyes were rolled up, and their tongues were hanging out. Pinned to each chest was a note, "We are together at last." By the time Mother finished her story, we had reached the church.

After Mass, we took a shortcut home. On our way, I spotted a persimmon tree, full of ripe fruit. "May I stay behind for a while, to pick fruit?" I asked Mother.

"Yes, but you'd better not get your ao dai dirty," she warned.

"Yes, Mother," I assured her.

I waited until she was out of sight and headed for the tree. It was overloaded with ripe, yellow persimmons. I filled my stomach, then used the flap of my white dress for a basket and picked as much fruit as it would hold. I climbed down, eager to go home and share the fruit with my mother.

As I approached our fishpond, a large and beautiful dragonfly darted in front of me. I wanted it for my pet collection and gave immediate chase. I stalked him and tried to grab his tail, but as soon as I got close to him, he flew, so I chased him back and forth. My cunning didn't fool him, though, and he flew away. Afraid of losing him, I took off after him at full speed, but I tripped over a tree stump and fell flat on my face, squashing most of the ripe, yellow fruit beneath me, some rolling into the pond. I got back on my feet just in time to see the dragonfly disappear behind the bushes. Then, I looked down at myself and thought, "What a mess!" The sticky yellow fruit was all over my white dress, and the juice soaked through my clothes—I had ruined it. I tried to rub the stains off, but that just made it worse. I knew Mother was going to punish me. I thought about those bamboo sticks and decided to blame the entire incident on the dragonfly. After all, it was all his fault.

I walked into the courtyard, keeping a wary eye out for my parents. Luckily, Cay saw me first and rushed me into the kitchen. She ran to the closet, returned with clean clothes and told me to change, so she could wash the soiled one. She reminded me of how lucky I was that she spotted me first, and I replied with a thankful look and a big smile.

Returning to the courtyard, I saw Mother carrying something in her hands. Without knowing what happened to me, she drew closer. She opened her hands to show me a tiny, yellow baby chicken. "A hawk flew by and dropped the chicken right in front of me," she said. "Would you like to have it?"

"Of course!" I said. I scooped the chick from her hands and held it close to my chest. I was so happy to have such a beautiful pet of my own. The poor little thing didn't look more than a couple of days old.

I thanked Mother for the gift and went to the kitchen, looking for something to feed the chick. But before I found food, I looked it over and noticed one of its legs was broken. I tried to fix it, but I couldn't. I was concerned and ran to Mother to show her what had happened. "It will be fine," she said. "Chickens can survive with one leg." Even with its broken leg, I still fell in love with it. I took the chick to the rice bin, chewed up a hand full of rice, and fed it to him.

"It's eating!" I yelled. "I think it's going to live!"

For the rest of the day, I carried the chicken with me wherever I went. I was so proud of him and showed him to everyone I saw. "I bet it's a boy," I thought, and I named him Chip-Chip, because he chirped all day, calling for his mother. I took him to a pile of bricks, selected a few good ones, and built a house for him inside my room. When Mother realized where I had built the house, she made me move it outside. I did as she said but built it right in front of my door. When darkness fell, I put him in his house and covered him with my old clothes to keep him warm. I sat with him until he stopped chirping and went to sleep, then I went to bed. From then on, I was never apart from my Chip-Chip.

Weeks passed and Chip-Chip got bigger. Chip-Chip turned out to be a "he" as I had suspected. He started growing feathers, but, at first, they were no more than short, stubby quills—he looked more like a porcupine than a chicken. He got around by hopping on one leg, and he followed me everywhere I went. When I was up a tree, he would sit underneath. While I was in the pond, he would sit on the edge of the water to wait. I wasn't supposed to swim in the pond, but my parents had many ponds and trees, and they couldn't watch them all. The maids loved and protected me, and they never told on me. They looked away and let me do whatever I pleased. I loved them, and I loved my chicken. I spent most of my day protecting him from dogs and cats and finding insects to feed him. He ate too much and got very fat, so sometimes his leg couldn't support him, and he fell over like a ball. I always laughed when that happened, but then picked him up and comforted him.

I teased him sometimes by hiding and then calling to him. He would look around for me, with his neck stretched up high, and when he couldn't find me, he panicked, hopping around searching for me. Then, feeling sorry for him, I would come out of my hiding place, pick him up, kiss him, and hold him close to my heart.

The older he grew, the more colorful and beautiful he became. We were never apart from each other—he was my best friend, and I loved him more than anything in the world. To have more time to spend with

Chip-Chip, I cut down my collection of other pets. I devoted every waking minute to him, except for school and church.

As the fighting grew worse, we often had to go to the bunker during the day to escape the bombs and bullets. My poor chicken was not allowed in the bunker, and he had to sleep outside. The bunker dried out a little, and although we no longer had a problem with leeches, we still had to deal with frogs and snakes. By then, my little brother had grown accustomed to the bunker and seldom cried. Mother was pregnant again, and it was very uncomfortable for her to be in the bunker, but she had no choice.

We awoke to a loud banging from above one morning. Thu, one of our field hands, yelled, "The French and Viet Minh are fighting near the edge of town, close to my house! You should all leave while there's still a chance!" Poor Thu had run all the way from his home to warn us.

He helped my stepfather lift the bunker cover, and we all scrambled out. My stepfather thanked Thu, who then rushed back home to take care of his own family. Mother grabbed some gold and money, picked up some clothes, put it all in a bag, and told me to carry it. She then told the maids, who were at her doorstep, to go home to their families. Mother carried my brother, I carried the bag, and we ran out of town before dawn. When we got to the main road leading to the big city, I looked for my stepfather, but didn't see him, and guessed he was running ahead.

"My chicken! Oh, my God, I forgot my chicken!" I screamed. "I have to go back to get him, Mother!"

"There is no way you can go back," Mother said, "They are probably fighting near our house right now."

I got weak in the knees. Tears rolled down my cheeks as I slowed to let the others go ahead. I was so concerned about Chip-Chip that I didn't want to take another step.

"How could he survive with only one leg?" I cried. "Besides he is still locked in his brick house. Who will let him out and take care of him?" I took off toward our house, determined to save him. Mother saw what I was doing and asked one of the men in the group to get me. I struggled with him as he grabbed my arm and dragged me back.

"Please let me go," I begged. "I have to go back for my chicken."

He laughed and said, "Right now, your life is more important than some chicken's." He left me with my mother and ran ahead of us.

The stranger didn't understand how much the chicken meant to me. He was my only friend, and I loved him. Rejoining Mother, my tears streamed so heavily, I could barely see where I was going.

Gunfire erupted all around us. Someone shouted, "Take cover!"

We were all so confused and didn't know which way to go or which side of the road to jump to. Mother carried Kinh in one hand and held me with the other, as she jumped from the road and ducked into a rice field. I saw the man who had taken me back to Mother running back in our direction. I didn't understand why he would run in the opposite direction. Perhaps he saw a single, pregnant woman, with two kids, and ran back to help. Before he could get very far, a bullet stopped him, and he fell flat on his face. He twisted and turned for a few seconds and then lay still.

My little brother started to cry, so Mother forced her breast in his mouth to keep him quiet. Far ahead, I saw another man running along the edge of the road. I heard a shot and watched him fall into the field. He cried for help, but no one could come because everyone was too scared to move. A few minutes later, he also fell silent.

When the shooting calmed down, a member of our group went over to examine the two men. "They are both dead," he said. "We should move on."

Hastily, we got back on the road and ran for our lives. Mother carried Kinh, which slowed her down. I wanted to help her, but Kinh was too big for me to carry. Luckily, another man who was running with us offered to carry him, and Mother was happy to let him. With her hands free, Mother then carried my bag.

The man told Mother, "The reason we were being shot at is because neither side wants us to leave the town. They want us there, so they can use us as pawns in their senseless games."

We got farther away from the sound of bullets, and with the excitement behind us, I started thinking of my chicken again. "I'm so sorry," I cried. "I wish I could have taken you with me. I hope and pray you will be fine and will be waiting for me when I come back."

The burning sun was over our heads, and I was hot and hungry. I turned to Mother and exclaimed, "I can't walk another step. I'm hot, I'm tired, I'm thirsty, and I'm hungry."

Mother looked at me with tender eyes, and I knew she was feeling sorry for me. "It will only be a little longer," she said. "We're getting close to a city. We'll have something to eat, and we can rest there. I've been there before, and I know we are very close. We would have been there much sooner if we didn't have to stop so many times." A man walking behind us saw how tired I was and offered to carry me, but I declined.

When we reached the outskirts of Dong Nam that afternoon, those ahead of us split off in different directions. I heard strange noises but could see nothing in the distance. We drew closer to a paved road, and I saw all sorts of strange machines on wheels. I was excited and curious about all of these strange-looking things that kept whizzing past us.

"What are all those?" I asked Mother.

"Those are cars, trucks, and cyclos," she replied.

I'd never seen anything like them in my life. I thought my stepbrother Den's bicycle was interesting, but this was unbelievable. I stared at all the moving vehicles, while Mother said goodbye to our walking companions and thanked the man who had helped carry my brother.

"Hurry up and come along," she said, as she walked down a paved road. "Cyclo! Cyclo!" Mother called and waved at a three-wheeled vehicle. The driver stopped and Mother told him where she wanted to go. After some bickering over the price, we got on the cyclo, and the driver peddled away.

I looked around in amazement. Everything was so fascinating. Even the road we were on was black and smooth, not like the dirt and clay roads I was used to. The buildings along the road looked different, too. They were built very close to each other—some even shared the same wall. Mother told me that most of them were small businesses or stores. People were walking around everywhere. I had never seen so many people before, and they were dressed so differently from us. Pointing out all the differences to Mother, I shouted "Look at that, Mother! Mother, look!" I fell in love with the excitement. If it hadn't been for my chicken in the country, I would have wanted to stay there forever. Obviously, Mother had been to this city before. She knew where to go and didn't share my excitement and enthusiasm.

The cyclo stopped in front of a store. "This house belongs to your father's friend," Mother said, as we climbed down from the cyclo, and she paid the driver.

She carried my brother, and I dragged along behind her, toting a bag. We walked through a room lined with shelves of Chinese herbs and medicine, into the back of the building. My stepfather was already there. I don't know how he got there so fast. He was already having dinner and drinking tea with his friend's family. There were a dozen or so people there, not counting my stepfather, who all smiled as we walked in. We greeted the owners, and they greeted us in return. I glanced around the small place for a few seconds, then ran outside and began counting cars. I was so excited about everything that for a moment, I forgot how tired and hungry I was.

I pointed to each passing vehicle, counting "ninety-eight, ninety-nine ..." Then, I heard "Loan Oi!" My mother was calling me. "Come inside and wash up for supper," she said as she walked toward me.

I turned around and said, "I'm not hungry, Mother. I want to stay here and count cars."

Mother glared at me and said nothing more, but I knew that look and realized I had to do what she said, so I followed her to the bathroom. The house was built of brick and wood. The front was used for selling Chinese herbal medicine, and the back was divided into smaller living quarters by curtains.

Mother turned on the water faucet for me. I'd never seen one before. "Where does the water come from?" I asked.

She ignored my question and told me to hurry up; people were waiting for us, so they could eat. There were ten or more people seated at the table. Except for my brother and me, there were no other children. The table was too small for all of us, so Mother asked if some of us, including herself and me, could sit on a grass mat on the floor. The food was then divided between the two groups. There were too many strangers. I was confused and wasn't sure where to sit or how to eat. Mother told me to sit next to her, and she would guide me.

I waited until everyone else started eating before I picked up my chopsticks. The food looked good, and I was very hungry, but I was afraid to eat what I wanted. I ate what I needed, then asked to be excused to go back outside. I intended to continue counting cars, but I stood up and realized how tired I was. I asked Mother to point to a place where I could sleep, and she directed me to a corner where our bag of clothes already sat on the grass mat, on the floor. "You can sleep next to the clothes," she said. I walked toward the corner, but I don't remember lying down; I think I was asleep before hitting the floor.

A lot of people had fled to the city when the fighting started in our village. The house where we sought refuge was very cramped. There were too many people in the small space to begin with, and my family of four just added to the already crowded conditions. We had to eat and sleep on top of each other.

We were there for several days, but I seldom saw my stepfather. He often disappeared somewhere, while Mother stayed behind to help cook, clean, and keep an eye on my little brother.

The city helped keep me amused—it was so interesting. There were French soldiers stationed nearby, and they often walked up and down the street. They looked different from any humans I had ever seen. Many of them were hairy, with blue eyes, pale skin, and yellow or red hair; some were black, and their skin was dark as night. They had teeth so white they must have shined in the dark, and they seemed very nice—nothing at all like I had heard or imagined.

I'll never forget the first time I saw a Frenchman. I was standing in front of the house counting cars when a group of about six or seven black and white French soldiers appeared out of nowhere. They stopped right in front of me, then one of them said something to me in their strange language. I took a quick look at them and ran inside, trembling in fear. I was curious, however, and didn't go far. I stood just inside the doorjamb and stuck my head out to stare at them.

One black man smiled and signaled for me to come to him. I shook my head no and hid my face behind the door. He said something to the others, and they all laughed. I was too scared to even smile. I hid until they left, then stepped out to watch them walk away.

"What kind of people are they?" I wondered. "They look and act like humans, but they talk like birds."

A week passed, and I became friends with four or five boys and girls in the area who were about my age, and we played games together. We often went to a huge French garbage dump, looking for things to play with. Among the treasures we found there were dozens of white balloons. We took them home, blew them up, and marched up and down the street.

A stranger stopped us right in the middle of our parade and pointed to the balloons. "You should throw those nasty things away," he said.

"Why?" I asked, "We didn't steal the balloons. We found them in the garbage dump."

The stranger shook his head in dismay and replied, "Those are not balloons. They are dirty condoms that French soldiers use for protection."

We looked at each other in puzzlement. Realizing we didn't understand, he took us aside and explained how they were used. When he finished his last word, we threw the balloons away and ran home to wash our mouths with soap, but before going inside, I stopped at the doorstep to look back at those balloons, bouncing up and down as cars passed. I wished they hadn't been so dirty.

Then one day as I was playing, Mother told me the Viet Minh had driven the French from Luong Dong, and that we were going home. My stepfather had already left to see about the house. This was good news for me, because, at last, I could see my Chip-Chip.

Our journey started the next morning. We took a cyclo to the dirt road leading home, and from there we walked. I carried a bag of clothes and food for lunch while Mother carried Kinh. In my haste to see my chicken, I left Mother far behind. I ran until my legs were too tired to go any farther, then found a shady tree, sat down, and waited for Mother to catch up. I dozed off. When she arrived, she woke me, and we had lunch.

"Where is the rest of our family?" I asked.

"They all went in different directions when the fighting started," she replied, "but most of them should be home by now. With the French gone, things should be back to normal." We drank water from the rice field after we ate, and started walking again.

I could tell Mother was tired and asked her if I could carry Kinh for a while.

"No," she said, "your brother is almost as big as you are. You're doing enough to carry yourself and the bag of clothes."

It was almost dark when we arrived home. I left the bag of clothes at the gate and climbed over into the courtyard. I started looking and calling for my chicken, but there was no sign of him. The house I had built for him was empty. I sat with my back against the wall, wondering where he could be. I heard Mother at the gate and ran to open it.

"I can't find my chicken anywhere," I told her, as I picked up the bag of clothes.

"Chickens go to sleep early. Wait until tomorrow. Finding him in the daylight will be easier," she said, and we walked into the courtyard.

I went to bed very worried about my Chip-Chip but was so tired, I was able to fall into a deep sleep. The following morning, voices outside of my room woke me, and I jumped out of bed. Somehow, the maids knew we were home, came back, and were preparing breakfast. Instead of eating, I resumed the search for my pet.

Mother walked up to me and said, "If you want to see your chicken, go to the front pond. You'll find him at the corner of the step."

I was so happy! I thanked her and ran like lightning to the pond. I climbed down the steps, my heart beating with excitement. I couldn't wait to see him.

I looked around, but all I saw was a pile of feathers. I didn't realize what I was seeing until I looked closer at the feathers—they belonged to Chip-Chip! My fears rose as I poked through the feathers, and to my horror, found a decomposed chicken head. Someone had killed my poor Chip-Chip! I cried as I picked up a handful of feathers and held them to my chest. "Oh, God, why did you let him die? He was the only friend I had. From now on, who will run after me, who will watch me swim in the pond, and who will sit under the tree, waiting for me to come down?"

Mother and the maids took turns checking on me, but they knew I was upset and left me alone to grieve. I knelt by my poor Chip-Chip and cried until my knees hurt, then I got up to gather what was left of his feathers and his head, took them to the tea garden behind the house, and dug a deep hole with my bare hands. I placed his head and each of his feathers in the hole. Tears flowed as I filled it with dirt. "It's all my fault for not taking you with me," I said. "Why didn't you run and hide? Why did you let them kill you? You are my only friend, and now you're dead too, and I will never see you again."

Standing up, I looked for tea sticks to make a cross. I tied two of them together with banana string and placed it on the end of his grave. "I will miss you and will never forget you," I mumbled. I sat and let the tears dampen my clothes. I heard someone sigh behind me. When I turned around, I saw Mother standing there with tears in her eyes.

"How long have you been standing there?" I asked, as I stood up and dusted my clothes.

"Not long," she replied.

My dead chicken reminded me of my father and my hometown, and I had an urge to visit them. Looking up at my mother, I asked, "Would you mind if I went back to see Father's grave and visit my relatives?"

"That would be fine," she answered. "I'll find someone going that way and ask them to take you along." She held my hand, as we walked back to the house.

When we returned, I let go of Mother's hand and walked toward the pond. I sat under a large jackfruit tree and watched the fish swim back and forth, and up and down in the water. They seemed happy chasing each other. Now and then, they would grab an unfortunate bug that fell from the air. The sky turned dark, and it started to rain. It must have rained a lot while we were gone, because the pond water was high and was level with the road.

Raindrops hit the water, and the fish disappeared. I didn't even move, I just sat there staring at the water for what seemed like hours, as the rain started coming down harder. The surface of the pond became rougher. The raindrops created bubbles, and the fish thought they were something to eat. Some swam to the surface and grabbed the bubbles, and when they popped, the fish sank back, embarrassed by their folly. Their antics put a smile on my face. I watched this peaceful scene and let the rainwater run down my face.

My stepfather's angry voice shattered the quiet. "Loan, come in here!" he yelled from the house. "Do you know it's raining out there?"

I obeyed, tiptoeing toward him. When I got within reach, he slapped me hard across the face and said, "Go to your room and change your clothes. Don't let me catch you sitting in the rain like that again."

"Yes, Father," I responded, and walked toward my room. Tears mixed with the raindrops running down my face.

Suddenly, I heard a commotion outside the gate. I stopped at the doorstep and turned to see what was going on. People were running around, trying to catch traveling fish. When heavy monsoon rains filled the ponds, the fish tried to move from one pond to another to find a mate or fresher water by crossing the road that divided the ponds. People in our village knew this, so they waited for heavy rains to catch the fish. I watched people having fun, fighting over the fish. They screamed and laughed, as they stumbled and fell on the slippery road. I laughed out loud though the tears were still damp on my cheeks.

I heard my stepfather's stern voice again. "What are you waiting for?" he questioned. "Why haven't you changed your clothes yet? Do you need for me to show you how to change your clothes?" I stopped laughing, dried my tears, and walked into my room.

A week after burying my chicken, Mother called me to her room and said, "I just heard that Uncle Ky moved to Cao Moc, an independent town, where we once lived for a few months, while we tried to escape from the Viet Minh. Remember? I know two women friends of mine are going there tomorrow. Would you like to visit him?"

Delighted to have the chance to get out from under my stepfather's rigid thumb and see my favorite uncle and his family, I accepted without blinking an eye. Early the following morning, Mother helped me pack and made a big rice ball for me to take on the trip. While waiting for the two women to come for me, Mother gave me a handful of money for the trip and said, "Be careful and tell your uncle and aunt that I said hello and share some of this money with your cousins."

"Yes, Mother."

The two ladies came as the sun was rising—one was about thirty and the other a little older. While they were talking to Mother, I said goodbye to everyone and made a quick visit to Chip-Chip's grave.

"Loan Oi!" Mother called. I went back to my room and picked up my bag of clothes. I said goodbye to Mother and followed the two strangers. As I walked away, I could hear Mother crying behind me.

Chapter 6

CHAIN OF TEARS

I WAS HAPPY to be on my way to my Uncle Ky's house and away from my stepfather's watchful eye for a while. On our way, we walked to the edge of a river, stopped to eat lunch, and waited for a boat to take us across. A few hours later, a small boat arrived. After we boarded the boat, the operator paddled it against the current to reach the other side; we paid him and started walking again.

The younger woman told me about the conditions in Cao Moc as we walked. "The people there dug huge trenches and built high walls to keep both the French and the Viet Minh out," she said. "They mined the fields surrounding the wall. There's only one small entrance, overlooked by a guardhouse. The guards allow people to come and go during the day, but at night the gates are secured with explosives and barbed wire."

"Villagers grow food inside the wall," she continued, "and an occasional plane drops food and medical supplies."

"Who do the planes belong to?" I asked.

"I have no idea," she replied. "The townspeople drew a large white cross in the church courtyard, and planes drop supplies there."

We walked for two days, stopping in various towns along the way, so the two women could visit their families. We approached the village of Cao Moc one afternoon just as the sun was setting. The two women argued about whether we should enter the city or wait until morning. Eventually, the younger woman, who lived in the village, convinced the other one to continue. The sky darkened as we drew closer.

"I know a path that will avoid the land mines," the younger woman said. "Follow me and be careful. If your foot happens to touch a string or anything strange, stop at once, don't move, and wait for my instructions."

This made me very nervous, so I crossed myself and prayed. My heart was pounding as we took each step and slowly ventured toward the gate.

Suddenly, a loud gunshot stopped us in our tracks, and a man's voice shouted from the lookout tower, "Stay where you are and don't move, or I'll shoot!" A guard shined a bright light in our face and asked, "Who are you?"

The younger woman replied, "We live here and are just coming home a little late. Please let us in."

"You're all fools!" the guard yelled. "You could have been blown to bits by the land mines out there. What are your names and where do you live?" The younger woman told the guard who she was and where her home was located.

Satisfied with her answer, he yelled to another guard below to open the gate, and we entered. The second guard pointed his gun at us as he closed the gate and said, "Walk towards me, one at a time, with your hands up."

We dropped our belongings, held up our hands, and did as he asked. He patted us down, searched our possessions, and then he checked our papers. He was just finishing with the inspection, when a loud explosion almost shattered my eardrums.

"Another rat just blew himself up," the guard said. "It's nothing to worry about. Now go on about your business and be more careful the next time."

After we thanked the guard and walked away, I told the two ladies who escorted me how much I appreciated their help and asked the younger one for directions to my Uncle Ky's house. Thankfully, he lived only a couple of houses from the gate, and I walked alone to his home in the darkness. I knocked on the front door, but no one answered. Assuming they were all asleep and being extremely exhausted from my journey, I found myself a comfortable spot on the porch, lay down, and shut my eyes.

I was in a deep sleep when Uncle Ky woke me. He had just come from guard duty. He smiled and rubbed my head, and we exchanged pleasantries. Then he grew serious and said, "I just helped clean up what was left of a man's body. He stepped on a mine last night and was blown to pieces. We put him in a bag, and he will be buried later this morning."

Uncle Ky's words made me realize how close we had come to being blown up—the young woman's idea could have killed us. I told Uncle Ky what the guard said about a rat being blown up. He shook his head, and explained, "When we have a war like this, human life becomes meaningless. We say our dead are sacrificed for a good cause; the enemy looks upon the same death and says it was just another rat in the field." The thought of people dying gave me the chills.

Uncle Ky pushed the door aside and said, "You didn't have to sleep outside last night; the door was open."

"I arrived late," I said, "and didn't want to disturb anyone, so I decided to sleep outside."

I followed him inside; our conversation awoke my two cousins. To my delight, when they saw me, they jumped from their bed and ran to me, yelling, "You're here! You're here!"

We were very happy to see each other again—cousin Tuan smiled, and his younger brother rubbed my hand. It had been too long since we'd seen each other, and I couldn't believe how much they had grown.

Since his wife was out of town buying food, Uncle Ky asked me to help him make breakfast. After our meal, we cleaned up and went to the garden to work. When it got too hot, my cousins and I jumped into the pond to cool off. We always had such a great time together.

I loved Uncle Ky and his family, and I would have been happy to live with them for the rest of my life. He was a kind and gentle man who taught us to love and respect others and didn't treat us like animals who needed training. His wife was a very quiet woman, who cooked our meager meals, cleaned house, washed clothes, and tended to their small garden. She seldom smiled or talked to me, or to her husband and her own children. In spite of her quiet personality, I knew she was sweet and she loved us.

Conditions in the village grew worse; people were getting hungry and were near panic. And while the village leaders met often and tried to figure out how to deal with the lack of food, there was nothing they could do. For several days, all we ate were boiled weeds, dipped in fish sauce, without rice.

The fighting reached a critical stage in March of 1954 when the French challenged the Viet Minh at Dien Bien Phu. Both sides were hoping for a decisive victory before the Geneva Convention. The French underestimated the Viet Minh and were defeated. France lost more than a battle at Dien Bien Phu—it lost the war and the last remnants of its Indochinese Empire.

In May of 1954, delegates to the Geneva Convention decided, over objections from both the north and the south, to partition Vietnam at the 17th Parallel. Bao Dai was to govern the Republic of South Vietnam, with Ngo Dinh Diem as his head of state. Ho Chi Minh and key leaders of the Viet Minh were to govern North Vietnam.

The delegates also agreed to allow voluntary relocation to and from both North and South Vietnam. Elections to unify the country were to be held in July of 1956.

When they carried out the agreements, about 50,000 Viet Minh sympathizers left the south and moved north. Almost 900,000 people, most of them Catholic, moved from the north to the south, under the most difficult of conditions. This southern exodus caught the North Vietnamese officials by surprise, and they stopped many of those who tried to leave. The plight of those who made it to South Vietnam was pathetic.

Uncle Ky took me aside one morning and said, "You must go back to your mother, because I don't have enough to feed you. I'll send you back when I find someone going there."

"Oh, Uncle!" I cried, "I don't want to leave you."

He looked at me and said in a gentle voice, "I'm sending you home, because I love you and want you to have a better life than I can give you."

"I don't care about the food," I argued. "I'm so happy here. Can I please stay?" He said nothing, as tears welled in his eyes. It was only on very rare occasions that I saw my uncle cry.

He was right, of course. He couldn't feed his own family; how could he feed me? A few days later, he found a couple who was traveling to Luong Dong and asked them to take me to my mother. They agreed, and before leaving, we all got together on the front porch and had a tearful goodbye. Thankfully, the trip home didn't take as long as the trip to Cao Moc. When we arrived, I thanked my traveling companions, said goodbye, and walked into the courtyard of my stepfather's home through the back gate.

As I entered, I saw maids emptying my stepfather's fishpond by dipping water from the pond and depositing it into another. They all smiled and waved at me as I walked by, and I smiled and waved back. I drew closer to the empty pond and was shocked to see them throwing my stepfather's rare fish collection into bamboo baskets. But I didn't mention it because at the moment, I was more interested in my mother than in the fish.

"Where is my mother?" I asked Cay.

"She's in her room," she replied. "She's been waiting for you. I'm sure she'll be glad to see you."

I ran to Mother's room where I found her sitting on the edge of the bed, fanning my baby brother. Then I noticed her stomach had gotten bigger and was protruding. She signaled for me to be quiet, so I wouldn't wake the baby, and she got up from the bed, motioning for me to follow her outside.

"I'm so glad you're back," she said. "I sent a message to your uncle, asking him to send you home. I've been waiting for you to return. I thought about going to get you, but I couldn't. The rest of the family has already left for South Vietnam. Your father wanted me to come with him, but I convinced him to let me stay behind and wait for you. I was afraid if I left, I'd never see you again." I understood then why my uncle sent me home—my mother wanted me.

I listened to her as we walked toward the pond. "Why are they catching all of Father's fish?" I asked. "Won't he be angry when he comes home?"

"I don't think we'll ever be back here again," she replied. "And since we are leaving, I decided to give all the fish away. I told the maids they can take all the fish they can carry and take anything else in the house they can use. We won't need them anymore."

"Where are we going?" I asked Mother.

"We are moving to South Vietnam, for good." she replied.

I let her words sink in. I was sad and concerned about leaving, but then I became distracted by the maids and what they were doing—laughing and yelling and having a good time chasing the slippery fish in the pond.

"Can I go help them?" I asked.

"Go ahead," Mother said with a smile, "just don't hurt yourself. We have a long walk ahead of us."

Excited to be able to join in the fun, I rolled up my pants and walked into the mud. But it was slippery, I stumbled, fell on my butt, and slid all the way to the middle of the pond. The maids laughed as they watched me struggling in the mud. When I finally got to my feet, I started flailing around trying to catch a fish. Cay saw what I was doing and stopped me. She showed me how to catch a catfish without being stung. I learned fast and was able to capture a few catfish on my own. The maids' faces were so muddy that I couldn't tell them apart until they said something. We had so much fun. And we didn't just catch fish; we also took turns throwing mud at each other. Mother stood at the steps and laughed at our antics. I wished the moment would never end, but when all the fish were caught, I was forced to get out of the muddy pond.

After we were out of the pond, the maids separated the fish and shared them with each other. They tried to give Mother the largest fish, but she wouldn't accept it. She told them we were leaving soon, and we would not have time to eat it. The work was done and most of us went to another pond to scrub off the mud and change clothes.

After getting dressed, I went back to the tea garden and looked for my chicken's grave. I found the cross I made, but the rain had washed the mound of dirt away, so I built the grave back and sat next to it, letting my tears flow.

A warm hand on my shoulder brought me back to reality. "Your mother says you'd better get ready to go." It was Cay. I got up and hugged her. It is not our custom to hug each other, but I couldn't help myself.

"I'll miss you when you are gone," she said, in tears.

"I don't want to leave you," I sobbed.

She looked at me and replied, "I hope you will grow up to be as nice as your mother. I'll pray for all of you." We let our tears flow as we walked hand-in-hand back to the house.

All the maids loved my mother, and they were always very good to me. Cay and Nhan, I felt, loved me the most. When they cooked good food, they always saved special parts for me. I knew Mother and I would miss them just as much as they would miss us.

After we walked back to the house, Cay was helping me pack my clothes when Mother came into the room. "Don't fold your clothes," she said. "You can't carry anything with you. We'll have to wear all the clothes we take. The only thing we dare carry is a little food."

"We must leave early in the morning, through the back gate," she cautioned. "We have to be careful and not let anyone know where we're going, because they might stop us. Just in case we are stopped, you must remember to say we are going to the next town to visit relatives and nothing more. It will take us a long time to get to Kien An, depending on how fast we walk. We'll meet your father when we get there."

Cay listened to Mother and said, "I want to go with you and help you find your family. You're eight months pregnant, and you're going to have a hard time walking alone, much less carrying another child."

Mother smiled and refused her help. She told her it was just too much to ask, but Cay kept insisting, until Mother finally accepted her offer. After it was decided that Cay would come with us, they left my room, and I started putting on layer after layer of clothes until I couldn't button them anymore. I went to bed and lay there like a stuffed scarecrow. Every time I took a deep breath, another button would pop open. At first, I tried to button them back, but soon, I got tired and gave up. Thinking about the exciting trip, I tossed and turned for a long time before I was able to fall asleep.

The following morning, as we said our goodbyes, Mother reminded the servants that if anyone asked about us, they should say we had gone to visit relatives in another town, and we would be back soon. No one was without tears.

We left before sunrise, stopped midday long enough to eat lunch, and walked until sunset. We walked from village to village and from rice field to rice field as there was no other transportation available. We traveled by day and rested by night. Some nights we found shelter in homes, but often we had to sleep by the roadside under the open sky. At first, I tried to keep count of the days we walked, but after a week, I lost track; it seemed like forever.

Armed soldiers stopped and searched us often. When they asked, "Where are you going?" the answer was always the same, "We are going to visit relatives in the next town."

Food was another problem; some days we ate very little and filled our stomachs with only water. Mother didn't carry too much money, because she was afraid she might be caught with it, so she carried only gold. I had no idea where she hid it, and I never asked.

Finally, we crossed the last river and boarded a bus, which took us to Kien An. It was a large city, full of people and thick with vehicles. We left the bus, entered a taxi, and told the driver to take us to the Catholic church where my stepfather said he'd wait for us. We found him there.

After arriving in Kien An, things settled down, and Cay asked Mother to let her return home. Mother tried to talk her into coming with us, but Cay chose to stay behind with her family. Mother gave Cay money and some of her jewelry. She thanked her for helping us, and with tears spilling from her eyes, she told Cay to take care of herself. Cay was too choked up to talk. She just nodded her head and let her tears flow, as she combed my hair with her fingers.

We were all heartbroken and let our tears stream down our faces. Finally, Cay pulled herself away from me and walked as fast as she could, without looking back. I watched her until her shadow disappeared into the crowded city. "I will miss her the most," I thought. "Who will take care of me now?"

* * *

Kien An was different from any place I had ever been. It was big and dirty and garbage was everywhere. But the big city, the uncountable people, and the endless vehicles excited me. And, of course, there were so many different kinds of food I had never seen before, such as ice cream, cookies, and cake.

We waited in Kien An for my stepsister, who was supposed to meet us there. Her husband arrived days earlier. We stayed together in the basement of an old church with several other refugees. Conditions were crowded and unsanitary, and every time it rained, water and garbage came in from the street. The basement was wet, dirty, and it smelled bad, but we were lucky to have a place to stay.

Our family shared the experiences of our trip with others who were staying in the church basement, and I discovered we were lucky to make it with our possessions intact. In fact, we were lucky to have made it at all. According to other refugees, many people were forced to turn back, and some had all their belongings taken away.

My stepfather's niece, whom I called my stepcousin, was a widow with a five-year-old son. One night, she shared her story, "I heard some female guards were checking women in their private places, looking for jewels. I swallowed mine and retrieved them when I went to the bathroom. I repeated this process until I arrived here. It's a good thing I did, or I wouldn't have them now," she said.

"I didn't have to," Mother told them. "I hid my money and jewels in my hair turban and in the hems of my clothes."

Mother's hair was long, and she combed it to one side, like a long ponytail. She used a black rectangular piece of velvet to roll her hair and draped it around her head, making a turban, as traditional North Vietnamese women wore.

A week passed, and my stepsister still hadn't shown up. My stepfather decided we could not wait any longer and took us to Hai Phong, where we would board the ship to South Vietnam. Once there, we stayed in one of hundreds of tents built for refugees near the harbor.

My mother at about age 37, with her hair turban, at the refugee camp.
This was from her ID card.

We found our living conditions in Hai Phong to be just as crowded as they were in the basement. There were about ten or fifteen families in each tent, and at night, we had to sleep almost on top of each other. Many of the young children didn't like sleeping with strangers in a strange place, and they cried all through the night—my brother was one of them. Poor Mother looked like she was going to have her baby at any moment, but she still had to care for and breast-feed my brother, who was only about a year old.

Open Mouth ship used during operation "Passage to Freedom."

Thousands of us waited for the ships to come, but there were too many people and not enough ships. Each time a ship arrived, there was yelling, fighting, and a rush to get to it. The chaos and turmoil in the tents can't be described—it was both exciting and terrifying. Those who didn't make it onto a ship had to line up for food three times a day. Sometimes, we had cooked food; other times, we only had bread and canned sardines. We used temporarily dug outhouses, surrounded with only sheets and blankets for privacy, but there were too many people and not enough holes. Some people could not wait and relieved themselves in the field. We didn't bathe, because there was not enough water.

Like the others, when we heard, "The ship is here, the ship is here," we ran as fast as we could, with our possessions in hand, trying to fight our way to the ship. Mother held my hand, and a relative carried my brother; my stepfather and his son-in-law carried the bags. Everyone was screaming, yelling, and pushing their way toward the water. I saw some people stepped on and then struggle to their feet, just in time to see the ship pull away from the shore. Again and again, we had to come back to the tent.

One day, my stepfather decided to stay at the dock and wait there, rather than go back to the tent. His method worked, and we boarded the "open mouth" ship the following morning. We called it the "open mouth," because the front hatch swung down to take on people, and when full, the ship's "mouth" closed.

After struggling to get on the ship, my stepbrother decided to stay behind and wait for his wife. Tears streamed down everyone's faces as we watched him walk into the oncoming throng. I cried out to him not to go back, but my voice was lost in the crowds, and he couldn't hear me.

My stepbrother-in-law was very dear to me, and I feared we would never see him again. I remembered that once, when he visited our family, my stepfather was punishing me for something I did, and he had the courage to step between my stepfather and me, rescuing me from further punishment. He received a few accidental whacks from my stepfather's stick in the process. It was scary to me then, but as I thought about it, I smiled through my tears.

The ship's blaring horn roused me from my daydream, and I watched as we moved out to deeper water. Many in the crowd on shore panicked. Some jumped into the water, trying to swim out to the ship, while others on board jumped and tried to swim back to shore to be with their loved ones.

The conditions onboard the ship were almost intolerable. People were packed in like sardines, and the noise was unbearable. Some shouted, while others sang, prayed, or cried. I could hear the loudspeaker giving instructions, but nobody listened. They sandwiched me in so tight that it was hard to breathe, and I wondered, at the time, if I could stand like this, all the way to South Vietnam.

The chaos of refugees trying to board a Navy ship, during operation "Passage to Freedom."

As the ship moved farther from shore, I thought of my relatives who were left behind and wondered if I would ever see them again. Mother began praying and told me to join her. I prayed for my relatives and for our uncertain journey.

As we stood praying, to my complete surprise, we drew alongside another huge ship. It appeared from nowhere, and, as small as I was, I could see it above people's hats. I stared at it in disbelief—it was bigger than any building I had ever seen.

Rope ladders hung down from the larger ship, and people began climbing them. I followed suit, after almost being knocked in the water by an impatient refugee. As I climbed higher, a white-skinned man appeared above me and held out his hand. He smiled as he picked me up and stood me on the deck. Once I felt secure, I looked around for several moments, transfixed by all of the foreign surroundings. I watched people being hoisted up from the smaller ship, and to my surprise, I saw Mother and Kinh being lifted with the cargo.

I was happy that she didn't have to climb the rope ladders, but before I had a chance to join her, my relatives and I were led to a different section of the ship, where I saw mountains of boxes of different sizes, stacked behind tables. Open boxes were on top of the tables, and between the boxes and the tables were women and men of differing nationalities. Some were Vietnamese nuns and priests, but most were white, with different colored hair and eyes, and some wore white uniforms.

"What is in the boxes?" I asked my stepcousin.

"Cookies, chocolate, French bread, and cans of sweet condensed milk," she replied, "and they're very good." She acted as if she had eaten them before. We then lined up, passed in front of the tables, and received a gift from each one.

"Do you know who this ship belongs to?" my stepcousin asked. I looked at her with a blank stare and shook my head. "It belongs to Americans," she continued. "All those people behind the tables, with white skin and light-colored hair, are Americans." I don't know how she knew so much—perhaps someone told her, or she read about it somewhere. Anyway, I was glad to see American people who were willing to help us.

At the end of the line, my hands were full, and my gifts were stacked up to my chin. A sailor with curly, bright-red hair led our family to a big open room, two or three levels below the deck. He spoke in broken Vietnamese but managed to tell us that we should stay there. He gave us a stack of white towels and several small, brown, empty bags.

After he left, I looked around at the crowded quarters and climbed into an empty bunk on the highest tier. My stepcousin and her son were in the middle bunk, just below me. I opened one of my gift boxes and discovered something that looked good to me—it looked like white cream sandwiched between two black cookies. I took a big bite, chewed it for a second, and spit it out. The bitter taste disappointed me. I put the remainder back in the box and tried the chocolate bar— it tasted even worse. I tried a few more things that were made of chocolate, but I didn't like them either. I stopped and wondered why Americans made cookies and chocolate so bitter instead of sweet. I put all of them away, but not before I licked the white cream between the two black cookies. I wanted to try the milk with bread because I heard they tasted good together, but I couldn't find a can opener, so I ate the bread by itself.

I lay down to rest, but couldn't get my mind off the can of milk. I was curious to see how it tasted, so I took the can and walked up several flights of steps to the deck. I wandered around, hoping to find an opener, but all of the excitement on the deck distracted me, and I forgot what I went up there for. I went to the edge of the ship, leaned against the rail, and watched the white caps break as the ship moved through them. My attention then turned to the people, who all seemed to be on the move. Some formed small groups and were praying, talking, or crying, while others just walked back and forth. I recognized their songs and prayers and knew that most of them were Catholic. I found the scene to be both interesting and disturbing.

Standing there, I realized I hadn't seen Mother since coming on the ship and became worried. I got lost several times as I hurried back to our room, and when I finally made it back, I asked my stepcousin about my mother. She said Mother had gone to the ship's hospital and was ready to have her baby.

"Where is the hospital on this ship?" I asked.

"I don't know," she replied. "You have to wait for your father and ask him when he comes back here."

"Do you know where my father is?" I asked.

"He must be with your mother," she said. "He was here and told me about your mother's condition and left."

"Where is my brother?"

"He must be with your mother as well," she answered.

I didn't wait for her to finish, before I took off running with my canned milk in hand. I headed back for the deck again, looking for Mother, and with all the running around, I began to feel dizzy and nauseated, so I went back to our room, climbed up to my bunk bed, and collapsed. The room seemed to spin, and I felt like vomiting. I tried to get up, but before I could, I threw up on my bed and my clothes. I moved to the edge of the bed, intending to throw up toward the floor. Instead, I made a mess on the bunk below me.

From under me, my stepcousin jumped out of her bed and screamed, "You're supposed to get sick in the empty bag they gave you earlier!" Of course, I had used the bags for storing my cookies. I thought that was what they were for.

She continued, "You better get down here and clean up your mess!" I was so sick I couldn't even answer, but she wasn't about to let up. The next thing I knew, she reached up and dragged me down.

"Clean up this mess!" she demanded.

I cried and called for my mother, as I took off one layer of my clothes and began cleaning the floor. When I finished, I went back to bed. I didn't remember ever feeling so sick.

Soon after, an American in a white uniform brought in food. Each family received a tray full of fish, cheese, milk, and other treats, but I was so sick that I didn't want to even look at the food, much less eat it. All I wanted was to lie down and die.

From my bed, I heard everyone eating and commenting on how good the food tasted. Listening to them made me even sicker. I tried to throw up again, but all I could do was heave; there was nothing left in my stomach. Those who were eating yelled at me to stop making those awful noises and to be quiet, so they could eat in peace. After everyone finished eating, the room quieted down, and I dozed off.

I awoke to the sound of someone throwing up below me. It was my stepcousin and her son. Soon, everybody in the room was vomiting. The smell of cheese, fish, and sour milk, and the heaving noises were killing me. I wanted to get up and leave the room, but I was too sick to move. So I just lay there, trying to cover my ears and my nose, and eventually dozed off again.

The next morning, the call of nature woke me. I climbed from my bed and asked my stepcousin, "Do you know where the bathroom is?"

"I don't know," she said.

I ventured out of the room and asked around for directions to the toilet. Some pointed down, others pointed up, but no one seemed to remember for sure. I followed the last direction given and found what appeared to be a bathroom.

Inside, several American sailors were sitting side-by-side on two lines of white stools, with their pants down. I really had to go, so I pulled down my pants and squatted in the middle of the floor. The men sat there looking at me, and then at each other. They frowned but said nothing. I finished, pulled my pants up, and walked out of there, acting as if I knew what I was doing. Later, I discovered that I had wandered into the men's bathroom.

I tried to find my way back to our room but kept getting lost. Instead, I ran all over the place, crying my eyes out, until a Vietnamese priest witnessed my plight and asked me what was wrong. I told him I was lost and didn't know how to get back to my room.

"What is the room number?" he asked.

"I don't know," I sobbed. "I think it's on the third level down."

"My mother is in the ship's hospital, having a baby, and I really want to go there," I said.

He smiled and instructed me to follow him. To my relief, he took me to the ship's hospital and led me to a desk, where a white-skinned man sat. The priest told the man to take care of me and left. With a strong accent, the man asked for my mother's name and took me to her. There were a few small beds in the room, all occupied by women and their babies.

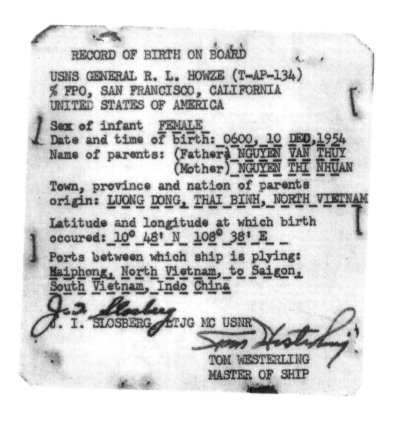

Birth record for my sister, Nho. She was born on the ship.

"This is your mother's bed, and this is your sister," he said as he pointed to a small baby in the bed alone. "They've taken your mother to another room to be washed and examined, but she should be right back. You can wait here for her."

I turned to him and smiled but said nothing. He patted my head and walked away. I climbed on the bed to play with the baby, and moments later, two American men helped my mother back into the room. She smiled at me, and I could tell she was surprised to see me. I waited until the two men left to explain how I got there.

Mother pointed to the baby and said, "This is your sister. She was born early this morning, right after I boarded the ship." I realized I had slept longer than I thought.

"What is her name?" I asked.

"We will wait until your father names her," she replied.

"Where is my baby brother?"

"He is with your father in the nursery. I haven't seen him since yesterday," she said. I felt happier with my mother and my new sister close by.

*   *   *

It took me three days to get used to the ship and to find my way around. I always carried the can of milk with me, snuggled under my arm—it became my pet, my friend, my security blanket, and my companion. I no longer looked for an opener.

I didn't go to the sailors' private bathroom anymore but used the one provided for the refugees instead. I spent most of my time wandering around the ship, watching the ocean waves. I was not free from dizziness and nausea, but I managed, and I learned to eat all kinds of strange foods—the French bread and the cheese were my favorites.

I still had not seen my little brother since we got on the ship, and each time I asked a family member about him, he always seemed to be with someone else. I just hoped he had not fallen in the ocean and disappeared.

We saw land on the fourth day, and almost everyone crowded on deck as the ship docked. An American sailor carried my mother, a Vietnamese nurse carried my baby sister, and my stepfather carried my brother to the deck. I was very happy to see my brother, Kinh, as I had been worried about him.

Our family grouped together as we got ready to leave the ship. Along with the thousands of others on board, we carried our belongings and lined up. I saw how excited everyone was as we prepared to leave. Almost everyone was in tears, either singing or praying. I held on to my clothes, my towel, a bag of chocolates, and the cookies, which I had not yet developed a taste for, but didn't want to part with, and of course, my milk can.

We followed a line of people, walking the steel plank that led to land. We went through lines of tables again, as we did when we boarded the ship. The same kind of workers gave everyone another loaf of bread, a bag of uncooked rice, a can of sardines, and a can of milk. Since I already had a can of milk in my hand, they wouldn't give me another. But I didn't mind. It felt good to be on land after being at sea for so long.

As I took in my surroundings, I noticed there were rows upon rows of buildings with brightly colored signs in front, and moving vehicles packed the bustling streets. People were rushing, horns and engines blared, and the air was full of the smell of gas and kerosene.

"Where are we?" I asked the man standing next to me.

"We are in Saigon, the biggest city in South Vietnam," he replied.

I jumped up and down as I shouted at Mother, "We're in Saigon! We're in Saigon!" I had never heard of Saigon before but that made no difference; we were there, in the biggest city in the south! It was so exciting that I kept jumping up and down, annoying my tired mother. She turned around, gave me a stern look, and told me to calm down.

I learned later that the Americans had indeed been involved in the relocation of civilians from North to South Vietnam. From August 1954 to May 1955, the U.S. Navy moved about 310,000 people on American ships, in a military operation called "Passage To Freedom." Our ship, the USNS *General R. L. Howze*, left North Vietnam on December 9, 1954. The ship had the distinction of holding the record for the most births onboard during the entire operation. The total was thirty-eight, and my sister, born on December 10, was one of them.

Chapter 7

TIGER'S CLAW

WHEN WE ARRIVED in the city, Saigon's harbor was overflowing with refugees. People were running around like ants, trying to find lost relatives or arranging for transportation. Our group waited amidst the chaos for the trucks that would take us to our new settlement, somewhere.

We waited for hours under the hot, midday sun. My bare feet burned on the scorching cement surface, and I had to stand on my bag of clothes to find relief. My poor, tired mother sat on her bag of clothes holding my three-day-old baby sister. Kinh was over a year old and wasn't walking yet, but he sure could crawl, so everyone had to keep an eye on him.

Unfortunately, there were too many people and not enough trucks, and there was no organization to the trucks' movements. No one knew where the next truck might stop or where it would be going. Everyone was impatient to be on their way, out of the boiling heat. It was hot and humid, and the air felt so different from North Vietnam.

My stepfather was no exception. He moved our family from place to place, trying to guess where the next truck would stop, so we could get on. After one of our moves, a truck stopped right where we had just left, and everyone yelled at him for moving us.

"If you hadn't moved us, we would already be on the truck," Mother complained.

"If you're so smart," my stepfather retorted, "why did you decide to have a baby right in the middle of nowhere?"

Just then, my stepcousin joined in. "I agree with her," she said, pointing to Mother. "It was all your fault," she said to my stepfather, angrily. "We could be on our way now, if you hadn't moved us around."

He turned to my stepcousin, gave her a stern look and said, "You too. If you're so smart, why did you have a baby without a husband?"

She gave him a dirty look and walked away.

I was tired of listening to their fussing, and reached for my loaf of bread. I broke it in two and gave Mother half. I asked her to hold the bread while I looked for a can opener for my milk, but I still couldn't find one, so we ate the dry bread by itself. Mother ate only a few bites and gave the rest back to me.

Later in the afternoon, a truck finally stopped right in front of our group. Before the driver had a chance to open the tailgate, men, women, and children were fighting to get on. We managed to climb aboard, but it was so crowded everyone had to stand. We were squeezed in so tightly, there was barely room to breathe. Even so, the driver had to push and shove people together, just so he could close the tailgate. Then he jumped into the driver's seat and drove away. A few people took advantage of the slow-moving truck and climbed onto the tailgate of the vehicle, but they had to hang on outside.

My poor mother couldn't stand with my baby sister in her arms. With some maneuvering, she found room to sit, but every time the truck turned or hit a bump, those standing near Mother would fall on her, sometimes hurting the baby and causing my sister to cry. They apologized as they got up and struggled to keep their balance, but with the next curve or rough bump, down they went, and the baby began crying again. Mother tried to crouch over the baby to shield her from the unstable crowd above, but that didn't help much. Mother's hair turban constantly fell, and she had to push it up from her face. She ended up holding the turban in one hand and my baby sister in the other. The ride was hard for everyone, but it was particularly hard for her. I was sandwiched in the middle of the truck and couldn't see out. I wondered if those who had been hanging on the outside of the truck were still there.

Just before getting on the truck, I was lucky enough to find an opener for my milk can. I was able to open the can of milk but didn't have a chance to taste it. We were packed so tightly that I couldn't get the can up to my mouth. I just cradled the open can of milk to my chest, and when I fell, which was often, the sweet, sticky, condensed milk spilled out, dousing me and anyone nearby. Those who were doused yelled at me to throw it away—but how could I? That can of milk was my support and comforter. I had become attached to it and guarded it with care. I wouldn't part with it, even though it had become a nuisance.

I was so busy dealing with all of the chaos, I had no idea how far we had come or how long we had been on the road. After what seemed like forever, I felt the truck slow down and come to a final, bumpy stop. I could hear excited shouts from inside and outside the truck. I heard someone yell, "We are in Ba Loi, near Tay Ninh!" and everyone started piling out. A kind stranger helped Mother to her feet and assisted her off the truck. I jumped off the truck and raised the milk can to my mouth, but it was empty. I tossed it aside and took a quick peek at my messy clothes.

I looked around at my surroundings and saw dozens of huge tents, scattered throughout newly cleared land, right in the middle of a thick forest. There was an older man who seemed to be in charge. He asked each family to stay together and then counted each group. Our family of seven was assigned to one of the tents nearby. When our family marched inside of the tent, I saw that many other families were already there. Some people slept, while others coughed, sounding very sick. Many of the children were crying, and the rest sat talking to each other. The people looked at us as we entered, but they didn't smile. They all seemed sad with void expressions.

We found a spot in the corner where our blanket would fit, and all seven of us made our home on the one blanket. My stepfather went outside with his niece, while Mother lay down with my sister in her arms. I dropped my sack of clothes and plopped down on the blanket beside her. She took one look at me and said, "Get off this blanket right now. Go find water somewhere and get yourself cleaned up." I looked down at my sticky clothes and walked outside to find somewhere to wash up.

I found a well not too far away, with half a dozen women taking turns dipping water from it to wash their clothes and bathe. I watched them for a few minutes and asked one of them to let me use the bucket and she handed it to me. I drew water from the well and poured it over my head. The murky well water, mixed with the milk on my clothes, ran down to my feet and made a chalk-white puddle beneath me. I scrubbed myself with my clothes on until I felt clean, and then I undressed. I wrung my clothes until they were almost dry, rolled them into a ball, tucked them under my arm, and ran back to the tent naked.

The entire settlement shared one shallow well. The water was muddy and smelled like sulfur, and there were no bathrooms or kitchens. We cooked over open fires outside the tent and used the forest as our toilet.

The settlement was in an area known for man-eating tigers. A few weeks after we arrived, a young boy relieved himself in the jungle and never came back. The search party found a few of his remains, confirming their suspicions about the tigers.

Because of the boy's death, no one was allowed to go into the jungle alone. Only groups of three or more could venture away from camp to use the toilet, and each of us had to carry a pot and pan, or a can and stick to make noise and scare the tigers away, while taking turns relieving ourselves. At night, we slept very close to each other and posted lookouts.

Often, the sound of growling tigers and the screams from refugees, followed by the sounds of pots and pans banging together, shattered the still night. The noise started a chain reaction of yelling and banging throughout the camp. The fear of tiger attacks was very real.

Early each morning, members of our family took turns lining up to get our daily ration of food. The one exception was my stepfather, who did not have the patience and had too much pride to stand in a line. When his turn came, I took his place. Sometimes, they gave us uncooked rice and dried fish, and other times, they gave us French bread and canned sardines. Now and then, we received a can of condensed milk and sugar. They also gave us clothes, but most were too large and too heavy for our hot weather, so we used them for blankets at night. I spent most of my time in a long line, waiting for one thing or another. I even had to line up at the well to get a bucket of murky water for my family to cook with and to drink.

As time went by, my stepfather grew weary of living in the settlement, and after a while, decided we should move. One day, he said to Mother, "If we stay here much longer, we will either starve to death or become food for tigers." Several other families felt the same, and they all got together with my stepfather to plan a trip.

The morning of the move, we packed our belongings into three large bags. My stepfather, my stepcousin, and I carried the bags outside to join the families who were leaving with us. Mother carried my baby sister, who was about two months old and very small. Mother did not have enough food for her and was unable to produce the milk my sister needed for nourishment.

As we gathered, preparing to leave, I heard the man who was in charge talking and making plans for the trip. He said he knew a shortcut, but we would have to walk through the forest to get there. The majority of the people agreed that we should go through the forest if it meant the journey would take less time. As we were standing there, I felt anxious and ran back into the tent to take one last look. All that remained of our stay in the settlement was a bare patch on the ground where our blanket had killed the weeds and grass.

About a dozen families, each carrying their own possessions, prepared to leave. We followed the middle-aged man, who knew the way through the forest, to the village of Ba Nha, a larger settlement with more decent homes.

We walked deeper into the woods, singing and praying out loud. At the same time, we banged on pots, pans, and empty cans to make a lot of noise, hoping to scare the tigers away. Tigers really frightened me, so I walked in the middle of the group of some forty-five or fifty people.

An old lady walking next to me noticed my fear and tried to comfort me. "You have nothing to be afraid of," she said. "Tigers are smart and choose their prey with great care. They can smell and hear from far away." She patted my head as she continued, "They like to attack only those people born in the year of the pig, because tigers like to eat pigs, just like the boy who was killed a few weeks ago."

But her attempt to comfort me didn't help, because I was born in the year of the pig! I didn't say anything though, as I was afraid a tiger might hear me. Before our talk, I was just scared. After listening to her, I was terrified. It was then I knew the dead boy was my age. At noon, we stopped to rest and have lunch. Because of our fear of tigers, we never stopped making noises, whether we were resting, eating, or walking. The sound of cans, pots and pans clanging together, and the praying of Catholic Rosaries, mixed with the cries of tired children, produced a weary melody of fright that will never be erased from my memory.

It was late afternoon before we reached the village of Ba Nha. The families we traveled with separated and started looking for homes. My stepfather asked around the village and was directed to a house that had just been vacated. Almost all of the homes there were built for refugees, and were made out of tree trunks, on clay floors, with king grass roofs. The homes all looked new and similar to each other, and the refugees used them until they could find better places to live. The doors were made from tree limbs, which could be picked up and moved aside. My stepfather picked up the door and pushed it out of the way. He stepped inside, looked around, and said, "It's livable." We followed right behind him.

I climbed rough and crooked stairs, which led to a gnarled, uneven loft, built about halfway to the roof. Although it was quite rugged, the house appeared to be in good condition. My stepfather pointed to the loft and announced, "Mother and the three kids will sleep in the loft. The rest will sleep downstairs."

Thinking I was one of the three to sleep in the loft, I started climbing higher, but my stepfather stopped me and said, "Not you Loan. You are old enough to sleep downstairs and help watch out for tigers." I realized that he meant my stepcousin's son, who was a little younger than I, the third kid. The thought of tigers coming into the house and attacking people terrified me.

"Please let me stay in the loft with Mother," I begged.

"You're too old to sleep up there," he said. "I don't want to hear any more about it."

I didn't like having to sleep downstairs, but I knew better than to argue. Soon, everyone settled down. We were very tired, but before resting, we gathered wood, cooked rice, and ate it with the canned sardines we brought with us. After eating, I climbed on a rough, wooden bunk in the lower level. I prayed for God to protect us from tigers and fell asleep.

In the middle of the first night, the roar of a tiger woke us. It got closer, and we started banging on anything that made noise. After that, the roaring got softer and then it was silent. Everyone else went back to sleep, but not me. I was too scared.

My wooden bunk was not very comfortable. The rough, uneven bed was too hard for my back, and the knots in the wood kept poking me. I wished I could have slept on the floor; it would have been better for my back. Instead, I twisted and turned for the rest of the night and thought of our journey and of the struggles we had experienced. It was scary and sad, but it was also exciting. I was thankful we had found a decent home.

Several months passed, and we realized that although we had a roof over our head, the living conditions were just as bad as Ba Loi. My stepfather struggled to provide enough food for our table. Since moving from the last settlement, we were on our own. There was no Red Cross or anyone else to help us with food or supplies.

My stepfather made several trips to Tay Ninh City each month to buy herbs and medicine for his practice, though he had little money and could buy only a few supplies each trip. The sick he cared for were also poor, so they did not have much money to pay him, if at all.

The house we were staying in didn't have electricity or running water, and there was no well in the village, so we had to walk to the river, almost a mile away, to bathe, wash our clothes, and carry water back to the house for cooking. Carrying water and watching my baby sister were my chores. My parents named my little sister Nho, which means "to remember."

Not long after reaching the village of Ba Nha, I turned eight years old and was able to attend a real school near our house. The school was built from a few crooked poles that held up a roof made from king grass, and about thirty or forty students of all ages and both sexes attended.

The tables and benches in the school were also made of rough wood, from which I received my share of splinters. Because there were no walls, strong winds blew leaves and trash in, and blew our books and papers out. Students often had to chase after their papers in the wind. Sometimes, the students' papers got mixed up, and chaos ensued. Our teacher just stood there and smiled patiently, as he watched us trying to sort out our papers.

One morning, a few days after school started, we were ordered to line up. A nurse told us we were going to be vaccinated to keep us from getting diseases. When it was my turn, the nurse gave me a shot in my shoulder, then applied a white liquid on the upper part of my arm and scratched it with the sharp point of an old metal writing pen until it bled.

If one vaccination was good for me, I thought, two would be twice as beneficial, so I covered my bleeding left arm and got back in line. The nurse didn't recognize me and vaccinated my right arm. When I went to class, I showed the girl who sat next to me my two vaccinations. She rolled up her sleeves and showed me that she had done the same. We agreed to keep this our secret.

Right then, we became friends. Her name was Hoa, and she was about three years older than me. She wasn't very pretty, but she had long beautiful hair. One day, during break time, she and I were playing hopscotch in our bare feet. Suddenly, I felt a sharp pain in my big toe. I screamed as I watched a scorpion crawling away.

The pain was unbearable. Hoa suggested I go to the clinic, and she ran to get an excuse from my teacher for me. Together, we walked as fast as my throbbing foot would allow me to the nearby clinic. I was surprised that the clinic looked no better than our school. A nurse gave me a shot on my bottom and told me to stay off my foot for a while. We went back to school, but I was grimacing so much from the pain that the teacher sent me home.

Mother was in the little shack, built for cooking outside the house, when she saw me limping home. "Why are you home so early?" she asked.

"I was stung by a scorpion," I replied, "and my teacher sent me home."

Mother looked at me and said, "If it had been a scorpion, you would be dead. An ant must have bitten you."

"No, Mother," I argued, "I saw the scorpion crawling away after it stung me."

She looked at my dirty foot but saw nothing. "I think you just misbehaved in school," she said, "and your teacher punished you by sending you home."

I didn't feel like arguing with her anymore, so I limped inside. My baby sister lay crying on a hammock that hung from two poles next to the uneven wall. I sang to her, and as I swung the hammock back and forth, it caught on a limb that stuck out from the wall, and she was thrown to the floor. She cried even harder as I picked her up and tried to comfort her.

Mother ran in when she heard Nho crying. She was very upset, took her from me, and began breast-feeding her to calm her down. My stepfather walked in, looked at the hammock, and without asking, realized what happened.

He grabbed my arm, took me outside, and tied me to a tree. I was scared and crying, and begged him to forgive me for being clumsy. He was very angry and ignored my pleas. He dug a hole in front of me, and said he was going to bury me alive.

"I'm afraid to die," I pleaded. "Please forgive me, Father. I didn't mean to hurt my sister. It was an accident, and I'm sorry she fell." He was too angry to listen and kept digging.

When he thought it was deep enough, he untied me, picked me up, and tried to put me in it. I was terrified of being buried alive and started pushing and kicking, as I tried to keep myself out of the hole. He was too strong for me, and managed to lower me in, feet first. He shoveled dirt around me, until it came above my waste. He stamped the dirt solid and walked away with the shovel. I realized he did not bury me all the way and was thankful he spared my life.

In the excitement, I had forgotten all about the scorpion sting, and then the pressure of the dirt caused more pain in my foot. I cried and begged for release, but no one dared help me. A sympathetic neighbor had to wait until my stepfather left the house before he came over and pulled me out.

Everyone saw the way my stepfather mistreated me, but there were no rules or laws against spousal or child abuse at that time. Parents had the right to teach their children, no matter how hard or how rough the lessons were. If a woman married a wife beater, she would suffer for the rest of her life. Divorce in the Catholic church was simply unheard of.

* * *

Every weekend, with a group of about six or seven of my friends, I went deep into the forest to gather wild fruit. We each carried a knife to cut fruit from the tree, a bag to carry the fruit in, and a stick and an empty can for making noise to scare tigers away. I was the best climber in the group. Even though some of my friends were older, they were not as agile. I climbed the fastest, the highest, and always picked the most fruit.

One day, as we filled our bags with delicious, ripe fruit from several different kinds of trees, we heard an ominous roar nearby. Everyone grew quiet as we watched a huge tiger walking beneath us. I had heard tigers roar before, but I had never seen one. I knew we were all going to die, and I was certain that I was more scared than anyone there. I remembered what the old lady said about being born in the year of the pig, and I held my breath as I hoped and prayed the tiger couldn't climb trees.

I was so scared that my whole body started shaking. I trembled so much that I lost my grip on the branch I was holding. I grabbed another limb, but it broke and down I went, screaming and yelling as I fell from one limb to another. My friends saw what happened and started yelling and banging on their cans, hoping to scare the tiger away.

I lay there dazed under the tree, and for a moment, couldn't move. My friends stayed in the tree and continued yelling and banging cans. They were too scared to come down to help me. Some of them yelled for me to hurry up and climb back up the tree. "I'm in too much pain! I can't move!" I cried. I glanced around for the tiger, hoping it had run away.

When I realized the tiger had gone, I crawled to a tree stump and rested my back against it. I examined myself and saw I was cut and scratched all over. Blood was oozing from some of the wounds. Judging from the pain in my chest, I was sure I had cracked some ribs.

My friends kept begging me to climb back up the tree, but there was no way I could. I had no choice but to sit on the ground. Assured the tiger was gone, my friends resumed their fruit picking.

I glanced at the ripe, yellow fruit scattered all over the ground. Some were still in one piece, while others were smashed from the fall. The thought of going home without fruit worried me, and I crawled around in pain, trying to gather as much as I could, stuffing the good pieces in my bag.

Later that afternoon, when everyone had filled their bags with as much fruit as they could carry, we prepared to leave. I made them promise not to tell my parents what happened. I picked up my bag, but I was in too much pain to carry it, so my best friend Hoa carried it for me. Even without the bag, I still couldn't keep up with them. Hoa hung back with me for a while, but as I got farther behind, she left me with my bag to catch up with the rest of the group. The bag of fruit was too heavy for me, so I ended up dumping out the fruit, found a stick to support myself, and dragged the empty bag behind me. My injuries slowed me down, and I had to stop often to catch my breath. I hoped and prayed the tiger would not come back, as I made the scary walk home. It was almost dark when we got back.

Mother expected me to bring fruit home and was disappointed when I showed up with an empty bag. "Why don't you have any fruit?" she asked. "I saw your friends come home earlier with full bags, and I don't understand why you have none. You've wasted the whole day for nothing."

I tried not to show my pain, because I was afraid she would be angrier if she knew I had hurt myself. Instead of answering her, I smiled and walked away. Weeks later, I still felt pain whenever I had to carry water from the river. I was determined not to return to the forest to pick fruit again.

As time went by, conditions in Ba Nha became desperate. There was no work, and many families moved away. Those left behind were poor, sick, and hungry. The cemetery filled with victims of disease and malnutrition, most of them children. Our home was not far from the cemetery, and we witnessed a funeral almost every day. Even my little sister got very sick, and we all thought she was going to die. My stepfather bought wood and made a small box, which would serve as a coffin in preparation for her death. We were all so worried about her. I heard my stepfather mention many times that we needed to move away from the village, but he didn't know where to go, and that was why we were still there.

I carried a bucket of dirty clothes to the river one day, but before washing them, I sat by myself at the riverbank, watching the water flow by. I let my mind wander to my birthplace and thought of my relatives, my father's death, my old friend, our maid, and my chicken. Where were they now? After all the struggling to leave North Vietnam, I wondered how my stepfather felt now. He was once among the richest and most powerful men in the village and now was little more than a pauper. The price of freedom was indeed dear.

I thought most about my poor dying sister. She was so skinny, and so weak that she could barely cry. I felt guilty, because I had caused her to fall from the hammock. I loved her and prayed that God would spare her life.

I stood up, wiped my tears, dragged the bucket full of clothes to the water, and began washing them. A large black object floated down the river and almost hit me. I jumped back to avoid it. When I calmed down, I tried to see what it was, but the water was too swift. It looked like a human body, and it smelled terrible. I was scared, so I grabbed all the clothes, dirty and clean, and stuffed them into a bucket. With the bucket bouncing against my leg, I ran home as fast as I could.

Shaking like a leaf, I told Mother, "I think I just saw a dead person floating in the water!"

"That can't be," she said. "Maybe some animal drowned while getting a drink. Now go on and get your work done." She didn't want to believe me.

"Mother, there's no one at the river today, and I'm scared," I pleaded. "Can I wash the clothes tomorrow?"

"We need them today," she replied. I had no choice but to take the clothes back to the river and continue washing them. The following day someone found the body of a man farther downstream. When I realized how close I had been to him, I began having nightmares. I asked Mother to let me sleep in the loft with her, but she refused and told me to be strong.

One morning, I overheard someone telling my parents that a tiger had broken into a nearby house and dragged a young girl into the forest, and a group of people were searching for her. To my surprise, the missing girl was my best friend, Hoa. I was very worried and asked my parents if I could go with the search team to help look for her. Mother said I could go but told me to be careful. I ran as fast as I could to Hoa's house. When I arrived, I found Hoa's mother was crying hysterically. I asked her which way the search team had gone, and she pointed toward a path leading into the jungle. I ran to catch up with the twenty or more people who were looking for her. After several hours, I heard someone yell, "I found her!"

I felt relieved and hoped that she was all right.

I ran to where she had been found, and to my horror, saw that there was not much left of her. Her beautiful, long black hair was tangled and matted. Her eyes were half-open, and blood covered her pale face. I stood in silence, with tears rolling down my cheeks, and my heart pounding in pain. I watched the men pick up her remains and place them in a bag. I followed them as they carried her home.

Hoa's mother was at the doorstep, waiting for news of her daughter. When she saw the searchers carrying a bag toward her house, she realized what had happened. She ran to the searchers, cradled the bag to her chest, and sobbed. I felt so sorry for her. Her husband had been killed in the war, and Hoa was the only family she had. "From now on she will be alone," I thought. Tears streamed down my face as I watched her. She reminded me of my mother, crying over the body of my dead father years ago.

"I can't take any more of this," I said to myself, and I turned and walked away. They buried her in a tiny wooden coffin the following day.

By that time, everyone in the village was trying to move away. The school closed, and the village was becoming deserted. My stepcousin and her son who lived with us had already gone. My stepfather made several trips to search for a new home. Then one day, he found one and announced that we would be moving to the coastal town of Nha Trang. "It's very far from this terrible place," he said, "and it will be a better place for us to live and for me to practice medicine."

Immediately, we started packing. We put most everything we owned into three large bags and stuffed the rest of our meager possessions into the tiny coffin. The next morning, we ate breakfast and said goodbye to some of our neighbors. My stepfather and I carried a heavy bag, while Mother carried my sister in one hand and led my brother with the other. We walked to the main road to wait for the bus. Mother stayed at the road to watch our things, while my stepfather and I went back to the house for the rest.

We waited for hours until a small, pale blue bus arrived. It looked like it was about to fall apart. Most of the metal was rusted and wooden parts were chipping off. Inside the bus were three unstable benches that were already filled with people. Thankfully, with the help of the driver, we managed to squeeze on.

The bus moved down the bumpy road, leaving a cloud of dust behind it. As we drove away, I looked back at Ba Nha and thought, "Except for the tigers roaring every night, I loved the place, with its beautiful river and fruit trees. I hope wherever we are going, it will be just as nice, but without the tigers."

Along the way, the bus stopped now and then to let us relieve ourselves behind the bushes or to pick up some food from roadside vendors. We went through many forests and over rugged mountains. The condition of the roads was bad, and at one sharp turn, our front wheels fell into a hole right on the edge of a cliff. We were left suspended, our bus tilted to one side, ready to plummet into the valley below.

Everyone aboard the bus panicked, but the driver calmed us down, as he got off and said, "Just sit still, and everything will be all right, as long as you do what I say. I've never turned a bus over before." With great care, he helped each one of us through the window on the opposite side of the cliff. We all held our breath and tried not to shake or disturb the vehicle. When we were all safe, the driver ordered the women and children to move away from the bus, while the men helped the driver push it out of the hole.

Using trees and branches for reinforcement and leverage, they maneuvered the bus back on the road. When the bus was steady, we climbed on and continued on our way. It was many restless, dirty, and hungry days before we finally arrived in Nha Trang.

Chapter 8

BLACK INK

NHA TRANG WAS different from any place I had ever seen. Tall, magnificent mountains stood in one direction, and the ocean glimmered in the other. The town was alive with vehicles and people on the move. The bus eased into the station and stopped. We climbed down from the rickety bus, my stepfather paid the driver, and we unloaded our belongings. He hired a horse-drawn carriage to take us to our new home. I sat in front of the carriage, watching the poor horse pull the heavy load, dragging its hooves on the hot tar road. Although I felt sorry for the horse, it was an interesting ride. I lost track of time, until we arrived at a small, empty wooden house, with a tin roof, built at the foot of the mountains. It was a beautiful location, and I fell in love with it at once.

I took care of the kids, while Mother helped my stepfather unload our things. I carried my sister and kept an eye out for Kinh, as I investigated the surroundings. "I can't wait to live here," I thought.

Thankfully, my sister's health improved after a few months, and my stepfather tore up her coffin and made it into a small table. We filled the house with humble, but necessary furniture.

The friends I made in the area all attended school, but each time I asked my stepfather if I could go, he said no.

"Girls don't need a higher education," he said. "If you can read and write, that's enough. Besides, when you grow up and get married, you'll become a housewife, and you don't need more education. Look at your mother. She cooks, cleans, and has babies. Who needs an education for that?"

Knowing that it wasn't my place to argue with him, I asked Mother to intercede. She tried, but in the end, she could do nothing. I resigned myself to staying home and caring for my brother and sister, but I felt bad whenever I saw my friends carrying their books to school. I wished I could go with them.

My stepfather's reputation with medicine grew in the village, and as it did, our financial situation improved. I had to help Mother prepare and process the herbs my stepfather used for medicine, and patients circulated through our house all day. When they asked why I wasn't in school, I replied, "I'll be going to school later, but right now my parents are too busy preparing medicine, and I have to stay home to help them."

Although the city was large, we didn't live close enough to benefit from city services. Like many others who lived near us at the outskirts of the city, we didn't have electricity or running water. Instead, we used wells for water and wood or kerosene for light and cooking. After we moved in, I had to help my stepfather dig a well by hand. We had trouble at first, because of the sandy soil, but we managed. Lucky for us, the water table was high, and we didn't need to dig too deep before we hit water.

Our house was very open, and mosquitoes easily found their way in. My parents and the kids, who slept together, had one large mosquito net covering their bed for protection. But I had to sleep without one, on a small bench that was used for patients to sit on during the day, and the hungry pests fed on me every night. Each morning, I saw them resting on the wall, their stomachs bloated with my blood. Red spots, souvenirs from the mosquitoes, covered my face. When asked if I had the measles, I would smile and say, "No, they are just red freckles."

My stepfather spent a great deal of time and money trying to find relatives who had come to South Vietnam. He found his mother, his son, Den, and a teenage niece. They all moved in with us, and our little one-room house became so crowded that we had to sleep almost on top of each other. I had to give up the bench I was sleeping on to my step-grandmother, and three of us slept on one grass mat on the floor.

When I wanted some peace and quiet, I took the kids for a walk to our favorite spot, at the foot of the mountains, away from the house.

There, a small waterfall molded a little stream that filled a beautiful and serene pond. Without disturbing the surface, I could see the blue sky and the mountains mirrored in the reflection. The pond was full of living creatures like fish, frogs, water bugs, and tadpoles. I loved to catch them; they made great toys for the kids.

I let the two- and three-year-old kids play in the pond one day, and all I had to do was keep an eye on them. I sat with my back against a tree trunk, daydreaming. The little pond reminded me of North Vietnam, and I recalled making my own fishing gear. I used a bamboo stick for a rod, the string from a banana plant for line, a piece of bent wire for a hook, and flies for bait. Of course, fishing was forbidden, and since I got into such trouble for fishing, I had to hide my gear from my parents. When no one was around, I fished in the larger pond behind our house. I caught many fish there, but I always threw them back. I would never forget the time my stepfather almost killed me for catching his fish.

The sound of someone struggling in the water aroused me. My little brother was thrashing around, trying to keep his head above water. I jumped in the water and pulled him out as quickly as I could, but his face turned purple, and he couldn't cry. Not knowing what else to do, I picked him up by his legs, turned him upside down, and shook him as hard as I could, trying to get the water out of his lungs, as I had seen others do before. To my relief, he began to cry. I stopped shaking him, turned him right side up, and held him close to my chest to comfort him. I felt so bad about the incident but was too afraid to tell anyone what happened, so I kept the secret to myself.

*   *   *

Unhappy with the crowded condition, my step-grandmother left with her granddaughter and went back to her daughter's home. My brother Den still stayed with us; he slept on the bench, and I took the floor. We got along a little better as we got older.

Mother insisted we attend Mass every morning, but I didn't like getting up that early. One morning, Mother called me several times, but I was too sleepy to get up. She pulled me up, pushed me out the door, and threw my dress on top of me.

"Put your ao dai on while you walk to church and hurry up. You are late!" she demanded.

I rolled the dress into a ball, put it under my arm, and dragged myself to church. I found a pew where no one could see me and went back to sleep, but when I awoke, the church was deserted. As quickly as I could, I slipped my dress over my pajamas and ran all the way home. As I sneaked into the house, Mother spotted me.

"Where have you been?" she asked.

"I stayed behind for extra prayers," I lied. "Can I go crabbing today?" I asked Mother as I took off my dress.

"Who will you go with?" she asked.

"The couple next door is going to the bay," I replied. "They told me yesterday it would be all right if I went with them. May I please go?" I begged.

"Go ahead," she said.

I found a bucket and ran next door where the couple was still waiting for me. It took us almost an hour to walk to the bay. When we got there, we saw thousands of colorful fiddler crabs basking on the sandbar, giving it the appearance of a rippling rainbow. They were fast, however, and not easy for us to catch. When we approached, the crabs disappeared into holes in the sand, but I was quick and managed to capture a small bucketful by midday. They tried to escape, but I stopped them from crawling out by packing sand on top of them. The couple was slower, and their bucket was larger, so I helped them fill it. I noticed they topped their bucket with a lot of seaweed and grass to stop the crabs from crawling out. I didn't ask questions, and I didn't change my technique.

We headed home about midafternoon during the hottest part of the day. The hot tar roasted my bare feet, and I had to hop on the weeds that grew sparsely along the road.

Mother was in the kitchen when I arrived. "Help me with the crabs, Mother!" I said. Kinh and Nho heard me talking to Mother about the crabs, and they got so excited they couldn't wait to see them. They began jumping up and down, and clapping their hands.

"Be careful and don't let them get away! They crawl as fast as lightning," I warned Mother.

"I'll watch my side, and you watch yours," Mother replied, and we positioned ourselves on either side of the bucket. Kinh and Nho stopped dancing and watched us with eager attention. We picked up the bucket and turned it upside down into a large bamboo basket. To our surprise, none of the crabs were moving. They were all dead and had begun to smell.

"We can't use them," Mother said with obvious disappointment. "They have been dead too long. Take them out back and bury them before your father comes home."

"No, Mother!" I said, "They were alive just a few hours ago."

"Crabs turn bad as soon as they die," Mother explained, "I know from experience."

I stood in silence, staring at the crabs for a moment. I looked up at Mother and at my brother and sister, and felt terrible. Then, I gathered the dead crabs, and while I was dragging them to the back of the house, Mother yelled, "Wait! Just hide the crabs for now. I want you to watch the rice, while I run to the market to buy something to make the soup your father is expecting."

I took the crabs behind the house and walked back to the kitchen. I watched over the food and told the kids about how I caught the crabs. Since moving south, we no longer used clay for cooking. We still cooked on the floor, but we used aluminum pots and pans, a three-pronged metal stove, and wood for fuel. Mother came back soon with fresh crabs in a paper bag and told me to take care of the dead crabs out back. I grabbed a shovel and motioned for the kids to follow me. I dragged the crabs farther behind the house and started digging. When the hole was deep enough, I dumped the crabs in and covered them with sand. The kids were silent, watching me until all the crabs were buried.

I often took Kinh and Nho to school and let them play in the schoolyard, while I sat under the window outside the classroom. I kept an eye on them as I listened to the teacher lecture inside. Although not in class, I could still learn.

Now and then, the kids would start to fight or cry, and the teacher would stick her head out the window and yell, "Go away and take those kids somewhere else to play! This is a school, not a playground for children." I took them away but came back when they stopped crying.

I thought of how lucky my stepbrother Den was. After a short stay with us, my stepfather sent him to a boarding school for his education. When Den was home, he never had to watch the kids, cook, do dishes, or any other chores. When I complained, my stepfather always said, "That's because he's a boy." In our culture, as well as some of those in China and other Asian countries, boys were more important than girls. Boys carried the family name, made important decisions, and therefore received more respect.

Time passed and soon it was time to prepare for Tet, the Asian New Year celebration. It was our tradition to prepare a variety of food for the occasion. We also bought dried, red, roasted watermelon seeds as well as many cookies and candies. The candy was often made from preserved fruit or dried fruit pieces. We cleaned and decorated the house with bright, lucky, red colors, then waited for the New Year celebration to begin.

During the three days of the New Year, friends and relatives gathered, exchanged gifts, and wished each other good luck for the coming year. Tet is also recognized as everybody's birthday, no matter when we were born. We are all a year older at Tet, and since I lived in ten different years, I was then considered to be ten years old, even though I was actually still nine. It is a time to start anew, improve relationships, to change bad habits, and take precautions to secure a more prosperous, lucky new year. Tet is considered very sacred, but it is also an exciting and very happy time, especially for children, as food, gifts, and money for birthdays are more abundant than usual.

In 1956, Tet fell on February 12, a Sunday. I woke up without Mother having to urge me and went to church. Instead of dozing off as I usually did, I found a seat in a front pew and knelt to pray. After church, I went home, entering through the back door like everyone else in the family, except my stepfather.

On the first day of Tet, most of us believe that whoever enters the house first will set the pace for the whole year. So the front door should be reserved for someone who we hope will bring us luck, someone stable, happy, and cheerful. My stepfather decided he was the one that should enter first.

He returned from church, walked through the front door, and we treated him as if he were a guest. He greeted us in return and acted very cheerful. Of course, that was hard for him, but he didn't want to be blamed for a year of bad luck. I offered him hot tea and food. After tasting the food and sipping tea, he gave us children lucky money for our birthday, as is our tradition. From then on, the door stayed open for other guests.

Our family had many visitors; most of them were my stepfather's patients. They all gave us kids money for luck and for our birthday. During this period of celebration, my friends and I ran back and forth between each other's homes, showing off our money, comparing to see who had the most. By the end of the third day into the New Year, I had a nice stack of money.

On the fourth day, we took down the decorations and cleaned up the house. Mother saw me with a pocket full of money and suggested I give it to her for safekeeping. "If you don't give it to me, I'm afraid you might lose it," she said.

"Please let me keep it myself," I replied. "I want to buy a mosquito net and school supplies, just in case Father lets me go to school this year. If there's any left over, I'll give it all to you, I promise." Reluctantly, she accepted my argument.

We hadn't swept the floor for three days, believing that doing so would bring us bad luck. The more trash, the better the luck, money, and fortune. To sweep the floor on New Year's Day meant we would sweep away our fortune. I didn't know what kind of luck the garbage brought, but it was not lucky for me because I had to clean up the mess! It was easy to sweep the candy wrappings and the fruit peelings from the sandy floor, but the little, red watermelon shells blended with the sand and were very difficult to sweep, and because I couldn't sweep them, I tried picking them up by hand. In desperation, I used a bamboo basket to strain the sand to remove the shells.

Mother saw my futile gestures and took pity on me. "You can stop now," she said. "You've done your best, so quit worrying about them. The empty shells will soon fade, and in time, they'll look like sand."

With relief, I thanked her and threw away the shells I had already collected. Later that afternoon while eating dinner, my stepfather looked at the floor and said to me, "Why didn't you clean the red shells off the floor? When you're finished eating, I want you to pick up every one of them."

I looked at Mother and said, "Yes, Father."

Two weeks after Tet, school was back in session. I sat on our doorstep with my brother and sister, watching my friends and the other students walk to school. My friends waved to me as they passed by, and some asked, "Why are you still sitting there and not getting ready for school? Come with us!" I waved back with half a smile, wishing I could be with them. I wanted to go to school so much it hurt me. I sat there until the last student passed, then stood up, wiped my tears, stretched my arms, and took a deep breath. I was planning to take my brother and sister to the schoolyard.

"Loan Oi!" my stepfather called. With apprehension, I walked in, as I always did when I heard him call my name. He was sitting at the table, drinking rice whiskey and eating boiled pig stomach dipped in nuoc mam, a fish sauce mixed with lemon. I approached him fearfully, because I might have done something wrong, but I wasn't sure. "Yes, Father." I said.

He looked at me for a moment but didn't say a word. He picked up his glass of rice whiskey, took another sip, and set it back down. He took another bite of food as I stood there, silent and nervous, waiting for the expected accusation or scolding. My brother and sister were standing behind me acting timid as well.

He looked at me again and in a low voice said, "Get ready. You can go to school today."

His words startled me. I was so happy that I wanted to put my arms around him, hug him, and kiss him, but I didn't dare. I let out an unexpected whoop and quickly covered my mouth. I didn't want to disturb his breakfast. I thanked him, ran outside, and began jumping up and down. I was going to school again! Nothing could have made me happier.

I turned around and saw Kinh and Nho trying to imitate me and laughed at their antics. "School supplies," I thought, "I must get school supplies!" I stopped dancing, gathered my brother and sister, and ran to the nearby bookstore. "I am going to school," I announced to the store clerk, "and I need a notebook, a pencil, a pen, and an ink jar."

The clerk handed me what I asked for, but when he asked me for money, I realized I had forgotten to bring any. I apologized and asked him to keep my supplies until I returned with the money. I ran home, Kinh and Nho running far behind me.

I looked all over the house for my money but couldn't find it. I had forgotten what I did with it. The last time I recalled seeing it was when I showed it to some of my friends and bragged about how much I got during Tet. I knew I would have to wait until they came home from school to ask them, and I missed my first day.

Mother came home from the market, and while helping her with the groceries, I told her the good news. She was very happy for me. "With all the money you have from Tet, you can buy all the school supplies you need," she said. "You won't have to ask your father for anything."

I smiled and said nothing. I couldn't tell her about misplacing my money. I hoped to find the money before she knew the truth. After the meal, I took the kids to the foothills to play. I was anxious for the day to pass and could hardly stand still. I walked around the pond, thinking about the events of the day.

Near the water's edge, I noticed a pile of small black balls, about the size of large peas. They looked like the herbal medicine pills my stepfather made. I picked up one and smelled it. There was no odor, so I cleaned off the sand and sampled one. To my surprise, it tasted like medicine. I ate a few more and took a handful back to my brother and sister on the other side of the pond to share with them. I was certain they were medicine and would therefore be good for us. We finished those I had gathered, and I went back to look for more, taking Kinh and Nho with me.

I found more pills and wrapped them in my shirttail. I looked around and saw more piles of the black pills. There were more pills than I could carry. I ended up making my brother and sister help me carry them in their shirttails. We headed home, confident we would be rich from selling the pills to my stepfather's patients.

I ran home first, letting the kids run behind, and showed the pills to Mother. She looked at the pills and warily tasted one. "They look like your father's medicine, but they taste funny," she said. "Besides, what in the world are they doing in the middle of the forest?"

"Maybe someone dropped them," I replied. "I'm going back and collect more."

I grabbed a large bamboo basket and ran out. Mother was skeptical, but she didn't stop me from going. I returned to the hill by myself, passing my brother and sister on the way. I told them to keep on walking to the house and I'd be home soon. Surprised by my hurried state, they stared at me for a moment, and then continued their way down the hill, still holding the pills in their shirttails.

I began gathering every pill I saw, placing them in the bamboo basket. The farther I walked, the more I found. My basket was almost full when I came upon a herd of strange looking animals. A rugged and bearded, middle-aged man was caring for them. He frowned at me and my basket and asked, "What are you picking those up for?"

"This is medicine," I said, as I tilted my chin up with pride. "My father is a doctor and makes pills like these. They make sick people well."

He looked at the basket again and broke out in uncontrollable laughter. He tried to tell me something, but he was laughing so hard he couldn't talk. He finally stopped laughing long enough to point to the animals. "My goats made those medicine pills," he said, and he broke out laughing again.

I stared at him in confusion, but I wasn't about to believe him. I'd never seen goats before, but I knew they were not capable of making a round little ball of medicine. I looked at him and said, "Only my father or another Chinese doctor like him can make medicine like this."

Through his roaring laughter, he pointed to a goat that had its tail raised and said, "Look, look, one of my goats is making the pills right now."

I looked at the goat, at him, and then at my basket. I thought about what I had done with the pills earlier. "I ate them! I not only ate them, I fed them to my brother, my sister, and my very own mother!" Cold chills ran down my spine. I began gagging and tried to spit out those I had in my mouth. I hesitated for a moment, then turned the basket upside down, my eyes glued to the stranger who found the incident so enjoyable. When the basket was empty, I picked it up and ran as fast as I could, spitting all the way home. I could still hear the man's hysterical laughter as I ran. I promised myself I would never tell anyone about the incident as long as I lived.

I arrived home, gathered all of the balls I collected earlier, and threw them far from the house. I went to the well, scooped up water, and cleaned my hands and mouth with soap. Then I found the kids and began cleaning them. When I told them to open their mouths, I could still see the black residue on their teeth. Luckily, Mother had forgotten about my brief experience with medicine, and I wasn't about to remind her.

That afternoon, I went from door to door, looking for my money, but none of my friends remembered seeing it. I had to tell Mother what happened, and I knew it would upset her. If I didn't tell her, I couldn't get the supplies I needed for school. My burning desire to go to school was stronger than my fear, so I decided to face her.

Mother was in the kitchen roasting herbs when I walked in the house. "I lost my money, and now I can't get school supplies," I said.

She didn't look at me, but I could tell she was angry. She didn't create a scene, because she too was afraid my stepfather wouldn't let me attend school if he had to pay for it. "You will pay for this later," she said, as she handed me the money. I ran to the bookstore, bought what I needed, and gave her back the change.

I loved my school so much that I would often skip breakfast just so I could go early and sit and wait for it to start. Months passed by, and I still couldn't locate the money I had misplaced. I didn't have pretty clothes to wear, and I didn't have as many books and supplies as other students, but I was happy. It was enough for me to be in the classroom, instead of sitting outside listening through the window. I was the oldest in my class and soon became known for breaking up fights and creating new games. My school had few, if any, rules, and there was little or no record keeping.

My education was not important to my stepfather. However, my mother was happy because she wanted me to have the same opportunities as the other children. My, stepfather, however, didn't share her feelings. My mother was one of those Vietnamese women who walked behind their husbands and did whatever their husbands told them. By tradition, that was how a good wife was supposed to act. If Mother said anything, my stepfather would cut her off and tell her she didn't know anything. When Mother didn't obey him, our home became a war zone. In the end, she always gave in to whatever he wanted.

I didn't have a high opinion of this "master and slave" relationship between my parents. Mother often wept, because she felt trapped in her marriage. Whenever I asked her for a favor, she always told me to ask my stepfather, because her voice was not loud enough, and her opinion didn't count for much. I almost never asked my stepfather for anything, because I was too afraid of him.

My stepfather was a proud man. When I look back, I think he was a good provider, but he wasn't a loving husband to my mother or a good father to us children. But I still had to obey and respect him, because he was my stepfather and he was raising me.

Five months after starting back to school, Mother called me into the kitchen one afternoon. "I have some bad news," she said. "We are moving to Qui Nhon in a few days." I stood in shocked silence as she continued. "Your father just found your oldest brother, Hen. He is a supply sergeant in the army and is stationed in Qui Nhon. Your father wants to move there and be close to his son."

I was heartbroken. I had been in school for only a short time, and I was being told that I had to move to another strange place. I didn't know if I would ever go to school again. That week, our family packed everything we owned and prepared to move. I heard my stepfather tell Mother that his son had arranged for someone to move us with a big truck.

While Mother was getting ready, I asked for permission to go to school for a few minutes, so I could say goodbye to my teacher and my classmates. There were thirty or more students in the class and most of them were my friends. Class had already started when I arrived to say farewell, and the teacher was cleaning the chalkboard. When I walked in, they all looked at me. I waved to everyone and then walked up to my teacher.

"My family is moving," I said, with a lump in my throat, "and I have come to say goodbye."

My teacher rubbed my head, and with tears in her eyes, said "Good luck, I hope you will find a good school wherever you go."

I looked around the room and all of my classmates were crying, too. I was too choked up to say anymore, so I walked out of the classroom and cried all the way home.

When I got there, a military truck was parked in front of the house, and our possessions were being loaded. When it was done, my stepfather sat in front with the driver. The rest of us squeezed into the back of the truck and made room between stacks of furniture. The truck pulled away from its parking spot, and I stood up to look back at the house and the magnificent mountains that I would miss. It was sad to see the beautiful place fade away in a cloud of sand.

Chapter 9

HOT SAND

WHEN WE ARRIVED at our new home, and the truck slowed to a stop, I stood up to look around. Over and through the shacks and shabby houses, just a short walking distance away, I saw white caps on a turquoise blue ocean. The trip to Qui Nhon was not as bad as the one coming to Nha Trang. The military truck was larger, and it carried only our family, unlike the small, old wooden truck that carried dozens of people, plus dogs, cats, ducks, chickens, and pigs.

I tried to get a feel for the place when I heard my stepfather bellow, "Out, out, out of the truck!"

Mother was getting my brother and sister ready, and I jumped to the ground just in time for the violent, hot, sandy wind to blow in my face, welcoming me to Qui Nhon. I turned away from the wind, covered my face with my hand to prevent sand from getting in my eyes, and followed my stepfather.

He unlocked the door, and we walked into our new house. Except for the king grass roof, it was similar to our house in Nha Trang. My stepfather saw me following him with empty hands and told me to go back to the truck to help Mother. The driver opened the tailgate, and let Mother and the kids out. I loaded my arms with as many possessions as I could carry and reentered the house. I noticed dozens of small, funnel-shaped depressions in the sandy floor made by tiger beetles. I sat our belongings on the floor and rushed to dig one up. My preoccupation with bugs soon caused me to forget the chores, until Mother brought me back to reality by calling, "Loan Oi, come help me." The kids were running back and forth, as we dragged bags and pieces of furniture from the truck to the house. The wind continued to blast us with hot sand and caused our faces to burn. Before long, we all had red faces and sandy eyes.

My eldest brother, Hen, appeared from nowhere. I had seen him only once since I was seven years old, and I didn't recognize him at first. After a brief but happy greeting, he helped his father put the furniture together while Mother and I arranged a few knickknacks. We then went to the kitchen, built behind the house, to prepare a meal for everyone. We had rice with scrambled eggs and leftover dried meat she had prepared for the trip. Mother cleaned the dishes, and I took Nho and Kinh outside. From the back of the house, I could see mountains in the distance, shimmering in the heat, and miles of white sand with an occasional small, dry bush. From that vantage point, it looked as if we were living in the middle of a desert, but on the opposite side of the house was the ocean. Other than digging for tiger beetles in the sand, there was nothing to do, and the strong wind kept blowing sand in our eyes and faces. We grew tired of fighting the wind and went back inside. I thought to myself, "Qui Nhon seems hostile and boring, and it isn't a likeable place for me."

Weeks went by, and I saw there were no signs of a school, nor did I see any students in the area. I didn't know if there were any and didn't bother to ask. The only activity of interest to me was playing on the beach with my brother and sister or plucking my stepfather's gray hair for money. He paid me fifty cac, about five cents, for every one hundred gray hairs I plucked. When I had enough money, I walked more than a mile to rent a bicycle, which cost me one dong and fifty cac, or three hundred grey hairs. Most of the bikes I rented were old and about to fall apart, but when I got one, I pedaled home as fast as I could, because I didn't want to waste time. Even though the bikes were in bad shape, I wished I had one of my own.

While giving the kids a ride one day, my stepfather called me. Afraid I had done something wrong, I approached him in fear. He looked at the bicycle for a moment and said, "I want to try it." Having never ridden one before, he asked, "Can you hold the bike while I pedal it?"

I realized I wasn't going to be punished for something and replied happily, "Oh, yes, Father." The bicycle was made for kids, and he was so big and tall that he looked like King Kong on wheels, but I was happy to help him ride.

His balance was terrible, and he fell a lot. Most of the time, I managed to get out of his way, but sometimes he fell on me, and we both laughed. We were both scraped, cracked, and bleeding, but he did not want to stop riding.

Mother saw us and said to my stepfather, "You are too old and too big for that small bicycle; you look silly trying to ride it."

He ignored her and kept going. Finally, his bleeding knees and elbows forced him to stop, and I had just enough time to take the bike back to the rental place. Good times with my stepfather were rare; I treasured them and wished I had more.

Hen lived at the military base, but now and then he would come to spend the night. He had a girlfriend, but he never brought her home. I heard she was older than he was and had three children from a previous marriage. My stepfather did not approve of her and said he would never allow a widow with kids to marry his virgin son. In fact, my stepfather forbade Hen from bringing his girlfriend home. His strong, controlling nature always caused feuds to flare between him and his son. Mother tried to keep the peace between them, but neither listened.

After one of their big fights, my stepfather stormed out of the house. He didn't say where he was going, but Mother told me he had gone to Long Phuoc, where he heard that a number of my relatives, including Uncle Ky's family, had relocated. I was hoping it was true and couldn't wait for my stepfather to return to find out.

At midday, while my stepfather was still away, I took Kinh and Nho to the ocean to play on the beach, which was normally deserted. I told the kids to stay put and not to wander off. The cool, refreshing water was so inviting, I dove right in and swam away from shore. Without warning, a strong current pulled me under, and I struggled to get my head above water.

I fought the current for what seemed like an eternity, and just as I was about to give up, the current let me go. I looked around and realized that I had drifted a considerable distance from where I started, and I was too tired to swim back. I floated until I felt strong enough to swim to shore.

I ran to where I had left the kids, but they were nowhere in sight. In a panic, I ran all over the beach calling for them. "That's it!" I thought. "My brother and sister have drowned!"

I cried and prayed for them as I ran home to tell Mother. I went to the kitchen to look for her, and to my surprise, Kinh and Nho were in the kitchen by themselves playing with fire at the wood-burning stove. I put the fire out, said, "Thank God!" and hugged them both.

*   *   *

I was sweeping the floor one day, when Hen and his girlfriend walked into the house. Surprised, I bowed and greeted them. They smiled and greeted me back. She wasn't beautiful, but she was nice and friendly. I called for Mother to come greet them, and the three of them talked. While they were talking, I overheard Hen telling Mother he was going to America for military training.

"Where is America?" I asked Mother after Hen and his girlfriend left. "Somewhere near Germany or France," she replied.

Six months later, Hen returned from America. He brought a single gift: a doll for my sister. It was a beautiful doll, with blond hair and blue eyes. I was so envious and wished it were mine. My stepfather took charge of the doll anyway, and my sister wasn't even allowed to play with it. He kept it locked up in a cabinet, and the only time he touched the doll was to show it to his patients or our guests. Whenever the doll was taken out of the cabinet, all of us kids had to stand at a distance and watch. He showed his guests the different things the doll could do; it could close its eyes and move its arms and legs. The guests looked and touched, as they puzzled over this strange-looking doll, and sometimes they turned the doll upside down to see under its dress. When the guests left, the doll was locked up again.

Hen married his girlfriend not long after he returned from America, but there was no wedding party. My stepfather was furious that his oldest son had disobeyed him—this was an unpardonable sin. It was traditional that marriages be arranged, or at the very least, approved of by the parents. Without this parental blessing, couples were sometimes disowned by their families.

With a solid rift between my stepfather and Hen, there was no reason for us to stay in Qui Nhon any longer. "We are moving to Long Phuoc," my stepfather told us during dinner one evening. "We will travel to Saigon by train," he said. "Then we must take a bus to Bien Hoa and ride a boat to Long Phuoc."

I was so excited to be leaving Qui Nhon. It was definitely the most boring place I had ever lived. I could not wait to see my relatives again, especially Uncle Ky and his family. Den was back on summer break, but he didn't want to go with us, and chose to stay behind with his brother. My stepfather left almost everything for his two sons. We left Qui Nhon, taking only our necessities and our clothes with us.

We spent several days on the train, before arriving in Saigon. My feet hit the ground at the train station, and I was fascinated by the commotion surrounding me. I fought a crowd of people coming from and going to the train and ran to the front gate. It was incredible. There were countless people and noisy vehicles going in every direction. I was captivated and knew then that I wanted to be a part of the thrilling excitement of Saigon. I watched in dazed silence much longer than I should have.

Suddenly, I remembered that I had arrived there with my family. I ran back into the station looking for them, but they had disappeared. I ran around asking every stranger I bumped into if they had seen my family. But they would give me a quizzical look and rush off about their own business.

I spotted my stepfather walking toward me in the distance. I was so relieved to see him. "Father! Father!" I called and ran to his side.

"Where were you?" he shouted, and he slapped me so hard my teeth rattled. Then he turned around and walked away. I followed him in silence, rubbing my face to ease the pain.

He took me back to the bus station where my family was waiting.

The bus motor was running, waiting for the last passengers. I jumped aboard after my stepfather and sat next to my mother. She slapped me right where my stepfather had, and shouted, "We almost missed the bus because of you!" The second we were seated, the bus left the station. I could hear the driver complaining about the delay, and my tears flowed as I felt the imprints of ten fingers crisscrossing my cheek.

Bien Hoa is not far from Saigon, but because of the bad roads, the heavy traffic, and the bus constantly stopping to let people on and off, it took us an hour and a half to get there. We carried our belongings to the Dong Nai River, just in time to see the last boat leave the dock. My stepfather said that because of the delay I had caused, we missed the boat. I felt bad for causing so much trouble.

Since we missed our boat, we had to sleep on the riverbank that night. The following morning, we had breakfast, which consisted of French bread and sweet milk. The boat arrived early to drop people off, but it didn't leave until noon. Then, finally, the wait was over, and we boarded the bright, multicolored wooden boat that was very old and looked as if it were about to fall apart at the seams. The deck was wet and slippery, and my stepfather had to help each of us on. We sat on a long, wooden bench that ran the length of the boat. About fifty people boarded, plus animals—mostly ducks, chickens, dogs, and small pigs. The passengers who were not fortunate enough to find a seat had to stand. After the boat was full, the roaring of the old engine pushed it away from the dock. The harder the engine roared, the thicker the smoke gushed out, causing passengers to cover their faces. Some coughed, while others gasped for air. The smell of the gas and kerosene that the old engine burned was more than we expected, and it wasn't until the middle of the river before the engine finally calmed down. Like the bus, the boat made many stops to let people and their animals on and off, and it took us more than three hours to get to Long Phuoc.

Chapter 10

BAMBOO BRIDGE

AS WE ARRIVED in Luong Phuoc, the boat honked its horn and slowed down as it prepared to dock. I stood up and looked over my mother's shoulder as it drew closer to the muddy shore and to the worn patch of dirt where they picked up and dropped off passengers. A half dozen people stood on shore, looking as if they were waiting for relatives or loved ones. Most of the passengers exited the boat, and I followed. I could hear my joints snapping and cracking from sitting in one position for so long. Carrying a bag, I walked with my family down a crooked dirt road.

The village of Long Phuoc looked very poor. Most of the homes were made from coconut leaves, and I saw no cars or any other forms of transportation. We approached the house my stepfather bought on one of his trips. He picked up a leafy door, set it aside, and we walked in. There were openings in the walls big enough to walk through, and the house lacked furniture, running water, and electricity, but the smooth clay floor felt good on my feet.

After I looked around inside, I walked out the back door. I noticed the house had been built over an large ancient cemetery. The rusty, old limestone grave markers were everywhere, including our yard. Some were still standing, but most had fallen into decay.

I saw two Catholic churches, each about half a mile away, in opposite directions. A clump of huge oil trees stood a hundred feet high, most of them scattered around an area near the house. Mother spread out the mat on the floor of our new home and called me to come eat. I was surprised we even had food. Mother had somehow managed to get some condensed milk, canned sardines, Asian baloney, and bread earlier in the morning. Over dinner, my parents discussed what they would need to make our new home livable, and then we settled in for the night.

The following morning, I asked Mother if I could take the kids to see Uncle Ky. "I don't know where he lives," she replied.

"He will be easy to find in this small village," I assured her.

"Go ahead," she relented, "but be careful."

I asked my stepfather for general directions and knew I could ask local residents along the way. We crossed the village and passed through several rice fields before coming to a small, unstable bamboo bridge, which crossed a deep creek. With great care, I helped the kids across, one at a time. Uncle Ky's house was just on the other side of the bridge.

This home resembles my Uncle Ky's, with the bamboo bridge;
they are common throughout South Vietnam.

My aunt and two cousins, Tuan and Bao, saw us and ran to the front yard to welcome us. We all held hands, dancing in a circle and laughing, except for Cousin Tuan, who was too old to join us. A minute later, I stopped dancing, looked around, and asked, "Where is my uncle?"

"I'll take you to him," Cousin Bao replied. I had not seen my cousins for several years, and both of them had changed. Before, Cousin Bao was shorter than me, but now he was taller, and Cousin Tuan was growing into a young man. He must have been fifteen or older, while Bao and I were only around ten.

Uncle Ky was working in the field, digging for sweet potatoes, when he saw us coming. He smiled, stopped what he was doing, and walked toward us.

"Hello Uncle," I said. "I've missed you and your family so much. That's why I came to see you as soon as I could."

He patted each of us on our heads. "Oh, you have grown so much!" he said. "Thank God you are here."

"Uncle," I said, "this is my brother and sister, Kinh and Nho." He smiled and patted them on their heads again. It was so good to see him, and we talked and laughed as we walked back to the house.

He lived on a narrow peninsula in a small shack made of leaves and sticks. "It wouldn't take a very big wind to blow it away," I thought. Surrounding the house was a garden, a watermelon patch, a rice field, a few fruit trees, and a small creek. It looked poor, but peaceful, and I fell in love with it.

"You must stay for lunch," Uncle Ky said.

"Thank you, Uncle, I will," I replied.

While my aunt cooked rice and prepared vegetables, we followed Uncle Ky to the creek. He threw out a small casting net and within minutes caught enough fish and shrimp for our meal. And what a meal it was! Everything was delicious and fresh, right from his backyard.

My uncle and aunt returned to the fields, while Tuan ran an errand. The rest of us ran off to play. We climbed trees, picked fruit, and swam in the creek, just as we used to do. We had fun playing until my aunt and uncle returned from work.

"Can you stay for supper?" Uncle Ky asked.

"I would love to, but I have to go home," I responded, since we had been gone all day. "Mother will be expecting us, but I'll be back to see you soon." They followed us outside, waving goodbye to us as we walked away. We waved back, smiling, and I left their house with a peaceful, happy heart.

It took almost a week to find and visit all my relatives who had moved to the village of Long Phuoc. My Aunt Ba and Uncle Tu were not among them, because they were unable to leave North Vietnam. All of their children were in South Vietnam with us, so I felt bad for them. Not long after moving to Long Phuoc, we received the sad news that Aunt Ba had passed away. I think she died from a broken heart and loneliness.

Every morning, Mother woke me before sunrise to go to church. We had to walk through the old cemetery to get there, and the dark bushes and old tombstones seemed to come to life whenever I walked by them. I was scared of ghosts, and most of the time I walked with my hand covering my face, peeking through my fingers at the road. Sometimes, I closed one eye. Other times, I ran with my eyes half open. Now and then, I stumbled and fell, but I didn't slow down until I reached the church. Once there, I caught my breath, dusted off my clothes, and walked inside, acting very respectful and nonchalant, as if nothing happened.

I often tried to find a place to sit in a back pew so I could sleep, but I was seldom successful. The churches were divided into sections by age and sex, and if I didn't sit in my designated area, a church supervisor or a nun escorted me by the ear to the appropriate pew.

The nuns watched the children and punished anyone who fell asleep or talked to their neighbor. I often felt the sharp sting of their sticks as I made halfhearted attempts to stay awake. Most of the time, I tried to avoid these problems by not going to church at all. I'd get dressed, and after Mother left I found a place to hide or would crawl under the bed to sleep. When I heard her return, I sneaked out the back door, then walked in the front door after her, acting as if I had just come from church. When she didn't see me at church, she asked where I had been, and I always told her I went to the other church—lucky for me, there were two.

One morning when I decided to skip church, I sat on the ground at the back of the house with my head resting on my knees, fully dressed and sound asleep. It was just my luck that she picked that particular day to come through the back door. She must have sensed I was back there. When she saw me, she gave me a hard kick, and I fell over. Before I had a chance to get up, she gave me a stern look and warned, "You will die and go to hell, if you don't go to church every morning and night, like you should." Her scolding, accompanied by the kick, was enough to scare me into going to confession with her the following evening.

Because there was so little to do in Long Phuoc, everyone attended church in the morning and at night. Once a week, the priest took confession before evening Mass. I couldn't understand why people had so much sin to confess when there was nothing sinful to do in town, but since my mother went to confession, I had to go too.

We found an empty pew that evening, dropped to our knees, crossed ourselves, and prayed. Mother was sobbing and begging God to forgive her sins, while I was having trouble concentrating on being sorry. I was trying to cry like her, but with little sincerity. She could tell I was not very remorseful and gave me a dirty look. I tried my best to think about something sad enough to bring tears to my eyes, but I was unsuccessful.

Instead, I just covered my face with both hands and leaned toward the front pew. I made what I thought were convincing sobbing sounds to please her, but she saw through my charade and gave me a hard slap on the back of my head, causing my forehead to hit the pew in front of me. I rubbed the painful spot on my forehead and found that a knot had risen there. I got up and ran outside, realizing too late that I had a real reason to cry.

Unfortunately for our family, my stepfather's practice suffered because the village was so poor, and the sick people couldn't afford a doctor. We were not much better off than they were. I didn't understand why he had left the beautiful city of Nha Trang and my stepfather's successful business there to move to Qui Nhon and then to Long Phuoc. I guess he felt that his family and relatives were worth the sacrifice.

In Long Phuoc, there was a small private school run by one of the Catholic churches. They charged tuition, which my family couldn't afford, and I knew better than to ask if I could go, because I knew what the answer would be. I just hoped the future would provide an opportunity for me to continue my education.

At that time, Mother was pregnant again, and when her time was near, she told me what to do while she was gone. She traveled three hours by herself on a boat to get to a public hospital in Bien Hoa to have her baby. Bien Hoa was the nearest city we could go to for food, medicine, hospital care, or anything else of importance. During the week she was gone, I took over her work like she asked. When I had time, I gathered leaves and sticks that had fallen from the large oil trees and used them to cook our food.

Each day, when the work was done, I took King and Nho to the boat landing to wait for Mother. On the eighth day, I saw her getting off the boat, carrying her newborn baby. I ran to her and helped her with the bag she was carrying.

"Is it a boy or girl?" I asked.

"It's a boy," she replied. We all wanted to see the baby, and Mother opened the thin blanket to show him to us. We all touched him and smiled; he was so precious.

I was worried about my new baby brother, because before Mother went to the hospital, my stepfather told her, "Don't come home with a boy, because I'll give him away. We've got too many boys already!" Mother said nothing to him, she just picked up her bag and walked away. I was happy my mother was home. I just hoped my stepfather didn't mean what he said.

We walked in the door, and I said, "It's a boy, Father."

"Now we have another mouth to feed," he grumbled. "Boys are worth nothing." To my relief, he didn't give the baby away as he had warned. Later, they named him Bay, which means the number seven, as he was the seventh child.

When Bay was two months old, I learned that my stepcousin Lam had started teaching at the Catholic school. To my delight, I learned that because I was a relative, I could attend for free. I begged my stepfather to let me go, pointing out he would not have to pay anything.

He bent his head and looked at me over his reading glasses, and asked, "Who will pay for your school supplies?"

"I'll find a way," I answered.

"Who will take care of your brothers and sister while you're in school?" he asked. "I'll take care of them somehow," I replied.

After running out of arguments, he finally gave me his permission. I had no idea how I was going to keep my promises, because I was taking care of three children, one of them an infant, and Mother could not take care of them and do all of her other chores by herself. But I wanted to go to school, regardless of the circumstances.

The first day of school, I asked Mother for money to buy one pencil and one workbook. She had enough for a notebook, but that was all. With more than a little anxiety, I asked my stepfather for money to buy a pencil.

This made him angry. "You said you would never have to ask me for any money."

"This is the first day, Father," I said. "I'll never ask you for money again."

He frowned for a few moments and handed me just enough for one pencil. "What are you going to do with your brother and sister while you're in school?" he asked.

"I'll take them to school with me," I reassured him. I took the money, ran straight to a nearby store and bought a notebook and a pencil. Then I went home, grabbed a knife, sharpened the pencil, and put it together with my notebook.

I woke the kids, took them to the kitchen, where I washed their faces, changed their clothes, and fed them. Mother said, "Since this is your first day of school, leave the children at home. I'll take care of them for you."

"Thank you so much, Mother," I said with relief. "I love you with all my heart."

I left the house and ran all the way to school, which was a small, concrete building next to the church. Stepcousin Lam saw me enter the building and led me to a crowded room. About fifty students shared the room and were divided into groups according to grade level. Although I was eleven years old, I was placed with the younger children in the third grade group. I felt somewhat out of place at first but soon forgot my discomfort as class got underway.

Stepcousin Lam taught three grade levels in one room—the second, third, and fourth grades. When everyone settled in, he looked around, counted the students, and checked our school supplies. "How many workbooks do you have?" he asked me.

"Just one," I said.

"You'll need eleven more," he told me.

"I can't get another workbook," I replied. "I was lucky to get this one." "You also will need a pen, and ink," he continued.

"I'm sorry," I said, "but there is no way I can get any more supplies. My stepfather told me that if he has to spend another cac on school, he will not let me go." Lam looked at me and shook his head in dismay. He was my stepfather's nephew, and I think he understood my situation.

For several months, my attendance was erratic, depending on the amount of work that had to be done at home. I had to take care of my brother and sister and often had to bring them with me to school. I sat near the window and watched them as they played in the schoolyard. Many times, I had to run outside the class to take care of the kids when they cried or needed me. That caused me to miss some of the lessons, and it distracted the other students. The teacher did not like that at all. He ran outside after me one day and yelled, "Tell your father to either let you go to school or keep you home where you can take care of your brother and sister." He just didn't understand. My longing to continue school was far more important to me than his scolding and criticism. After all, being inside the school was better than being outside listening.

It was also a challenge having to juggle many subjects into one work-book, and I often had to borrow a pen and ink from other students when the lessons required them.

In his impatience, Lam punished me with a heavy metal ruler for not completing my work as he expected, and I often went home with a knot on my head from it. Of course, he used the metal ruler on the other children when they misbehaved, too.

In less than two weeks, I filled the workbook my mother had bought me and asked her to buy me another, but she didn't have the money. When I asked my stepfather, he reminded me of my promise to not bother him for help. He was determined to keep me from going to school, because he believed girls didn't need an education.

In desperation, I had to steal school supplies from the store. Using these and other devious methods, I completed that school term, which ended in 1958.

During the summer break, my stepfather decided to dig a well near the house. He said, "With a well, we won't have to go to the river for water so often, and we can also use it to water our garden."

This sounded good to me, so I was the first to volunteer. "I just hope I don't dig up someone's grave," I thought.

After my stepfather selected the location for the well, we started digging. At first, my parents helped, but when the hole got deeper, I was the only one small enough to do the job. Using a small hand shovel, I filled buckets with dirt, and then my parents hauled them to the surface with a rope. They lowered me and pulled me up the same way each day, with a rope tied around my waist.

Days passed and conditions in the well worsened. The smell of limestone, sulphur, and mud caused nausea and gave me headaches. After several weeks, I hit a water pocket. "Water, water!" I yelled to my parents. They were as excited as I was. I kept digging until the water level rose above my knees and to my waist, and then I signaled for my parents to pull me up. I looked like a mud statue and smelled like rotten eggs. I was so relieved I had not dug up someone's bones and even more relieved to be leaving that nasty mud hole for the last time. The air on the surface never smelled fresher.

After the hole was dug, we cleaned out the well by emptying muddy water for the next few days, until the water was clear. Though it had been hard work, the well saved us innumerable trips to the river and, in the end, it was worth all the trouble. We used the water for bathing, cooking, and watering the garden. The fruit and vegetables were greener and healthier than they had ever been. What a difference the well made!

In my free time, I liked to go crabbing with my friends. My family always enjoyed fresh crab soup, especially when we didn't have to pay for it. One day, on my way home from church, a friend asked, "Do you want to go crabbing with me tomorrow?"

"Where?" I asked.

"On the other side of the Dong Nai River."

I had never ventured that far to go crabbing before, but I thought it would be a good idea. "I'll ask my mother for permission, and I'll let you know." I said.

Mother was reluctant to let me go, at first. She wasn't too keen on letting me cross a dangerous river in a crab boat. Many boats turned over because of the heavy current, and some people drowned. But I convinced her it would be safe because I was a good swimmer, and she agreed to let me go.

Before the sun rose on the following morning, my friend and I met up with a group of professional crabbers to cross the river. I took food and a large basket designed for holding crabs, and boarded a small boat, which already held four older women. The women took turns rowing the boat against the strong current in the very wide river, and it took us a long time to reach the bank on the other side. They tied the boat to a tree trunk, and we each got out and walked separately into the rice fields.

The narrow footpaths that divided the rice fields were not strong enough or wide enough to support more than one person at a time. Besides, if we all flocked together, there would not be enough crabs for each of us to be able to catch some. Therefore, we had to spread out, but before we left, we agreed to meet back at the boat dock before dark.

As I walked alone down a footpath, the fields seemed to stretch to the horizon, and the rice stalks were taller than my head. Only a few trees and tall bushes broke the monotony. I walked along a dirt path, looking for crab holes. When I saw one, I jumped into the field and stuck my arm into the hole until I felt something. I was often pinched by a crab or stuck by a fish fin, causing my fingers to bleed. Sometimes, frogs and snakes occupied the holes, but they didn't bother me. I just pulled them out, tossed them aside, and continued crabbing.

It was the leeches that gave me the most trouble. I didn't notice them until they had already drawn blood and fallen off. That's when I felt the pain. They left open wounds that I had to pack with mud to stop the bleeding.

The midday sun was getting hot, and I was hungry, so I stopped to rest and eat. I untied the food wrapped in a banana leaf, which I had tied to my waist. I looked around before I ate to see if I could see anyone else, but there was no one in sight. I wondered how far I had gone and where everyone else was. I sat down in the dirt and ate rice and little salty shrimp with their heads and shells still attached. I drank water from a pool in the field and went back to crabbing.

Before long, the sun went down, the sky turned dark, and my basket was full. I stuffed rice leaves on top to keep the crabs cool. I closed the lid back on the top and realized it must be time for me to go home. I dragged the heavy basket down the path, looking for the way back to the boat.

In my preoccupation, I forgot which direction I had wandered. I stood on my tiptoes but couldn't see over the rice stalks and bushes. "I'm lost!" I thought. I got nervous and dragged the basket behind me, wandering around in circles. I called for my friend, and when no one answered, I began crying. I searched for the way back to the boat until the sky turned black.

All alone in the dark, I was scared and tired. I sat beside the basket, hoping someone from the group would pass by. I stretched out and, sitting still, began to feel the pain from the leech wounds on my legs. I couldn't see the wounds but felt the blood oozing from under the dried mud I had packed over them earlier. I chewed a handful of rice leaves until they were moist and patted them on the wounds. The cuts in my hand caused by fish fins and the crab pinches were beginning to hurt and bother me, too.

I sat peeling dried mud from my face, peering through the dark, watching the blackness settle in. I listened to the wind blowing through the field, causing the thin rice leaves to sway in the air like a thousand green snakes trying to hold on in a gusting wind. The wind, whirling around my neck, felt like a cold hand touching me. The sinister noises from the rice stalks, combined with the cacophony of frogs and insects, produced haunting and frightening sounds in the night.

I tried not to think about the eerie noises as I rested my head on my knees and dozed off. Hungry mosquitoes took turns on the exposed parts of my body, and their swarming woke me. I looked around and hoped it was all just a bad dream.

But then when I stood to stretch my weary legs, the pain and stiffness assured me I wasn't dreaming. I tried to move about, but I tripped and fell on top of the crab basket. My terror got the best of me, and I scrambled to my feet and dragged the basket behind me, making another futile attempt to find the river. I was crying softly at first, but soon I was screaming for help at the top of my lungs. When there was no response, I crossed myself and prayed for God to protect me.

As I wandered, lost, my imagination started running away with me. I began seeing things and hearing what sounded like people laughing all around me. I thought I heard them whisper, "You are going to die." I sat back down, closed my eyes, covered my ears, and bent my head between my knees. I didn't want to see or hear anything more. Thankfully, because I was so tired, I was able to doze off again.

The sky started to lighten, and I discovered I was right next to the river, not far from where we had tied the boat the day before. I dragged my basket to the riverbank and waited for the professional crabbers. I knew they would return to the same spot to hunt for more crabs, and soon, the boat that had brought me came into view. I was relieved and happy to see the boat that held the same four women from yesterday, minus my friend.

The boat docked, and a woman asked, "What happened to you yesterday?"

"I got lost," I replied.

"That's too bad," she said. "We looked for you and waited as long as we could. You'll have to wait here if you want to go back with us this afternoon."

"I don't mind waiting," I replied. When they left, I stayed right near the boat. I wasn't about to get lost again. The day wore on, and as I sat waiting, my stomach grumbled, reminding me that I was hungry. I had not eaten since yesterday. I went to the river several times to scoop up water and drink it, to calm my stomach.

The group returned from the fields late in the afternoon. They helped me aboard and then rowed the boat back to the other side. When I finally made it home, I dragged the heavy crab basket into the yard. Kinh and Nho greeted me as I approached our house.

"Did you catch many crabs?" Kinh asked.

"I caught a lot!" I said with a smile, "And we are going to have good crab soup today."

My stepfather saw me and said, "You wasted two days of work for those stupid crabs?" I just smiled and said nothing.

I dragged the crabs to the back of the house. Then, I took a large bamboo basket from the kitchen and prepared to dump them out. I opened the lid and pulled the rice leaves from the top of the basket as Mother walked in.

"Where were you last night?" she asked with a frown and began to help me with the crabs.

"I got lost and missed the boat," I answered.

"You shouldn't be so careless," she said.

"I won't be careless next time, Mother," I said.

When we emptied the crabs into the bamboo basket, it was obvious that they were all dead.

Mother looked at the mess and said, "If you want to stay alive, you'd better hurry up and bury those crabs before your father sees them."

I was so upset. That was the second time I had gotten into trouble over stupid crabs. I apologized to Mother as I tried to explain how it must have happened. I had kept them out of the water and in the hot sun for far too long. She looked at me and said, "I don't care how they died, what killed them, or whose fault it was. The important thing now is for you to get rid of them."

With tears rolling down my cheeks, I dragged the basket into the backyard and buried the dead crabs.

I was exhausted and felt on the verge of starvation, but before I could eat, I had to wash up. I dipped water from the well, poured it over my head, and gave myself a good scrubbing. Once the mud was washed off, I examined the cuts and the leech wounds I received the day before and noticed that some of them started bleeding again. I made a solemn promise to myself that I would never go crabbing again. Then, in my wet clothes, I went to the kitchen, looking for something to eat. I found only a handful of rice and a few small shrimp, but it was enough to keep the hunger pains away and keep me from shaking.

* * *

Long Phuoc was a small village, and it was not important to the South Vietnamese government. The villagers were too concerned with surviving and trying to obtain food to notice the events that were unfolding, both in our country and around the world, which were to affect us so much in the years to come.

The 1956 elections to unify Vietnam, as called for by the 1954 Geneva Accords, never took place. President Diem, who had dislodged Bao Dai, refused to hold them, claiming fair elections would be impossible in either the North or the South.

The American government supported Diem's decision. They were convinced Ho Chi Minh was too popular, and the communists would win in a free election.

The Viet Minh had accepted the country's partition only because it was to be a temporary measure. They felt betrayed by Diem's refusal to hold elections. To achieve unification, they knew it would be necessary to overthrow the Diem regime, and that would require the support of the South Vietnamese. Thus, the program to infiltrate Viet Minh insurgents into villages in the South was intensified.

Consequently, America further increased its economic and military aid to the Diem government, setting the tone for the massive escalation that was to follow.

Chapter 11

LONELY CHOPSTICK

IT WAS TIME for school to reconvene, but my stepfather told me that I couldn't go. He didn't think his nephew would be teaching anymore, and if another teacher came, he couldn't afford the tuition. I was heartbroken.

During this time, Ly, a skinny distant cousin on my late father's side, visited us from Saigon. While eating dinner one night, he asked my parents, "Can Loan go with me to Saigon and help my pregnant wife and two kids?" He then added, "I will take care of her while she lives with us, and I will send her to school."

As soon as I heard the word school, my ears perked up. I looked at my parents, awaiting their response. They were taking too long to answer, so I decided to help them make up their minds. "I would be happy to help you and your family," I said. "Especially if you will let me go to school."

My stepfather didn't appreciate my voluntary remarks, and although he said nothing, he gave me a dirty look. Mother needed my help around the house, but she also knew how much I wanted to go to school and agreed to let me go. "You can go if it's alright with your father," she said. "It doesn't matter to me."

With some sarcasm, my stepfather replied, "Your mother's the boss. Besides, if you leave, there will be one less mouth to feed."

I didn't feel quite so bad about leaving, because my step-grandmother had moved back with us, and I knew she would help out around the house. My stepfather didn't care if I stayed or left, as long as someone other than he did the work.

It was settled then. I would be going to Saigon. Leaving my family would be sad, but the idea of going back to school filled me with excitement, and I certainly didn't mind the hard work. I left with Cousin Ly a few days later.

Cousin Ly and his family lived in a small wooden house on a narrow alley in Phu Nhuan, a few miles from downtown Saigon. At first, Cousin Ly and his wife were nice and friendly, but within a short period, they began treating me like an unpaid maid. Their two children, aged three and six, were well behaved, but I still had to take care of them. I helped with shopping, cooking, cleaning house, washing clothes, and anything else a maid would do.

Months went by without school being mentioned, and when I asked, they said I couldn't go to public school without a birth certificate. Cousin Ly told me he had applied for my birth certificate, but it would take some time to process. When I asked them to let me go back to my family, they reassured me I would be going to school soon. I felt trapped, but there was nothing else I could do but wait.

Ly's wife had her baby, and soon after, I received my birth certificate. However, before I had a chance to go to school, Ly developed tuberculosis and lost his job. We had to move to a cheaper place in Ong Ta, a very poor section of town. My cousin rented a shabby stilt house, built over a small creek. Garbage, dead animals, and raw sewage flowed down the creek, and the smell was noxious.

The house didn't have running water, and there was no well nearby. They bought water by the bucket from a delivery truck every morning, and Ly's wife used it for cooking and for bathing her family. She made me take a bath and wash my clothes in the creek water, where everyone dumped their waste and garbage. I smelled better when I didn't bathe, and I asked her why I couldn't use the clean water to bathe in. She said she couldn't afford the cost of more water.

Ly's wife began treating me worse as time passed. She not only made me work harder, but she often beat me as well. I was fed only leftovers and often went to bed hungry. When Ly asked her why she didn't let me eat with them at the table, she explained that since I had asthma, she was afraid her family would catch it.

Not long after moving, Ly's tuberculosis became worse. He coughed up blood all the time and lost a lot of weight. He was already skinny, but he began to look like a skeleton. He ate little or nothing, and his condition worsened. Finally, his wife took him to the hospital, and within days, he died.

After Ly's death, his wife grew meaner. She blamed me for her husband's death, claiming my asthma caused him to catch tuberculosis.

I worked very hard for her without getting enough to eat, and the lack of food caused me to lose a lot of weight. I started looking like my poor, dead cousin. She fed me less than she had before, and the little food I received was given grudgingly. A few times, she threw table scraps in my face and told me to enjoy my meal. I was hungry and had no choice but to pick up the food from the floor and eat through my tears. I never understood why she hated me so much.

She started working part time in a store while I stayed home to take care of the chores and her three kids. Out of sheer desperation, I decided to escape my prison. One day, after she went to work, I ran to the next-door neighbor's house. I knocked on the door, and a sweet lady of about fifty opened it.

"I live next door, and I need help," I sputtered.

She took one look at me and asked in shocked surprise, "What happened to you, child? You are as skinny as a chopstick." She motioned for me to come inside.

"You look terrible," she continued. "I heard you being beaten often, but I didn't know that you weren't being fed."

After listening to my story, she promised to help. "I'll try to collect enough money in the neighborhood to get you out of there," she said.

I was so relieved to know someone cared enough to help me. I ran back to the house just before Ly's wife came home. If she had caught me out, she would certainly have killed me.

Four days later, while Ly's wife was at work, the nice neighbor lady came to the door and gave me the money she had raised. "I hope this will be enough to get you home to your family, you poor child. If you stay here much longer, I'm afraid you will die."

"Thank you so much," I said with a lump in my throat. "I'll never forget what you've done for me. I hope God blesses you forever." She left as soon as I thanked her, to avoid being caught.

I packed my clothes and told the oldest child to watch the other two until their mother came home. Then I walked away as fast as I could. I felt bad about leaving the children, but I had no choice. The poor kids didn't know what was going on.

Before going home, I stopped at the cemetery where Cousin Ly was buried. I found his grave and sat down to talk to him. "I hope you understand. I had no choice but to leave your wife and children," I said. "Thank you for getting me my birth certificate, even though the birth date was wrong, and I didn't get a chance to go to school. I know you tried your best." I wiped my tears and walked to the street.

I hailed a cyclo, and after some haggling over the fare, the driver agreed to take me to the Bien Hoa bus station. On the way, I reflected on my experiences over the past year. I wondered why it was so difficult for me to go to school. Most of my friends' parents forced them to go to school. Did I really did have some kind of disease that caused my cousin to die? The horn from a passing car brought me back to the present moment, and I dismissed my thoughts and tried to concentrate on what lay ahead for me.

I was so happy to be going home. It had been a long time since I saw my family, and I wondered how much my sister and brothers had grown. I bought a bus ticket to Bien Hoa and made sure there was enough left for boat fare. Then I spent the rest of my money on cookies and candy for my brothers and sister.

When we arrived at Long Phuoc, I jumped off the boat, carrying my small bag of clothes and ran all the way home. All three kids were in the yard playing. I called each of them by name, but they didn't recognize me at first, because I had lost so much weight. They were afraid of me and moved closer to each other. Seconds later, Kinh recognized me and whispered my name, but he was too shy to come to me.

Mother heard me in the yard and walked out to greet me. She smiled and said to the kids, "This is your big sister Loan, go to her."

The kids remained shy until I opened the bag of candy and cookies. Then they walked toward me, and I gave them each a handful. They accepted their gifts, smiled, and lost all of their shyness. Mother watched this gentle exchange and then asked me to follow her.

The kids ate their candy and cookies outside while I went with Mother to the kitchen. I helped her cook and told her about my experiences with Cousin Ly and his family. She was in tears when she heard about my cousin's death, but her sadness was also because of my mistreatment. "I'm so sorry I couldn't take care of you and had to let you go live with them. Ly promised me he would let you go to school; that was part of the deal. Besides, he paid us some money for one year of your work," she sobbed. "Now look at you, you look like a skin-wrapped skeleton."

"Our family is also having serious problems," she continued. "Your brother Den is staying with us during his summer break, and your father makes barely enough to feed our family of seven."

I listened with sadness as she continued, "It's not just our family. The whole village is going hungry. We had to ask the government for help. They gave us things we can't eat or use; things from the American Red Cross and other international foundations," she continued. "We don't eat or use corn meal and wheat flour, and we don't know what to do with them. We fed them to the pigs, and they are the only ones getting fat and happy. The old clothes we got from good-hearted people were too big and too heavy to wear, so we cut them up and made blankets. I just wish we could get a bag of rice, a bag of salt, and a few bottles of fish sauce. That would be more helpful."

After listening to Mother, I regretted coming home. I realized I was just another mouth to feed for an already hungry family, and that night, I couldn't sleep. After giving it a lot of thought, I decided I had to go. I had learned one very valuable lesson—that I could take care of myself. I vowed I would not be a burden to my family. "When my visit is over, I will leave home," I promised myself.

I stayed home for almost a week. I visited my relatives and some friends, and I also got to know Den better. For years, he had been away at school living with Hen, his older brother. He came home now and then to visit during school break. Both of us had matured, and we developed a good relationship. This time, he even trusted me enough to deliver secret letters to the girl he saw and admired who lived nearby. Uncle Ky's living conditions had not improved, but he did have enough to feed his family. In some ways, his family was in better shape than my own.

As I prepared to leave, I thought a lot about what I was going to do. From what I had seen of Saigon, I believed I could find work there. Besides, I wanted to become part of the bustle of a big city.

The day then came when I felt it was time for me to go. We came home from church, and Mother went to the kitchen to cook. I went to the closet, packed my clothes in a paper bag, and got ready to leave home. I went to the kitchen, where Mother was preparing rice and vegetable soup for breakfast.

"I'm going to Saigon to look for a job," I announced, as I filled up my bowl with rice. "Father can't feed all of us by himself, and I'm old enough to work."

Mother frowned for a moment and then said, "I don't like the idea of you going to some strange place by yourself."

"Don't worry. I'm thirteen years old, and I can take care of myself," I argued. "I can make money and bring it home for the family. We both know that Father needs my help right now."

"What will you do in Saigon?" Mother asked.

"There are many things I can do," I replied, as I ate rice and fish sauce, trying to save the vegetables for the rest of the family. "I'm not sure just what right now, but I know I have to leave for the sake of our family."

Mother grew very quiet. I'm sure she was thinking of the journey I had just proposed, and I know she didn't want me to go, but she had no choice. I finished my breakfast, put my empty bowl in the wash pan, and drew closer to her. "I have to go now, and I don't know when I'll be coming back," I said. "I'll miss you."

"Good luck," she sobbed. "Take care of yourself and avoid bad places." I promised her that I would.

While most of my family was still asleep, I left the house. I could hear Mother crying behind me as I walked toward the river in tears. I didn't have any money, and I didn't know how I was going to get to Saigon, but I was determined to find a way.

On that foggy morning I followed a dozen people as they lined up to get on a boat going to Bien Hoa. Once on the boat, I found an empty seat and sat down. I went to the bathroom whenever I saw the lady come to collect money. Before the boat docked at Bien Hoa, the operator asked for the boat fare.

"Money, money for gas," she called.

"I'm so sorry, I don't have any money. I promise to pay you when I come back," I pleaded.

She cursed me and threatened to call the police or throw me in the river. This caused a few curious stares from other passengers, wondering what was going on. I was scared and embarrassed, and I continued to apologize. She finally left me alone and tended to the others, but not before she gave me a dirty look and made a few more growls in my direction. Lucky for me, she neither called the police nor threw me in the river.

I hopped off the boat, found my way to the Saigon bus station, and boarded a bus. I hoped I would be as lucky on the bus as I had been on the boat. We had just turned onto the highway when the conductor walked toward me, and I realized my luck was running out.

"How far are you going?" he asked. "To Saigon," I replied.

He smiled and said, "That will be fifteen dong."

"I'm sorry, but I have no money," I said.

The conductor stopped smiling and told the driver to stop the bus.

When it jerked to a halt, the conductor grabbed me by the collar and pushed me through the door. "Get out!" he yelled. "And don't try this again!" Before I could regain my balance, the bus sped away, leaving me in a cloud of dust holding my paper bag of clothes. I stood on the roadside waiting for another bus to come. It took several more tries, using the same trick, before I made it to Saigon.

"I've reached my destination," I thought. "Now what am I going to do?"

Chapter 12

CONCRETE PILLOW

WITH A BAG of clothes secured under my arm, I stood in front of the
bus station, watching the multitudes of people rushing around. "Where
are they coming from, and where are they going to?" I wondered as I
walked to the street, not knowing where I was or where I was going.
I stopped a well-dressed, middle-aged woman walking by and asked,
"Can you please tell me where I can find a job?"

"What kind of job are you looking for?" she asked.

"I'm looking for any kind of work."

"Go to the Saigon Market," she replied. "Most people go there to
find odd jobs; I found my live-in maid there."

"Where is the market, and how do I get there?" I asked.

"In that direction," she replied, as she pointed to one of several busy
streets. "You can take the city bus or you can walk."

I thanked her and started walking. The sun baked my head, and the
hot tar roasted my bare feet. I looked up at the sun and realized it was
afternoon. I was tired and hungry, and I could hear my stomach growling as I wove my way through the maze of rushing people.

I stopped to catch my breath outside a busy restaurant. Out of curiosity, I peered through an open window, and could smell the delicious
food being served inside. I watched the customers eating rice, meat, and
soup. My mouth was watering as I walked away.

I thought about trying to sneak onto a city bus, but I had no idea
where one would take me if I got on, so I decided it would be safer
to continue walking. Now and then, I stopped people on the street to
ask for directions, and I kept walking until I saw a large, square steeple, with "Cho Ben Thanh" (Saigon Market) written below a big clock,

which said fifteen minutes past four. Before going inside the market, I stopped at a circular park across the street to rest. The park was crowded with hundreds of people coming and going. Almost everyone in the park was engrossed in some activity, and those who weren't just sat and stared into space. Some tried to sell their merchandise to people who were passing through the park. Noisy vehicles and their horns blended with the voices of vendors, standing behind their wares, hawking their goods. It was all very exciting to me.

I had walked for quite a while, and I sat on one of the benches to examine my painful feet. They were red, swollen, and blistered from walking on the hot streets and the rough, rocky sidewalks. I was anxious to see inside the market, so I didn't rest too long. I limped toward a crowd of pedestrians who were waiting for the traffic light to change, followed them to the other side, and discovered it was too late. The market had already closed for the day, and the massive gate was locked. I peered through the iron bars and saw that the market covered a huge area. I decided I would wait until morning and come back when the market reopened. Disappointed, I returned to the park, found an empty bench, and flopped down.

All of the people and cars milling about created a hypnotic noise that lured me into a deep sleep. I woke up in the middle of the night, and for a few moments, wondered where I was. When I recovered my bearings, I stood up and stretched my weary body. I looked around and noticed it was much quieter. Fewer cars and motorbikes circled the park, and a smaller number of people wandered around. One poor old drunk with a bottle in his hand tried to cross the street, and I giggled as I watched him stagger from side to side, mumbling something to himself. He took a long drink when he made it to the other side, as if congratulating himself for not being killed by the traffic. Then I watched as he disappeared into the train station, like the last star before dawn.

In the streetlight, I saw a city bus station opposite the market. Between the bus station and the market on my left were several tall buildings. On my right was the train station. Together, they surrounded the park.

I looked up and saw that the clock in the market pointed to four. It was very early in the morning. I heard a low train whistle coming from the station. I was curious, so I crossed the street to investigate. I walked inside the train station, and after glancing around the huge room for a few moments, recognized it was the same exciting station we had come through from Qui Nhon a few years earlier. It was the same place where I got into trouble with my stepfather for being so careless. I saw people of all ages—some lay about sleeping with their children, while others sat talking to each other. Some people just walked back and forth with a cigarette in their hand, oblivious to the piles of luggage everywhere.

Animal cages were scattered throughout the station. There were dogs, cats, pigs, ducks, and a large number of chickens. I felt sorry for these poor creatures, because they would soon become someone's food. The moaning of those helpless animals, mixed with the crying of children, and the coughing of sick people, turned the scene into a place of horror. I couldn't take it anymore, so I left.

I walked out the front of the train station and faced the busy street. I stood there, like a body without a soul, and stared at the world around me. There were a number of vendors selling hot and cold food and drinks along the huge steps. Many homeless people of all ages and genders were resting or sleeping, while others just sat with an empty expression on their face, staring into the void.

I noticed a poorly dressed girl, not much older than I, who sat by herself on a step. Our eyes met, and we smiled at each other. There seemed to be an unspoken bond between us, and I walked closer to her and sat down.

"What is your name?" I asked, "And where are you from?"

"My name is Trang, and I'm from far away," she replied.

"Where are you going?" I prodded. "Or are you waiting for a train?"

"Nowhere," she said as she looked away.

A few seconds of silence passed, and she asked me the same questions

I asked her. I told her who I was and why I was there. She relaxed a little and began telling me her story. "I'm all alone," she said. "I have no family. Everyone in my immediate family was killed in the northern war. I followed a relative south, but a few days ago she kicked me out," she continued. "Her husband molested me, but she blamed me for it," she cried.

"I have no place to go and no money. I came here to look for work, but last night, a thief stole what few clothes I had. It happened right here in the train station."

My heart went out to her. I thought my plight was bad, but hers was so much worse. "I know how you feel," I said.

"I've been in the park and the market looking for work during the day but haven't found anything yet," she told me. "I eat whatever I find, and at night I come here to sleep."

"Boy," I thought, "I hope I'm luckier than she is."

I asked her age, which is our custom. We seldom call each other by name, but by rank and age instead. She told me she was fourteen. Since she was a bit older, I addressed her as "Chi," or older sister. She, in turn, called me "Em," which meant younger sister. We talked for a long time and seemed to have a lot in common.

As the morning grew brighter, my hunger and thirst increased. "I'm very thirsty," I told Trang.

"Follow me. I'll take you to a public restroom near the market, where you can get something to drink," she said. "But you'll have to pay for it," she added.

"I have no money, but I'll manage somehow," I told her, as we crossed the street and walked toward the public restroom in a corner of the Saigon Market.

A stout lady sat in the collection booth at the entrance of the restroom. She was busy writing or reading something, I couldn't tell which. "May I please go inside for a drink of water?" I asked.

Without looking at me, she said, "You can't go in unless you pay five cac." (The equivalent of a nickel).

"I'm sorry, but I don't even have one cac," I replied, "I'm so thirsty. Can I please have just a drink of water?" I pleaded.

She grew tired of my begging and looked up over her reading glasses. "You can drink the water, but you better not use the toilet," she warned.

"I promise I won't," I said and headed straight to a water faucet, where the water ran continuously into a large cement tub. Those who used the bathroom would dip water from the tub with an aluminum dipper to flush the toilet; I drank out of the same dipper. The water was so refreshing, I didn't care. After quenching my thirst, I used the leftover water to wash my face.

The guard saw me and yelled, "What are you doing? Hurry up and get out of there."

"I'm not using the toilet," I assured her. "I'm just washing my face."

"You're not supposed to wash your face either," she shouted. "I told you to only get a drink."

With my face only partially washed, I walked out of the bathroom and thanked her. She gave me a dirty look and told me not to come back unless I had money. I smiled at her and walked away.

Trang was standing outside waiting for me. "Did you have a chance to use the toilet?" she asked.

"No, I didn't," I said.

"Come with me," she said, and she took me to a secluded area at the market between two shops. It was too early for the vendors to open their businesses, and they weren't there yet. She looked around and said, "Go ahead, I'll watch out for you." I was reluctant at first, but my bladder was about to burst, and I couldn't wait any longer. We took turns relieving ourselves, and then ran out of there laughing as if we had outsmarted the bathroom collection lady.

We walked toward the entrance, and I asked Trang, "Where can we look for a job?"

"Follow me," she said, and then asked, "Why don't we tell everyone we're sisters, so we can work together?"

"That sounds like a great idea!" I replied, and followed her through the gate.

The market was much larger inside than I had imagined. There were hundreds of small booths scattered throughout the enormous area. The market was divided into specialized sections. Merchants sold dried goods in one area, while meat and seafood were sold in another. It was early, and the shopkeepers were just setting up.

We walked through hundreds of small shops, where everything imaginable was on display, such as fruits and vegetables and live animals waiting to be slaughtered. The bright lights, shining down from the high ceiling, illuminated the vendors as they scurried around trying to get their merchandise ready for that day's customers.

In an area near the meat stands, we joined several other poorly dressed women of various ages. It was obvious we were all seeking jobs that didn't require training or education.

One older lady took it upon herself to organize and supervise the process. She gave us a toothless smile and told the others to make room for us. She reminded me of my old, dear friend Ba Cu from many years ago. I kept staring until she told me to quit gawking at her. I squeezed into the crowded line and told her the reason I was looking at her was because she resembled an old friend who had passed.

She patted my head with a grin and said, "I might look like your dead friend, but I'm very much alive." We all laughed.

Trang and I sat with the other ladies, waiting to be chosen for a job. A few well-dressed people began circulating through the area looking for workers. The toothless lady ran back and forth between potential employees and employers, trying to organize rates and working arrangements. She got paid by those who hired her workers. Many were hired, but since we agreed to stick together, Trang and I turned down several individual job offers for maid work, baby-sitting, waitressing, and dishwashing.

A few hours later, the market started thinning out and the prospective employers quit coming. The place was empty, except for Trang and me. It was noon, and we had been sitting for hours. As we stood up to stretch, Trang gave me a disappointed look. We both realized we had to try again the following day.

"My bladder is about to burst again," I told Trang. "Can you watch out for me, so I can relieve myself behind those deserted meat stands?"

"Yes," she said, "but you have to do the same for me."

"Of course," I replied.

After trading places, we made our way back to the park, found an empty bench, and plopped down.

"Do you know if this park has a name?" I asked.

"I've heard it called Bong Binh Saigon," she replied.

The park was busier than the previous day, and we sat and watched the bustling commotion around us. I enjoyed watching the peddlers, who were trying to sell everything from food to toys. They intercepted people walking through the park and tried their best to sell their merchandise. If any of the prospective customers showed an interest in a product, there would be instant pressure from the seller, and the bartering competition would begin. If a prospect refused to buy the merchandise, the seller would yell and curse, but if successful with a sale, they would show off their profits to the other peddlers.

By late afternoon, my stomach was killing me. I hadn't eaten for almost two days. I told Trang to keep an eye on my clothes while I searched for food. I looked through the park's garbage cans and found a few mango seeds with some fruit left on them. I also retrieved a few ends of stale French bread. I wrapped them together in a newspaper and started back to our bench to share my bounty with Trang.

I passed a lady selling soup from her portable kitchen. She balanced her kitchen in two baskets from a yoke much like the one Mother used to carry me in when I was little. In one basket sat a small charcoal burner, and on top of it was a pot of simmering crab stock. The other basket contained rice noodles, surrounded by fresh herbs and empty soup bowls. I smelled the sweet aroma of my favorite crab noodle soup, and my mouth watered as I watched the sales lady serve several bowls to her customers. I wanted to beg for some of the delicious soup but didn't have the nerve. One patron finished eating and left a few spoonfuls in the bottom of a bowl. My hunger pangs overcame my shyness and my pride.

I turned to the soup lady and asked, "May I please have the leftover soup?"

She gave me an impatient look, and instead of giving it to me, she emptied the bowl on the grass behind her. "If you want soup, you will have to pay for it," she growled.

I waited for the next patron and tried again. "I don't have any money, and I haven't eaten for two days," I pleaded. "All I'm asking for are the leftovers."

With an annoyed glance, she pushed the bowl in front of me. I gulped down the remaining scraps. I hung around and was able to get three more leftovers before she chased me away. I thanked her and walked back to the park toward Trang.

Suddenly, a policeman stormed into the park. He grabbed the merchandise from the peddlers and threw it into one big pile. "I'm going to arrest every one of you!" he yelled at the peddlers. "This is not a market, this is a park, and selling goods here is illegal!"

Merchants scattered in every direction, some with their goods and some without. A terrified salesman ran into me, and we both fell down. The mango seeds and bread I had collected flew everywhere. The man jumped up and continued running, while I got to my feet and picked up the mango seeds and bread pieces. The policeman gathered all the merchandise he had seized and threw it into his white jeep. He drove away, leaving many angry merchants cursing behind him.

I glanced back and noticed the soup lady had also disappeared. Trang and I shared the meager food I brought back, and after talking almost all night, we slept in front of the train station. The concrete steps served as my pillow.

For several days, we tried to find work together but had no luck. No one wanted to hire both of us, even when we agreed to work for almost nothing. Some claimed they could not afford to pay both of us, while others said it would cost too much to feed us. Our diet consisted of any leftovers we could beg or whatever we could find in garbage cans that was edible. We slept on the cement steps in front of the train station and sneaked into the public bathroom to wash and drink. At first, the collector yelled at us, but later, Trang and I agreed to clean her toilets, just so we could use them. I also promised I would pay her when I had money. She gave up chasing us away and just rolled her eyes and shook her head whenever she saw us coming.

Though the conditions were not to my liking, it was good to have a friend like Trang. I was worried about us not being able to find a job and make money. But I said nothing about my concerns to Trang. I wondered if she was worried, too.

Many days went by, and I began to get tired of my living conditions—tired of sneaking into the toilet, tired of eating garbage, and tired of laying my head on a concrete pillow every night. I was determined to do something about it. That night, before I went to sleep, I thought about our situation and came to the conclusion that we were not going to be hired if we stayed together. I decided that I must tell Trang in the morning that we had to look for work separately. While thinking about how I was going to tell Trang about my decision, I fell asleep.

Before morning, I woke up with a start. I sat up, glanced down at the spot where I had left my bag, and was shocked to discover it was gone. I felt terrible about losing all my clothes, and I woke Trang to tell her about my bag being stolen. She felt sorry for me, and we both cried.

As we sat there crying, a white truck screeched to a halt in front of the station, and several policemen jumped out. They started grabbing anyone who was sleeping on the steps, including Trang and me, and pushed all of us into the truck.

Shaking like a leaf, I asked a young boy sitting next to me, "What's going on? We didn't do anything wrong."

"You were sleeping on the street, weren't you?" he responded. "That's why you're going to jail." I was terrified.

"What are we going to do?" I asked Trang.

"I don't know!" she said and kept crying.

We were taken to a nearby police station. A guard separated the men from the women and put us into different cells. As the jail door clanged shut, I looked around the crowded cell. There were more than a dozen women of all ages in the room with us, some of them with heavy makeup, big hair, high-heeled shoes, and low-cut dresses.

The floor was wet and smelled like vomit and urine, and I felt sick to my stomach. Trang and I found our way to a corner and stood there, talking in whispers. We were worried about what would happen to us, and we wished the morning would come quickly.

At nine the following morning, the police started fingerprinting and identifying all of us. Since Trang and I were in a back corner, we were among the last to leave. A flashy girl with caked-on makeup standing next to me whispered, "Don't give the police your real name. It won't be good for you. If you keep using a different name and address each time you get caught, they'll treat you like a first offender."

Although I didn't understand her thinking, she appeared to have gone through this experience before and knew what she was doing. I decided to take her advice. Trang and I agreed to trade names. A policeman called me into his office first and asked my name. "My name is Trang," I replied.

"Your full name?" he demanded.

"Tran Thu Trang," I said.

"Your address?" he asked.

I gave him a phony one I came up with on the spot, and he wrote something in a thick black book. He then motioned me to step aside and signaled Trang to come before him. She answered the same questions I did, but used my name with a make-believe address. After taking our fingerprints, they released us. We found our way back to the market, but it had already closed.

My clothes were dirty and were beginning to smell, so I sneaked into the public bathroom to rinse them out. I wore the wet clothes and sat in the sun until they dried. We didn't return to the train station that night, and to avoid the police, we slept in a small alley not far from the market. Before going to sleep, Trang and I agreed we had to take work separately in order to get out of our current situation.

The following day, a lady offered a baby-sitting job to either one of us. Since Trang had been waiting longer, I told her to go first. She did not want to go, but I reminded her of our talk the night before, and she agreed to accept the job.

"Good luck," I said through my tears. "I hope someday we'll see each other again."

Trang was too choked up to say anything, and I could hear her crying as she walked away with her new employer. I watched her disappear through the crowded market, and I had the feeling I would never see her again. I bent my head and let the teardrops fall on my bare feet, creating brown spots on the dirty surface of my feet. Except for those owned by rich and important people in government, there were no telephones, and sometimes there were no home addresses. I didn't know how I would ever find Trang.

A heavyset lady, wearing expensive clothes and jewelry and a lot of makeup, stopped in front of me.

"How old are you?" she asked.

"I'm thirteen," I replied, as I dried my eyes.

"You're too young for the job," she said, with a big smile that caused her eyes to disappear under her fat eyelids.

"I can do any job older people can," I said, as I looked at her with my wide, red eyes.

"I need someone who can make men happy," she whispered. I stared at her, and she realized I didn't know what she meant. She whispered in some detail what I would have to do to make men happy. When I understood what she meant, I agreed I was too young for the job. She smiled again and walked away, leaving behind the heavy fragrance of perfume.

The market thinned out again, and I was still without a job. That evening, I returned to the same alley to sleep alone. It was very sad without Trang, and at midnight, a scream woke me. Startled, I sat up and saw the shadow of a man running toward me. I moved out of the way as he ran past. Behind him, another man was running with a stick in his hand, yelling "Thief! Thief!" When he saw me, he grabbed me by the shoulders.

"What were you doing in my house?" he shouted.

"I wasn't in your house," I said. "I've been sleeping right here all night."

"You're a liar!" he growled. He dragged me back to his house, located behind one of the stores. With his wife's help, he tied my hands behind my back with rope and told me to sit on the floor while he called the police.

"You're making a mistake," I pleaded. "The person you want is getting away." He ignored me and made his call.

The police arrived thirty minutes later and took me back to the same station I was taken to before. I was placed in the same cell, with the same smell, and some of the same kind of people who were there before. The next morning, the same officer who had taken my statement during my previous arrest asked me for my name. I was nervous and gave him my real name.

"I remember you," he said. "You were here before. Your name is still in my book."

It was then that I realized switching names with Trang had not been such a good idea. We should have used fictitious names instead. I tried to convince the officer I was innocent, but he ignored me. After writing something in his book, he took me back to the cell.

I discovered the prisoners who stayed more than one night had committed more serious crimes. We were fed two meals a day. Each of us had a bowl of rice, topped with a piece of dried fish, or a few pieces of vegetables. Any food tastes good when you're hungry. We were allowed to use the bathroom after each meal, but sometimes prisoners could not hold it and, in desperation, relieved themselves on the floor. I did, too.

The smell of urine mixed with vomit on the wet floor made me want to throw up.

I couldn't take it anymore, and I stopped a guard passing by and asked, "When can I get out of here?"

"How do I know?" he said.

"Can you find out?" I asked.

"Listen," he said, "they are processing your case and checking your record. It takes time."

"What record?"

"If it shows you are guilty," he said, "you will be locked up forever." Then he walked away.

Three days later, the guard took me to another office where I waited for more paper processing, and they took my fingerprints. To my great relief, that afternoon they released me. I walked to the market, but it was closed. I decided to take a chance and slept in the train station that night, mingling with the passengers coming and going.

To my surprise and great relief, the next day I found a job working as a maid for a family of five. The husband, a skinny man named Thuan, was about forty-five years old. His legs were paralyzed because of war injuries, and he was confined to a wheelchair. Thuan and his wife sold lottery tickets on street corners and were gone most of the day. I earned my keep by watching their three young children, washing their clothes, and helping to cook meals. Sometimes, I pushed Thuan in his wheelchair and helped him sell lottery tickets, so his wife could stay home with the kids. When I went with Thuan, we spent hours in front of market entrances in the mornings, but when the lottery tickets were not all sold, I pushed him from street to street, from store to store, and even from home to home to sell the rest of the tickets.

Though confined to a wheelchair, Thuan was domineering and cruel. His docile wife was little more than a slave. I was just a maid, but I had a stubborn streak. He could not dominate me, and I wouldn't let him get away with anything, especially when he tried to make a pass, kiss me, or touch me. I always yelled at him and gave him a few choice words, along with some dirty looks. It infuriated him, but he knew he could not do anything to me, except wink and crack a nasty smile. But he threatened he would get me later.

When his wife was busy, I helped him from the bed into his wheelchair. One day, he moved his upper body, and I helped him lift his skinny legs to the wheelchair. While I cradled his legs, he grabbed my breast. I pushed his hand away, and I dropped him. He lost his balance and fell to the floor. In anger and frustration, he picked up a metal cane lying near the bed and threw it at me. The cane hit me on the forehead and cut into my scalp. A fountain of blood gushed out, and I screamed for help.

His wife heard the commotion and ran into the room. She saw her husband trying to crawl back to his wheelchair from the floor and saw blood covering my face. In panic, she asked, "What is happening?"

"It's all her fault," he shouted.

She ran to the kitchen, came back with a rag, and told me to use it to stop the bleeding.

I heard him say to his wife, "She deserves to be punished!"

His wife told me to hold the towel tight against my head. She grabbed my arm, led me to the street, and hailed a taxi to take me to a doctor.

The doctor looked at my cut, and asked, "What happened?"

Before I had a chance to answer, Thuan's wife replied, "She fell off a chair while hanging up wet clothes on a line." I looked at her and said nothing.

The doctor cleaned the wound and gave me shots to numb the pain. He then sewed me up with several stitches and wrapped my whole head with gauze.

"Keep the wound dry," he instructed, "and come back next week to have the stitches removed. And be more careful when you're on a chair the next time."

"Thank you, doctor," I said, and we left.

I got out of the taxi first, and Thuan's wife paid the driver. I walked in the house, and Thuan took one look at me and smiled with satisfaction.

"You'd better watch it from now on," he said. "If you don't do what I say, you're liable to have another accident."

My eyes couldn't hide the hatred in my heart as I glared at him. I made up my mind to get out of there as soon as I could. I waited for my cut to heal and then told them I wanted to go home to visit my family. Thuan's wife had no objections, but Thuan was against it. I kept pleading, until he finally agreed.

"Go," he shouted, "but I'm going to keep half the money you've earned. If you want the other half, you'll have to come back and work for me."

"I'll be back," I lied, knowing I would never return.

The following morning, after accepting my partial pay, I gathered my belongings and said goodbye. I walked down the street, caught a cyclo, and asked the driver to take me to the Bien Hoa bus station. We haggled over the price, and when he finally accepted my offer, he took me there. I bought a bus ticket, some gifts for the kids, and saved the rest of the money for my mother.

When I arrived home, Mother and my brothers and sister were very happy to see me. The reunion was enjoyable but brief, as my family's situation had not changed. My stepfather was still struggling to put food on the table, and Mother was grateful for the money I brought home. I stayed for three days, just long enough to visit my uncle and some other relatives, and then returned to Saigon.

For several years, I held a variety of jobs, from dishwasher to waitress and maid to cashier. When I gathered enough money, I would quit and make the trip home. I kept part of my earnings for transportation and a few necessary clothes and gave the rest to my family.

Once, instead of going back to work, I decided to take a break and visit a distant uncle. He was my father's first cousin, and he lived in Xuan Loc, about thirty-five miles northeast of Saigon. Although I didn't remember him, I heard Mother talk about him often. She said when he was younger, he used to live with us and take care of me. She told me I was the only living relative he had left, and he would be very happy to see me. For that reason, I decided to make the trip. I wanted to see him and thank him for taking care of me.

Mother gave me his full name and address. I didn't write it down, since I was good at remembering such details. I took the bus to Xuan Loc and, after asking around, was directed to the street he lived on. I went to the address Mother had given me and knocked on the door.

A stocky man opened the door and asked, "What do you want?"

I smiled and said, "Hello, Uncle."

"What did you say?" he asked in an annoyed voice.

"Hello, Uncle," I repeated.

"What is your name?" he demanded.

Continuing to smile, I replied, "My name is Loan. I'm your niece."

"I don't have a niece, and I don't want one!" he grumbled.

I was confused and quit smiling. I tried to explain who I was, but that just angered him more. How could a man reject his own niece? I was crushed. He was about to shut the door in my face, when a lady came to the door and asked what was going on. Before I had a chance to explain, the man said, "This crazy girl is trying to play games with me."

In desperation, I turned to the lady and said, "I'm his niece, and I've come a long way to visit."

"What's the name of the person you're looking for?" she asked.

"His name is Luu The Te," I said.

She laughed and pointed to the next door. "The family you're looking for lives at 145B, not 145A, but I think they are at work right now. They should be home this afternoon."

I was so embarrassed. My memory for details had failed me. I apologized and thanked the nice lady for helping me, then I walked to the next house and knocked on the door. When there was no answer, I sat on front of the porch and waited. Hours later, a middle-aged couple walked up to the house. I stood up and moved out of their way. They looked at me with curious half-smiles, as the man reached for the key in his pocket and opened the door.

"What is your name?" I asked the man, determined not to make a fool of myself again.

"Luu The Te," he replied. "Who are you?"

Relieved, I bowed and said, "Uncle Te, my name is Loan. I'm the daughter of your late cousin Thap, and I've come to visit you."

Uncle Te seemed happy to see me and explained to his wife who I was. She gave me a welcome look, and they both asked me to come in. My aunt went straight to the kitchen to prepare dinner. I followed to help with cooking, and my uncle put their garden tools away. We cooked the meal and the food was placed on the table, but before we ate, I followed my aunt to a neighbor's house to pick up her two children. Her son was five and her daughter was two. They appeared to be sweet children, even though they didn't notice my presence and were less than excited to see their mother.

My aunt and uncle were rather strange. They were nice but seldom talked to me, to their kids, or even to each other. They seemed neither happy nor unhappy about anything. It was hard to tell if they were happy or not. They went to work every day, but they never told me where, and I never asked. One day, I overheard them talking to each other about a coffee farm, and I guessed that their work had something to do with coffee. They didn't have much money, but they weren't poor either. They lived in a comfortable house, wore decent clothes, and had enough to eat. After a few weeks, I saw that they could use my help, and decided to stay with them for a while.

While living with them, I took over the cooking and watched their children instead of sending them to a neighbor's house. They often brought unusual food home to cook, such as snapping turtles, rabbits, squirrels, and even snakes. At first, I just helped, but later, they let me do most of the cooking by myself. Once, they brought home a big, dead flying fox, which is a kind of fruit bat, and a bag of fresh coffee nuts. They gave me some basic instructions on how to prepare the meal and then left the house.

I got to work on the meal as soon as they left. First, I shelled the coffee beans, while waiting for a pot of water to boil. Then I dipped the bat into the hot water. Moments later, I removed it, placed it on a chopping block on the floor, and scraped off the fur with a meat cleaver. I repeated this process several times, until all the fur was gone. The hairless fox looked scary. It reminded me of the ghosts I saw when my imagination got away from me. Its lifeless body drooped like a wet dishtowel. Its eyes were wide open, with no pupils. I felt like it was staring at me. Its tongue stuck out from its open mouth, and its sharp teeth appeared to be grinning. I collected myself before cutting its stomach open, removing its guts, and chopping its head off. Then I cut the body into bite-size pieces and sautéed them with onions. I used the head, wings, and legs to make rice soup. I opened the lid to check the progress, and I saw that the bat's eyes were still open, but this time, the eye sockets were filled with rice.

My aunt and uncle ate everything I placed in front of them, regardless of how it was cooked. They never complained about anything I did. I know they didn't dislike me, but they never indicated that they liked me either. We lived together amiably, but were almost like strangers. They were that way with each other as well as their kids. I wondered sometimes if I was really their niece.

We lived like that for three months, until it was time for me to go back to Saigon to work. When I told my uncle I had to leave, he didn't seem to be happy about it, but he didn't seem to be too sad either. The next day, I packed my clothes, said goodbye to everyone, and left.

When I returned to Saigon, I worked in a restaurant as a cook's helper for several months and was able to save enough money to go home. Instead of going home, I decided to look for my friend, Trang. I thought of her often and looked for her many times during our separation, but my efforts were in vain. Her whereabouts remained a mystery. I looked for her in the market and the train station but couldn't find her. Then one day, I decided to look for her at the public toilet. I saw the same old woman who had given me so much grief before and asked her, "Have you seen Trang, my friend who came here with me all the time?"

The guard shook her bent head, without looking up at me, and said, "I can't remember every person who comes in and out of here."

I prodded her memory by reminding her of the many times she threw us out for not paying, and the times she made us clean up the toilet, so we could go to the bathroom. She took off her glasses, looked at me closely, and said, "Maybe I do remember you now."

I was excited, because if she remembered me, she might recall seeing Trang. My enthusiasm disappeared when she said, "I remember that you owe me money for sneaking into my bathroom. Now that you're here and look as though you have money, why don't you pay me?"

"How much?" I asked.

"A lot," she said, "but pay as much as you can." I gave her a few dong and walked away, angry with myself for being so candid.

I went back to the train station, where I spent the night inside, sitting on a bench, pretending I was about to board a train. I didn't want to go to jail again and intended to go home the next day.

A young, pregnant woman walked up to me, we smiled, and she sat down next to me. She looked very tired.

"What is your name?" she asked.

"I'm Loan," I replied.

"What are you doing here?" she asked.

"I've been looking for a friend of mine," I told her.

"I've lived around here for years," she said. "Perhaps I can help you."

I was excited to find someone who might help me find my friend and began describing Trang. She looked at me and said, "Not long ago, a girl fitting that description was in the park," she said. "She was looking for a girl, too. In fact, you look very much like the person she described."

I realized Trang had also been looking for me. I smiled at the pregnant woman, but tears were flowing down my cheeks. I dried my eyes and changed the subject. I didn't want her to think her words had upset me.

"When is your baby due?" I asked.

"Any day now," she said. To me, it looked to me like it could be any minute. "Where are you going to sleep tonight?" she asked.

"Right here, inside the station," I said.

"Oh no!" she cried. "Haven't you heard about the recent trouble in the station?" I shook my head and she continued, "There have been terrible crimes committed here. People have been mugged, raped, and even murdered. I used to sleep here too, but I found a safer place. Come with me, and I'll show you."

Her story scared me, and I was glad she wanted to help me. I followed her to a quiet alley nearby. She pulled a stack of newspapers from her bag and rolled them out on the sidewalk. We sat down, and I said, "Thank you for being so nice. I hope and pray God will take care of you and your baby."

"Thank you," she said and then asked, "What are you going to do, and where are you going tomorrow?"

"I'm going to see my family," I said. "I can't wait to see them again."

"Do you have money with you?" she asked.

"Quite a bit," I said.

"Where do you keep it?" she asked.

"In my bag," I replied.

"You should put your money at the bottom of the bag, to be safe," she instructed. I followed her suggestion as she watched. I rolled up my large paper bag again, turned it upside-down, and used it for a pillow. She gave me another piece of newspaper to use as a cover. Before going to sleep, I thanked her again for being so kind and helpful.

She smiled and said, "You're welcome."

I felt safe with her, and after saying my prayers, I fell into a deep sleep. Something woke me in the middle of the night, and I sat up and looked around. The pregnant woman had disappeared. I assumed she had gone to the bathroom, and as I turned to straighten out my bag, I noticed a corner of it was torn. Upon closer examination, I discovered my money was gone. Then I realized what a fool I'd been.

I had trusted the woman to the point of showing her where I hid my money. She repaid my trust by stealing every dong I had. I felt terrible. It hurt to lose my money, but having my trust betrayed was even more painful.

Tears streamed down my face as I found my way back to the park, where I found a bench and plopped down. "I can't go home to see my family without money," I thought. "Now I'll have to go back to work instead, and it will take me months before I can go home."

I sat with my arms wrapped around my legs and rested my head on my knees. I rocked back and forth, like a ball, and thought about what I was going to do next.

A man came over and sat next to me. He made some lewd remarks, but I ignored him and continued rocking. He kept annoying me by trying to touch me, and I moved to another bench. He followed me from bench to bench, and when he realized I wanted nothing to do with him, he snatched my bag of clothes and took off running. I chased him for a few blocks, but he was too fast. I gave up and went back to the park in tears.

"I should have gone home days earlier," I thought.

Chapter 13

TENDER SHOOTS

IT WAS THE summer of 1962, and after being away for several months, I was anxious to see my family again. During the bus ride from Saigon to Bien Hoa, I noticed large numbers of Vietnamese soldiers and military vehicles on the move.

At Bien Hoa, I boarded the boat going to Long Phuoc, and when it arrived, I saw more soldiers near the police station. Politics held little interest for me then, and many years passed before I learned the truth about the events taking place.

In 1960, the National Liberation Front was formed in South Vietnam by North Vietnamese infiltrators, to unify opposition to the South Vietnamese government. Labeled the "Viet Cong" by President Diem, this unit was extremely effective. By 1962, the Viet Cong were established in eighty percent of the south.

The American government believed the Viet Cong could be stopped by supplying weapons and military advisors. In February of 1962, America sent US helicopters and army support units to Vietnam. The number of American foreign advisors jumped from the limit of 685, established by the Geneva Accords in 1954, to over 4,000.

The sight of all the soldiers frightened me as I jumped from the boat and hurried home. I walked into our house and was surprised to see that it was filled with new furniture. "My stepfather's practice must have improved," I thought. No one was home, and I started putting my clothes away. I was stacking them on a bedroom shelf, when I heard the strange voices of a man and woman as they entered the house. I listened closely but didn't recognize their voices.

A middle-aged couple I had never seen before walked into the bedroom. I was shocked to see them, but they seemed even more shocked to see me. Both of them yelled, "Thief! Thief!" The man jumped at me, grabbed my arm, and twisted it behind my back. "What are you doing in my house?" he demanded.

"I live here," I replied. He paid no attention, pushed me to the floor, and told his wife to get a rope. He started tying my arms behind my back, and a neighbor, who had heard the commotion, rushed inside.

"I caught a thief in my bedroom!" he shouted as he tied my hands. "I'm going to turn her over to the police."

I knew the neighbor, Mrs. Doc, and asked her to please help me clear up the misunderstanding. Mrs. Doc recognized me and started laughing. "She's no thief," she said to the man holding me. "She used to live here. Her father sold you this house."

The man let me go and untied my arms. He helped me to my feet and apologized. "What are you doing here?" he asked.

"I thought my family still lived here," I replied, still shaking. "I didn't know they had moved. I'm very sorry for disturbing you." We all had a good laugh about the mix-up and went outside.

I remembered my bag and asked, "Would you please get my clothes from your shelf? I'm afraid to go back in there." We laughed again, and the man went back for my clothes.

I asked Mrs. Doc, "Do you know where my family moved?"

"I don't remember the name of the town," she replied, "but I know it's far from here."

The man came back with my clothes, and I thanked both of them. I walked to Uncle Ky's house and found it vacant. I was growing more concerned and decided to go to my Cousin Ri's home. He was Aunt Ba's oldest son.

Instead of using the dirt road, which would have taken much longer, I chose a shortcut through a tidal creek at low tide. I took off my shoes, threw them in the bag, rolled my pants up above my knees, and headed down the muddy creek. Even at low tide, the water was above my knees in places. Rolling up my pants turned out to be a waste of time. I held my pants legs up with one hand and the bag with the other. Eventually, I made it to my cousin's dock. It was old and just about to fall apart. I climbed a set of fragile steps, but before I reached the top rung, they disintegrated.

I fell into the slimy muck, and it covered me from head to toe. Holding the muddy bag, I tried again to climb on the dock. Without the steps, it was difficult, but on the fourth attempt, I pulled myself up.

I looked for water to wash the mud off but found none. I felt pain in both legs. I pulled my pants up and saw several leeches attached to me. Blood poured from the bites as I pulled them off. The pain from the leeches was not as bad as the cut in my left foot. I must have stepped on a piece of glass while trying to climb the steps, and it was bleeding badly. I limped into my cousin's house, and to my surprise, it was empty, too. The dirt floor had turned green with mold, weeds were growing along the wall, and everything smelled musty. It appeared to have been deserted for some time. I was sad as I left the house, and I wondered where my family and relatives had gone.

I limped to a neighbor's house and knocked on the door. I recognized the old lady who opened it. I had seen her often when I visited my cousin.

"Do you know where my cousin has moved?" I asked.

She gave me a puzzled look and asked, "What cousin are you talking about?" "Cousin Ri," I replied. "My name is Loan. Don't you remember me?"

She laughed and said, "No, I didn't recognize you. You look just like a mudskipper. Before we talk, why don't you clean the mud off you? There's water in the barrel."

She pointed to a tar-lined, metal barrel used to catch rainwater. The barrel had been used to carry tar for road surfacing in bigger cities. Those who had such barrels were considered very fortunate. I thanked her and followed her suggestion. Using a coconut shell, I dipped water, one scoop after another, and poured it over my head. It took several minutes to get clean. I scraped mud from my wounds, and they started bleeding again. I wiped off the blood with my wet clothes, and changed into drier ones I found in the bag. Thank God, some of them were still dry. I wrapped the muddy clothes in a banana leaf, left them outside, and walked in. The old lady was sitting on a bamboo bed chewing betel nut and waiting for me.

I dried my hair with my fingers and asked her again about my cousin. "They moved to Mr. Tam's house, near your Uncle Ky's old house," she told me.

I thanked her and followed her directions to my cousin's house. This time, I wasn't about to take a short cut. When I walked into the yard, Cousin Ri's wife saw me and came out of the kitchen. We smiled and greeted each other.

"Where are Cousin Ri and the children?" I asked.

"Your cousin is working in the rice fields," she replied, "and the children are somewhere in the neighborhood."

"Where have my family and Uncle Ky's family moved to?" I asked.

"I don't know," she said. "You'll have to ask my husband."

I was disappointed with her response, because I had to wait to find out. I looked at her big stomach and thought to myself, "Again?" It seemed every time I saw her, she was pregnant. "When is your baby due?" I asked.

"Any day," she answered with a tired smile.

They already had too many children, and the oldest was only twelve. I don't know how she managed to care for her four kids while being nine months pregnant. They were poorer than my family. I sat the bag of muddy clothes in a corner and told her about the painful tour I made trying to find her house.

Just before dark, Cousin Ri returned from the rice field, and the children came home. They were all surprised and happy to see me. I gave the kids the candy intended for my brothers and sister. Soon, the dinner was set, with the food placed on a grass mat on the floor in the middle of the room. The food was simple. We had a large pot of rice with a few small, cooked shrimp mixed with fish in a chipped ceramic bowl.

During dinner, I asked Cousin Ri about Uncle Ky and my family. He told me my family was well and had moved to Chu Hai, near Vung Tau, about fifty miles from Saigon. He seemed reluctant to discuss Uncle Ky's family. After repeated prodding, he told me.

"Uncle Ky's family moved because of the fighting around here," he said. "The Viet Cong have attacked several times. The battles have been fierce, and both sides have suffered many casualties. Before Uncle Ky moved away, Cousin Tuan was killed in one of those battles."

"Oh God, no!" I moaned, "Cousin Tuan is dead?" I stopped eating and ran outside. I bent my head to my knees and sobbed. It was hard to believe my beloved cousin was dead. Cousin Ri followed me outside and put his hand on my shoulder. "After Tuan was drafted into the military," he continued, "he was sent on several missions. On his last assignment, he stepped on a land mine and was blown to pieces."

I looked up and saw tears streaming down Cousin Ri's face. "I loved him so much," he cried, then he paused a few moments to collect himself. "A few days after Tuan's death, his mother gave birth to a beautiful baby girl." I stopped crying for a second, excited at the news of the baby's birth.

"Uncle Ky was so happy with the precious daughter he had wanted for years. She was a little angel. It was too bad Tuan didn't live long enough to see his sister."

Cousin Ri was silent for a minute or two before he continued. "When she was just three months old, fighting broke out around Uncle Ky's house. Soldiers were shooting at each other and escape for his family was impossible. There was no place to hide, so they huddled in a corner of their leafy house."

"A bullet went through the walls and struck the baby in the head. She died in her mother's arms. When the fighting ended, Uncle Ky buried his daughter next to his son. His anguish was overwhelming. A few days later, they moved away, and are now living in Ho Nai, near Bien Hoa." My tears flowed like rain as he spoke.

"Many people in this town have moved away," he said, "but I can't afford to. God knows I want to, because the longer we stay here, the more dangerous it will be." My heart went out to him and his family.

"Can I stay with you and help your wife with the children until she gets on her feet?" I asked.

"You can stay as long as you want," he replied. "But remember, we don't have good food for you to eat, and sometimes we don't have any food to eat."

"Don't worry," I said, "I can find my own."

Cousin Ri's wife gave birth to a baby girl, and after a short period of recuperation, she went back to work with her husband in the rice fields. They let me name the baby, and I chose to call her Duong, which has many meanings, among them being "nurture and care." While their parents were working, I took care of the children.

One morning, I was in the small pond scooping for shrimp and fish for lunch while the kids ran around, when gunfire erupted in the woods nearby. I panicked, climbed out, gathered the children, and made a dash for the house. We hid under a bamboo bed. Of course, it was useless against a bullet, but it made us feel safer.

Between the explosions and gunfire outside, and the baby screaming under the bed, I thought my eardrums would burst. We huddled together, and I prayed for my cousin and his wife in the rice fields.

We stayed under the bed until the gunfire calmed down, and then we crawled out. I looked at my muddy clothes and remembered the basket of fish I had left near the pond. I put the baby on the bed and told her oldest brother to watch her. I ran back to the pond, but the little fish were all dead and had dried out under the sun. I dumped them out and started over.

When Cousin Ri came home, I asked him about the gunfire. He smiled and said, "It was just some soldiers practicing." I knew it was no practice, because I heard the bullets flying over my head. I guess my cousin didn't want me to be too concerned.

The next day, I took the kids to visit a neighbor. I overheard a man tell his friend, "Two Viet Cong were shot last night; one was killed and the other captured. They're holding the prisoner at the police station." My curiosity aroused, I told the oldest child to watch the younger ones, and I ran to the police station.

I saw a boy, who didn't look much older than I was, sitting at the bottom of a flagpole, his arms tied to the flagpole behind his back. His head was bent low, and his eyes were half-open. He had been shot twice, once in his shoulder and once in his right leg.

His wounds were still bleeding, and he was in obvious pain. Besides me, there were about a dozen other boys and girls standing around watching and taunting him. I watched him for a moment or two and asked, "What did you do to get shot?"

He looked to see who had spoken to him, and I guess he saw the sympathy in my face. He replied, "I was fishing with my older brother."

"What are they going to do to you?" I asked.

"I don't know," he said as he shook his head and bowed down.

I looked at him and somehow felt his pain. Meanwhile, the other children were spitting and throwing sand on him. I told them to stop, but they didn't listen. In anger, I pushed them away. Some fought back, but after calling me a few bad names, some of them left. Those who stayed behind quit bothering me.

I turned back to the young man and heard him groan, "I need help. I think I'm going to die." His light gray pajamas were covered with blood, and his dry lips were parched. His hair, his pale face, and his eyelids were covered with sand, thrown by the callous children.

I went inside the station and approached one of the uniformed men. "Would you please help the poor boy?" I asked. "He looks like he's dying."

The man looked at me and said, "Go home and blow your nose." In other words, I was too young to be sticking my nose in their business.

I went back to the flagpole, and the wounded boy cried, "I'm thirsty."

I couldn't stand there and do nothing, so I ran back inside the police station. "Would someone please give the boy some water?" I asked.

"I thought I sent you home already!" one of the uniformed men yelled. "Whatever happens to him is none of your business. You'd better go home before I tie you to the pole next to him."

"He's a Viet Cong, and he is our enemy! Do you understand?" another man scolded. "He deserves to be punished, and you'd better not help him unless you want to go to jail with him."

I said nothing and returned to the flagpole. "I want to help you," I cried, "but they won't let me."

He lifted his head and gave me just a whisper of a smile. Then he closed his eyes and bowed his head in silence.

According to the police, he and his brother were caught transporting ammunition to a nearby Viet Cong group. He looked so harmless. I found it hard to believe he was guilty of any crime. I was unable to watch him suffer any longer and said goodbye. I walked away feeling helpless, angry, and bitter inside.

I found out a few days later the boy died before he reached the hospital and never had the chance to go to jail. I discovered a mistake had indeed been made. He and his older brother were catching fish for their old, blind parents. The enemy was operating in the same area, and the soldiers thought the brothers were Viet Cong. No one ever admitted to the mistake.

"Why must there be war and so much hatred?" I thought to myself. "Who started this insanity, and what are they gaining from it? All I've seen so far is death, mutilation, and starvation. There are no winners in war, including the ones who claim victory. What do they win? Broken homes? Dead relatives? Environmental destruction? It is all so absurd to me."

I stayed with my cousin until their baby was three months old. I helped them move to a new settlement near Bien Hoa before I left them to look for my family. It was sad to say goodbye, but I promised I would come back to see them someday. My tears flowed as I walked out the door. I looked back at the squalid conditions and the hungry children and waved goodbye, promising myself I would never have children unless I was able to feed them.

I got to the highway and realized I had given all of my money to my cousin to help his family, and now I had only enough for bus fare. Without money, there was no way to go home to see my family, and once again, I had to go back to work.

I sat on an old termite hill waiting for the Saigon bus to come. I took a close look at myself, at my torn clothes and frayed shoes, and I thought about my life. Over the past few years, I had moved so often and changed my name so many times that often I forgot which name I was using and didn't respond when someone addressed me.

I don't know why I changed my name so often. Perhaps I didn't like my life and hoped it would change when my name changed. I missed my family so much I almost crossed to the other side of the road to catch a bus that would take me home. But I had no money to give to my family, and I didn't want to be a burden. I closed my eyes and sent them my love through the air. The bus horn startled me, and I motioned for the driver to stop. I hopped on and found an empty seat as the bus moved down the road.

Once in Saigon, I found work as a housekeeper and babysitter for a stage dancer who had two little girls, aged four and five. Her husband was a skinny man with a wooden leg. He sold tickets for a stage show called "Cai Luong" where his wife worked as a dancer. After work, his wife often went out with someone else, and the poor man had to limp home by himself.

He was no angel either. When his wife wasn't home, he'd sneak into the bedroom I shared with their two daughters. His intentions were obvious, and each time he appeared, I yelled and ran out of the room. The noise woke the children, and he went back to his bed.

I threatened to leave several times, but his wife kept promising to get me on stage, dancing or acting. The prospect excited me, and I continued to stay with them. In time, it became clear she was not going to keep her promise, so I quit. Besides, I had saved enough money for the trip to Chu Hai, and I was anxious to visit my family.

The stage dancer, her two children, and me at age 15. I was their housekeeper.

Chapter 14

BROKEN CHAINS

I BOUGHT GIFTS and a bus ticket, this time to Chu Hai, near Vung Tau, a town I had never been to before. I didn't even know where it was, but I knew I must find my family. I boarded the bus and told the driver where I wanted to go. The driver assured me he would stop for me, but I took a seat near him, anyway, to make sure he didn't forget.

Several hours and many stops later, the driver yelled, "The little girl who wanted to go to Chu Hai, get ready to get off the bus." The bus slowed down, came to a stop, and I jumped off. I looked around as the bus drove away and went to the nearest house to ask for directions. Lucky for me, the woman knew my family well and told me where they lived. I walked a short distance in the direction she had pointed. There was a line of simple wooden homes built together under one grass roof. Each home had a separate entrance, and the shelter appeared to accommodate six separate families.

Most of the doors to the wooden homes were open, and I chose to walk into the middle one. I looked inside, and to my surprise, I saw Mother sitting on the kitchen floor in the back of the house working with herbs. I ran through the open door and called, "Mother, Mother!" She stopped what she was doing and looked at me. At first, she gave no sign of recognition. I must have changed a lot since she saw me last.

"It's me, Mother!" I was laughing and crying at the same time.

When she recognized who I was, she was surprised, smiled, and asked, "Where in the world have you been?"

"I've been everywhere," I said.

"With all the fighting going on, I was afraid you had been killed," she said, with obvious relief. "Why have you been gone so long this time?"

"I'll tell you all about it later," I said with a big smile. It was comforting to know she cared. I opened a bag, took out a cooking pot, and handed it to her. "This one is yours," I said.

"Where is the rest of the family?" I asked.

"They are all out," she replied. "The kids are in school, but they'll be back soon." We chatted for a while, and Mother returned to her work. I walked around the house to take a closer look at everything. The furniture consisted of three beds and a table with six chairs. There was a small space with a cabinet where my stepfather practiced medicine. Behind the house, there were enclosures for chickens and ducks, and a pigpen containing five healthy looking pigs. Next to the pen were a vegetable garden and a well. Mother told me there was no electricity or running water in this town, and the well was a big help. I smiled at her and let my gaze wander beyond the house, where I saw a line of nearby mountains and hills, standing above the village's grass rooftops.

My brothers and sister came home, and as soon as they realized who I was, we had a happy reunion. They enjoyed the gifts I brought for them. When my step-grandmother and stepfather returned, they were surprised to see me, too. We exchanged greetings, and I gave them each a rosary, which they appreciated. After we said our hellos, Mother called me to the kitchen to help her prepare dinner.

When we were finished with dinner, I helped Mother clean up, We talked for a long time, and I told her about Uncle Te and Cousin Ri's family and all about my experiences in Saigon. It was good to be with my mother again, and she was very happy to have me home.

"There is so much to be done around here," she said. "I want you to stay home and help me from now on."

"I'd be happy to," I said. "I needed a break anyway."

I thought about the mountains I saw behind the house earlier and told Mother I couldn't wait to go up there to explore someday. "Those hills are loaded with wood," Mother said, "People go up there to cut wood for building homes, cooking fuel, and to sell. We have to buy it from these people ourselves," she continued, "Now you can go up there and get it yourself." I nodded my head in complete agreement.

Looking out the window, I saw numerous white mounds scattered over the flat fields nearby. "What are those white mounds?" I asked Mother.

"Oh, those?" she replied, as she pointed to them. "They are piles of unprocessed salt." She added, "The workers take salt water from man-made tidal ditches and pour a thin layer onto flat concrete fields. When the water evaporates, a thin layer of salt remains, and the workers scrape it into a pile. They continue this process until the piles become the white mounds you see. The salt is then bagged and taken to a plant somewhere to be cleaned and processed into sea salt."

The house that my family lived in was too close to the highway, and there was constant noise from the motors and horns of cars, trucks, and buses going by. Mother pointed to several rice fields on the other side of the highway and said, "Every morning I have to go to those fields and gather vegetation and rice missed by the farmers when they picked their crops." She continued, "I bring those leftovers home and feed it to our animals. Now you can help me."

It was getting late and it was time for bed. Mother pointed to the bed where my brother and sister slept and told me to sleep with them. The kids were still awake, and we talked until my stepfather told us to go to sleep.

Gathering wood and finding food for the animals became my chores. I went to the fields and ponds to pick water lilies, hydra, and any edible weeds that pigs eat. Most of the ponds were filthy and con-taminated, and some were full of leeches, but when I thought of the hungry animals waiting to be fed, I closed my eyes and walked into the nasty water.

When the large bamboo basket was full, I dragged it to the bank. I brushed off the maggots and leeches and waited for someone to help lift the heavy basket to my head. Sometimes the maggots and leeches crawled from the basket down to my face as I walked home. I picked them off and continued walking with the basket balanced on my head.

I became friends with five or six girls in the area, all of whom were about my age. We often went to the foot of the mountains to pick wood. We picked dead limbs from the ground, and sometimes, chopped down small live trees with machetes or small axes. We bundled the wood together with rope, and then helped each other lift it to our heads. I balanced the wood on my head and walked with my hands free.

Before going home, we always stopped at a small pool of water created by a nearby stream and waterfall. Each time we drew near the pool, we walked faster and faster and would often run to see who got there first. The clear water was inviting, and we couldn't resist the urge to jump in to cool off. We threw our wood down at the edge of the pool, took off our clothes, and jumped in naked. We swam around, having water fights, singing, screaming, and laughing so loudly that we could be heard from miles away. Those days were so much fun and carefree that I wished time would stand still.

While gathering wood, I also gathered wild fruit. There were many wild mangos and persimmons and other edible fruits growing there. Once, I made the mistake of picking fruit from a few poison palms and brought them home. I shared them with the kids, and within minutes, we all started to itch, and welts appeared all over our bodies. Mother saw us scratching and tried to help. She heated a rag over an open fire and rubbed our swollen bodies. I took turns helping her by rubbing the kids' backs as she rubbed mine. It was a chaotic experience, and it took days for us to recover.

When things calmed down, Mother told me, "Be more careful in the future. If you see birds eat the fruit, the fruit will normally be safe to eat. If in doubt, don't eat it."

Over time, I piled the stack of wood I collected as high as the house. I was happy to see Mother sell some of the wood to get extra money, and Mother appreciated my help and liked having me home.

My stepfather didn't share her feelings. Instead, it was as though he resented my presence. It didn't matter how hard I worked, I never satisfied his demands or expectations. Of course, my high-spirited nature didn't help matters any. He was used to complete submission and strict obedience. I didn't defy his authority, but I was unable hide my feelings and that kept me in trouble.

One day, I carried home a heavy bundle of wood and threw it into the pile. I was hot and tired, so I sat on the hammock in the house and swung high, back and forth, to cool off. My stepfather saw me and walked closer to the hammock. He pulled out the pin holding the hammock together, and it sprang like a sling shot, throwing me into the wall and then to the floor. I lay there in pain and shock and, for a moment, didn't know what had happened. Then I heard my stepfather growl, "A girl doesn't swing in a hammock like that! When are you going to learn?" Then, he threw the pin on the table, and I realized what he had done.

I sat up and felt a big knot rising on my forehead. My bones all felt like they had been separated at the joints, and I bowed my head to my knees, moaning and crying.

"You deserve it! Maybe you'll remember this lesson the next time!" he yelled, as he stormed away. My stepfather used this and other forms of punishment in his attempt to teach me lessons. His lessons were hard and painful, but I still loved and respected him, as a daughter is taught to do.

Before long, Mother was able to use the money from selling firewood that I collected to open a small vegetable and knickknack stand. She bought produce from the larger town of Ba Ria to sell for a small profit in the local market. It was a large open market, consisting of benches that were available on a first come, first served basis. It was located in front of our house, opening at dawn and closing at noon.

When Mother was busy at the market, I took care of the cooking, the cleaning, and caring for the children and the animals. When time permitted, I still gathered wood and picked wild fruit. It was hard work, but I was happy to be able to help my family and to be with them. Not long after I returned home, my stepfather started talking about moving again. He thought a town near Vung Tau was a better place for him to practice medicine. He said he was losing patients where he was, and he wanted to move. Mother didn't mind hard work, but the little she made wasn't enough to support the entire family. My stepfather, however, did not work hard, because he was raised differently. In fact, in all the years I lived at home, I never saw him go into the kitchen, not even to get his own food.

I didn't want to move, but I had no choice, so I said goodbye to my new friends, and we moved a week later. We moved to Rach Dua, a small town about three miles from the coastal city of Vung Tau. Most of the residents there were commercial fishermen and were rich by comparison. The house we moved into was on a busy street, and my stepfather's practice soon flourished.

In 1963, I was 16 years old.

By then, I was sixteen, and my body was well developed. Boys started noticing me, and I began to take an interest in them as well. My stepfather ordered me, however, to neither talk to or even look at a boy. He told me that when I was old enough, he would arrange for me to marry the right person. I therefore had no reason to pay any attention to any of them. When my oldest stepbrother married, he defied my stepfather's authority and was disowned. I was often reminded that the same could happen to me.

I left church one Sunday, and a young man stopped me at the door. He made a few remarks about how nice I looked and asked for my name. After telling him, I went home. Unfortunately, someone saw me with the young man and told my stepfather.

He confronted me and questioned me about the boy, but it had been an innocent meeting, and I told him what happened. He didn't like my answer and slapped me hard across the face.

"You had better not talk to any boy again," he warned. "From now on, if a boy talks to you, you better ignore him. Do you understand?"

"Yes, Father," I said as I walked away.

Another boy, named Chinh, lived and worked at his family's furniture store across the street from us. He saw me come in and out of the house all the time, and sometimes I walked in and out on purpose, just so he could see me. We smiled at each other when our eyes met. He knew of my stepfather's strictness but still communicated with me by writing silly notes and throwing them into the yard. One day, my sister found one of his notes and innocently gave it to my stepfather.

"Loan, come here!" he shouted, after reading it. "Who wrote this?" he asked.

"I don't know, Father," I lied.

He slapped me on the back of my head and yelled, "You had better stop flirting with boys!" He crumpled the note and walked away. I wished I had had the chance to read it.

Chinh would also come to our house on the pretense of buying medicine just to flirt with me. One day, he came in while I was alone, dusting the medicine cabinet. He walked up to me and was just about to say something when my stepfather walked into the room.

He looked at Chinh and said, "Hello, what do you need?"

Poor Chinh was so flustered he couldn't speak. He pointed to a medicine jar and said, "My mother wants some of those." The jar contained laxatives. I almost laughed out loud but was able to control myself. If my stepfather knew Chinh was there to flirt with me, he would have killed both of us.

About this time, Mother was eight months pregnant and, according to my stepfather, was too old to have a baby. She was forty-five, and my stepfather was almost sixty. Having a baby at their ages was embarrassing to my stepfather and as a result, Mother would hide or leave the room when my stepfather had guests, and she seldom left the house.

She was also forced to quit selling fruits and vegetables in the little stand she opened. For several months, I took over the stand for her. If I wasn't able to sell everything at the market by noon, I had to put the leftovers in baskets that I balanced with a yoke over my shoulders. I sang, as most vendors did, to identify their products, as I walked from street to street and from alley to alley, trying to sell the leftovers. I made enough money in the market for us to have extra food and some necessities.

When mother was due, she went to Vung Tau hospital by herself. One week later, she came home with another little boy. They named him Khai. He was so cute, and I loved to hold him but seldom had time to.

My stepfather refused to go near him until he was two or three months old. He was that way with all the children, and I asked him once why he didn't like little babies.

He made a face and said, "They are red and wrinkled like baby rats. I just don't like to touch them."

"What about infants who need your medical help?" I prodded.

"I don't like to touch them either," he replied, "but I treat them because I have to." This was the first time my stepfather and I had ever discussed anything that required more than ten words.

Poor Mother was confined to bed to recuperate, and I had to do most of her chores along with mine. I had to stop selling fruit and vegetables and stayed home to help her. Between caring for the kids all day, doing chores, and gathering wood, I didn't have enough time to even comb my hair. I also had to feed the kids, bathe them, and clean their clothes by hand. Mother tried to help, but I insisted she rest and do no more than care for the baby.

She didn't listen very well, and her standard response was, "We have too much work to do. You can't even do yours, much less mine, too." My stepfather never lifted a finger to help with anything around the house, and he never helped in any way with the children.

"A man is supposed to be that way," he would always say.

My step-grandmother helped some, but she always seemed busy with church activities, rolling her betel nut, or sometimes helping my stepfather with his medicine.

My efforts to help my mother didn't impress my stepfather, as he always found something wrong with whatever I did. His harangues grew more frequent and oppressive after the baby was born. He also started drinking more than usual and became very irritable. I felt like leaving home on many occasions but stayed because Mother needed my help.

Two months after Khai was born, Mother was cooking in the kitchen while I was busy doing all the other chores. Every morning after church, I had to stop at the butcher's shop to buy my stepfather's snacks for breakfast. I brought rice whiskey, and blood pudding, a delicacy called "Tiet Canh," and sat them on the table. Khai started crying, and I went to check on him. As soon as I picked him up, he stopped crying.

"Put the baby down and finish setting the table!" my stepfather shouted. "I'm hungry!"

"I can't right now," I replied. "The baby cries when I put him down."

My stepfather ran to the bedroom, snatched the baby from my arms, and threw him on the bed, then he grabbed my ear and pulled me back to the dining area. "Now you can finish your work!" he yelled.

But his actions only made the baby scream louder. It sounded like someone was torturing him. Between the baby's wails and my stepfather's shouts, I got upset, and my tears started flowing as I tried to do as he asked and set the table.

"What's wrong with you?" my stepfather bellowed when he saw me crying, but I was too distressed to answer.

He took my silence for belligerence and grabbed a stick. He whacked me a couple of times, and I lost control. I could no longer contain my anger. I picked up the closest thing to me, a leafy hand-held fan, and hit him back as hard as I could. For a moment, he was stunned by my rebellion, but he recovered quickly and pummeled me with renewed fury. The severe pain from his beating enraged me further, and I hit him back even harder. But with the flimsy fan, it looked as though I was just trying to cool him off.

Mother saw us hitting each other and started screaming. "Oh my God! Oh my God!" she cried. "Look at the father and daughter trying to kill each other! Where are my neighbors; come and help me!" Mother yelled.

I could take no more. I threw down the fan and bolted to the second floor. I grabbed my clothes hanging from a rope, threw them into a paper bag, and ran out to the street. A bus almost ran me over. I waved for it to stop and jumped on. I didn't know where it was going, and I didn't care.

My anger cooled off somewhat, and I asked the driver where the bus was bound. "We're going to Saigon," he replied.

"Good, I want to go there," I said. Lucky for me, I had enough money in my pockets for the bus fare. I cried all the way to Saigon. When we arrived, it was late, and I went to the familiar park. I found an empty bench, sat down, and planned to spend the night.

As I sat there, I overheard a couple arguing under a nearby streetlight. The girl was wearing a low-cut top, tight pants, high heels, and heavy makeup. The man was angry, and he accused her of not giving him all the money she made. He said he would kill her if she lied to him again, and then he walked away.

The girl sauntered over to where I was sitting and sat down next to me. The smell of her perfume was overwhelming. In the dim light, I could tell she was about my age. She gave me a harsh look and asked what I was doing there.

"I came to the market to look for work," I said. "I have no other place to go, and I'm going to rest here until tomorrow morning."

"What kind of work are you looking for?" she asked.

"I'm not sure," I answered. "Maybe a maid."

"Why do you want to be something stupid like that?" she chided. "It's hard work and pays nothing. You should work with me. You can make lots of money."

"What would I have to do?" I asked.

"All you have to do is make men happy," she said with a knowing smile.

I heard that before and shook my head no. "I'm afraid I am too young," I said, "and besides, it would be sinful."

"How old are you?" she sneered.

"I'm sixteen," I replied.

"I'm also sixteen, and I'm old enough," she said.

I didn't like the turn our conversation was taking, so I excused myself and moved to another bench. I could hear her laughing as I walked away. I laid my head down on the bench and went right to sleep. Loud voices woke me, and I sat up to see what was going on. Some four or five girls, including the one who had spoken to me earlier, were standing around my bench talking and laughing.

"Well, have you decided to work with me yet?" the girl asked.

"No," I responded, and shook my head.

One of the girls pushed my forehead with her finger and said, "What's the matter? Are you too good for us?"

Another pulled my hair and said, "You're so stupid!"

They all laughed and made fun of me, but I just sat with my head down and didn't say a word. I didn't feel like fighting, and besides, I was no match for all of them. When they didn't get any response from me, they got bored and walked away laughing and calling me names. I was relieved when they finally left me alone.

Thankfully, the following morning, I was hired as a housekeeper for a prominent middle-aged doctor, his wife, and their three daughters. The oldest daughter was in her teens, a little younger than I was. They lived in Cho Lon, a suburb of Saigon, in a huge three-story house, filled with expensive furniture and elaborate decorations. I had a private room in the servant's quarters, apart from the two other maids and separate from the main house. The family was of high society, and I felt secure there. My job was to run errands, clean and mop the floor, help set the table, and wash dishes, and although I had a job to do, I didn't have to work as hard there as I did in my own home.

One morning, I woke up with painful stomach cramps, and I was unable to do my work. The lady of the house told me to ask her husband for a checkup when he came home. So later, after the doctor arrived home, I asked him for some medicine to ease my stomach pain, and he said he would have to examine me first.

He came into my room that night carrying a stethoscope and a small cup of medicine. He closed the door behind him and, without turning on the light, walked toward me. He sat on the edge of the bed and asked where it hurt. I pointed to my lower abdomen.

"When did the pain start?" he asked, as he pushed up my blouse, lowered my waistband, and began feeling my stomach.

"This morning," I replied.

"When is your period due?" he asked.

"I haven't started yet," I told him.

"That's why you are having cramps," he said, and continued rubbing my stomach up and down.

His hand moved to my chest, and he asked if it hurt. "No," I responded, and wondered why he was examining my breasts. I had never had this kind of examination before and didn't know what to expect.

He squeezed each breast and then moved his hand down to my stomach. I grew suspicious when he started breathing hard and lowered his face to my chest. It was obvious he was doing more than just conducting a medical examination.

I was confused, scared, and angry. I jumped out of bed and told him to leave. He stood up and walked to the door. Before he left, he gave me a cup with pills in it and said, "Take the pills and if you don't feel better by the morning, let me know."

I didn't answer, and he turned to go. I shut the door and locked it behind him, feeling used and humiliated. I didn't take the medicine he gave me. Instead, I lay back on my bed, covered my face with a pillow, and cried myself to sleep. My stomach felt better after I started my first period a few days later.

Feeling ashamed, I didn't tell anyone about my incident with the doctor. Days later, I was helping the cook set the breakfast table one morning, and I overheard the doctor tell his wife he had a bad headache and needed to stay home and rest. After his wife and children left the house, and while the other maids were busy doing their chores, he asked me to come to his room and massage his head. I refused, telling him I had too much work to do, but he persisted, and I had to do what he asked.

When I entered his room, I saw him lying on a large fancy bed, wearing white pajamas. He was wearing his glasses, and he had a book in his hands. He had a big smile on his face when I walked in, and he didn't appear sick.

"Please close the door behind you," he said as I walked toward him.

"I'd rather leave it open," I replied. He wanted it closed, so he jumped up, closed the door himself, returned to the bed, and lay back down. I moved a small chair closer to the bed, sat down, and waited.

He took off his glasses and said with a smile, "It will be more comfortable if you sit on the bed."

I ignored him and sat on the chair next to his bed and began rubbing his temples. He inched toward the middle of the bed, and I had to move from the chair to the edge of the bed to reach him. As I did so, he put his arm around me and began rubbing my back. "Enough is enough!" I thought.

"If you touch me again, I'll walk out of here!" I said as I jumped off the bed. "If you want me to massage your head, move to the edge of the bed and keep your hands to yourself." My daring surprised me, but he moved back to the edge of the bed.

I sat back down in the chair and continued rubbing his temples. Without moving a hand, he started talking. "I've fallen in love with you," he said. "I want to rent a house for you and buy you everything you need."

I was shocked. He sounded serious, but I said nothing for fear of either encouraging or angering him. After rubbing his head for a few more minutes, I made up an excuse to leave. As I walked out the door, he asked me to think about what he had said. I was very confused. I liked working there, but I didn't know how to react to the doctor's advances.

During the following week, I tried to avoid him, but it was difficult. When I served a meal, he winked at me when no one was looking, and if we were alone for even a second, he said he loved me and asked if I had considered his offer.

I had to do something about the situation and decided it would be better if I just quit. I told his wife several times to find someone else, because I had to leave, but she kept insisting I stay and offered me more money.

One day, when his wife and I were home alone, I told her again that I wanted to return to see my family. Of course, I did not intend to go home, but it was a reasonable excuse for quitting, but she was happy with the work I was doing and kept asking me to stay.

Finally, I had no choice but to tell her the truth. "Your husband has been making passes at me," I said, "and I can't continue working here."

She was shocked, but her surprise quickly turned to anger. "It's your fault!" she yelled. "You must have done something to cause my husband to flirt with you!"

"I didn't do anything," I said. "Besides, I asked you to let me go many times, but you wouldn't listen."

She started crying, yelling, and cursing me, and she began breaking everything within reach. I got scared and tried to calm her. "Please stop destroying your furniture," I pleaded. "I didn't mean to make you so angry." She left the room, while I picked up the mess she had made.

In a few moments, she returned with some money in her hand. She threw it at me and screamed, "Get out of my house!"

Hastily, I picked up the money, went to my room, grabbed my clothes, and left. It was early in the day, but instead of going into the Saigon market to look for another job, I went to the park in front of the market, where I sat on a bench, feeling sorry for myself, and let the tears flow.

I left home because of the treatment I received there, and I quit a job because I had been taken advantage of and then accused of something I did not do. I had worked hard all my life, and I believed I deserved better than I had received. I wanted nothing more than to be treated as a human being with respect and dignity.

I felt both sad and angry as I thought about my life and all I had been through. I thought of what I had done, what I hadn't done, and what I wanted to do. I made up my mind that things had to be different from then on. I wiped my tears and sat straight up, determined to change my life.

Chapter 15

SAIGON TEA

AS I SAT on the bench reflecting, from out of nowhere, a beautiful, well-dressed woman walked by. Our eyes met, she smiled at me, and I smiled back, but she continued walking. She looked to be half-French, and a few minutes later, she returned and stopped in front of me. She smiled at me with bright, even teeth that sparkled in the sunlight.

"What is your name?" she asked. "Where are you from and what are you doing here?"

"My name is Phung," I replied. I picked the name just seconds before she asked. "I'm from Vung Tau, and I'm looking for a job."

"What kind of work are you looking for?" she asked.

"I'm not sure," I replied, "but I don't want to be a maid."

She looked at me and laughed. "I don't need any more maids," she said. "I already have two at home. If you will come with me, I have something better in mind for you."

"Oh no, not again," I thought. "What kind of work?" I asked.

"I just started a new meat stand at a small market in Cho Lon, and I need someone to give me a hand," she replied.

I didn't care for the idea of selling meat, but she seemed like such a nice lady, so I decided to take a chance with her. "I don't know much about meat, but I guess I could help you," I said.

With my bag of clothes under one arm, I followed her across the street to the market, and then on to Le Loi Street. The sidewalks were crowded with merchants selling everything imaginable, from local to foreign goods, and we had to battle our way through the mob as it surged up and down the street. She kept an eye on me and waited when

I fell behind. We were busy fighting the crowd and didn't have a chance to talk on our way. All we could do was exchange an occasional smile.

Then, she turned left, walked under an archway, and waited for me there. I followed her up the stairs to an older, French-style apartment on the third floor. She knocked and a woman, who looked to be about thirty years old, opened the door. From the way she looked and greeted us as we entered, I thought that she must be a maid. We went inside, and the maid locked the door behind us. It was a small studio apartment, with a beautifully furnished living area.

A younger woman, holding a five- or six-month-old baby, walked in from the kitchen. She looked at me and smiled, and I smiled back. "She must be the other maid," I guessed. The four of us gathered together, everyone looking confused except for the owner, who knew what was going on. I wasn't sure who the women were, and they didn't know who I was. I didn't even know the owner's name yet.

"This is Nam," the owner said, as she pointed to the older woman who had opened the door, "and this is Tam," she continued, pointing to the younger woman. "They are my maids, and they will be yours, too."

She turned to the maids and introduced me. "This is Phung, my niece. She will be helping me with my new business."

We smiled and bowed to each other. I had never seen the woman before in my life, and within a few minutes, I had become her niece. She wasn't a full-blooded Vietnamese, and I looked nothing like her. "How could she be my aunt?" I thought and began to wonder about my own identity. Whatever or whoever she was, I had a feeling I was going to like her.

After the introductions, with some of the confusion out of the way, the lady retired to her bathroom to take a shower, and when she finished, she told me to do the same. After bathing, I opened my bag and realized I had left many of my clothes at the doctor's house. It reminded me of the last time I had left home so upset and in such a hurry. I had stuffed my bag full of clothes, only to find out later most of them weren't even mine. They were Mother's, and some were my brothers' and sister's.

The lady waited for me to finish my shower, then she called me to the dinner table. I smiled at her as I sat down. While eating, she talked about herself and her family. She kept her voice low, so the maids in the kitchen couldn't hear what she was saying.

"My name is Lynn," she whispered. "I'm twenty-eight years old. My father was French, but I've never seen him. I got married when I was fourteen and had two children by the time I was sixteen. I divorced my first husband when I was seventeen and married his best friend."

She paused to catch her breath and then continued. "My two older children live away, and I have two others with my present husband. You've seen my little boy with the maid. My five-year-old daughter is in school now. She'll be home later. My present husband is a pilot. He flies a lot and is seldom home. Say nothing to the maids about what I just told you," she cautioned.

I wondered why she was telling me so many of her intimate secrets and why she didn't want the others to know. Whatever her reasons, I was glad she had confided in me.

I learned more about her and her wild lifestyle as each day passed. Lynn and I woke up before five o'clock every morning. We went to the Saigon Market and picked up the wholesale beef Lynn had ordered the day before. We loaded hundreds of kilos of different cuts of meat on a motorized cyclo and took our wares to a smaller retail market near Cho Lon.

We arrived early, in order to have our meat cut and displayed before the market opened. We separated the meat by cut, hung some of the portions by hooks on the steel bar above the table, and then organized the rest on the table. The meat would sell out about noon or a little after. We would count our earnings, saving enough for the next day's purchases, and then we spent the rest on ourselves.

Lynn and I shortly after we met. I was sixteen.

Lynn treated me like a good friend. To my delight, she took me shopping and bought me whatever I wanted and needed—the same quality of clothes and shoes she wore. She often tried to pay me for my work, but I didn't need the money and declined. Besides, I liked what I was doing and was happy to help her.

She introduced me to the English language and ballroom dancing. We dressed up and went to different nightclubs on weekends to have fun. While getting ready to go out one night, she confided in me at the makeup table, "The reason I go out so much is because my husband is seldom home, and when he is, he's not too good to me. Besides, he's like a chicken in bed."

I didn't understand what she meant, but I laughed at her joke anyway. It didn't matter. I liked her and enjoyed being around her. She was so much fun, and I was so happy. I was living a life that I never imagined.

One evening, we met one of her male friends at a nightclub, and we drank and danced until way past midnight. In the early morning hours, she whispered to me, "I'm not coming home tonight. I'll see you in the morning."

She left with her companion, and I went home by myself in a pedi-cab. The driver pedaled down the street, and, for a moment, I wondered how it might feel to be with a man, but my strong Catholic background took over and suppressed the fantasy, and I began praying for my sinful thinking.

I still went to church, but not as often as I had before. I went on Sundays only and sometimes not even then. Lynn was a Buddhist, and now and then, I went with her to the pagoda instead.

During that period, there was increasing dissension in the streets. Most of the unrest, at least on the surface, dealt with religious differences. Of the fifteen million people in South Vietnam, little more than one million were Catholic. President Diem and his family were Catholic, and they showed open favoritism. The Buddhists resented the regime's partiality.

A peaceful demonstration in Hue by Buddhist monks, in May of 1963, was disrupted by South Vietnamese troops, who opened fire, killing twelve and wounding many others. The unrest spread, and as the turmoil multiplied, I was drawn into it myself.

As the rioting and demonstrations intensified, unrest spread through Saigon like wildfire. During one demonstration, the police confronted a group of students who were protesting near the Saigon Market. When they refused to disperse, the police opened fire, and one of the female students, Quach Thi Trang, was shot and killed. She died in Bong Binh Park, the circular park that had been my home away from home so often. Her death caused such an uproar that the park's name was changed from Bong Binh to Quach Thi Trang, in her memory.

I learned only later that instead of resolving the real or imagined social injustices, the riots resulted in even greater suppression by the Diem regime. The American government watched these events with increasing alarm. They were convinced that to unify opposition to communist gains and resolve internal unrest, Diem had to step down.

It was rumored that Nhu, President Diem's brother, had made overtures to North Vietnam and had secretly planned to consider Vietnamese unification under a temporary coalition. The possibility of such a confederation was not acceptable, and it served to polarize American determination to oust Diem.

His regime did not intend to loosen its grip on the government, and top Vietnamese army officers, with support and assistance from the US Central Intelligence Agency, planned a coup.

On the evening of November 1, 1963, I was in a taxi on my way home from a party. Crowds of people were running in the streets, and sounds of gunfire echoed through the night.

"What is going on?" I asked the taxi driver in alarm.

"You should know what's happening," he said. "It's been going on for a long time."

"What do you mean?" I prodded. I had no idea what he was talking about.

"Let me put it this way," he said. "Someone is doing something about the mess this country is in. It's about time, too!"

I was still confused. "Would you please explain?" I asked.

"You haven't been paying much attention to what's going on, have you?" he responded, with some irritation. "A group of army officers is trying to take over the palace, and I hope they'll get rid of Diem, his brother, and his wife, Mrs. Nhu."

I was shocked. I sat back in the seat and asked no more questions. As we approached Le Loi Street, I saw army trucks and tanks parked everywhere. Except for the soldiers, there was no one else on the street. The taxi couldn't get close to my street, and I had to walk the rest of the way. Two armed soldiers stopped me and asked for identification. I showed them my ID card, told them where I lived, which was about a block away, and they let me go.

I raced up the stairs and knocked on the apartment door. Tam let me in. I threw my purse on the dining table and ran to the balcony overlooking Le Loi Street, which was just a short distance from the presidential palace. The street was quiet, and the soldiers sat like statues on their vehicles.

Tam came to the balcony and pointed to a soldier sitting on top of a tank. "Isn't he handsome?" she whispered. "I've picked him as my hero."

I looked at her and laughed. Lynn was not home, and the older maid and the children were asleep. Tam and I stayed up all night watching the soldiers. Now and then, one of them looked up at us and smiled.

As we looked out at the city, we could hear gunfire in the distance. Before daybreak, the gunfire got closer to us and sounded like Tet firecrackers. The soldiers, who had been relaxing on their vehicles, were now on the ground, ready for any necessary action.

I turned on the radio and listened for news. The announcer said an army officer, General Minh, had taken over the presidential palace and President Diem and his brother had been captured. The radio reception was bad, so I turned it off.

I was unable to understand the turmoil. I liked President Diem, but I didn't know much about his brother, and I knew even less about politics. I remembered that once the president had made an unannounced visit to the village where my family had lived a few years earlier. The church bells rang announcing the important event, and people came running to the church. He got out of his car and walked through the small throng gathered there. I was standing only a few meters from him. He smiled, talked to the villagers, and patted the children on their heads. He seemed like such a loving person then. I wondered what would happen to him.

Soon, Lynn came home with a newspaper. A picture of President Diem and his brother was on the front page. They had been shot in the head, and their faces were covered with blood. I was shocked. The accompanying article was full of critical accusations against the president and his brother, and there were long tirades about Nhu's drug addiction and alcoholism.

Lynn and I didn't work that day. Instead, we stayed home, listened to the radio, and played cards. We were anxious to hear news about the fate of our country, but all we heard were repeated announcements about how and when Diem and his brother died. The news grew repetitious, and we turned the radio off.

Throughout the country, many celebrated Diem's death while others mourned the loss of a brave, though stubborn, patriot. The military faction who ousted Diem lasted less than three months. This new government was overthrown in late January of 1964, and leadership was to change hands no less than six times during a period of one year.

Political and civil unrest was rampant, and corruption was the rule rather than the exception. Throughout this turmoil, the Viet Cong continued to wage war, inflicting severe losses on the South Vietnamese Army.

After alleged North Vietnamese attacks on an American destroyer in the Gulf of Tonkin in August of 1964, American forces were increased in Vietnam. By December, US military strength reached 23,000 troops. By the end of 1965, this number grew to 200,000.

Soon after Diem's assassination, Lynn and I were about to close the meat stand after a very busy day when she threw down her big chopping knife, turned to me, and said, "I'm sick and tired of selling meat. I'd like to open a nightclub with a restaurant and live entertainment."

Her announcement didn't surprise me at all, as she was always coming up with wild ideas. Lynn stood there, thoughtful for a moment, then continued, "I don't have enough money of my own, but I'm sure some of my rich friends will help. Madame Nhu is out of the way, and there is nothing to stop us from opening a dancing club."

Madame Nhu, President Diem's sister-in-law, had been appointed to top-level positions in the government and used her power to, among other things, outlaw public dancing. Private club owners who could afford to pay off authorities continued to maintain dance clubs, but they were expensive and risky enterprises. After Diem and his brother were assassinated, Madame Nhu fled the country, and public dancing was legalized.

Soon after, Lynn sold the meat stand, and with the help of friends, came up with enough money to lease a restaurant. It was located on the third floor of a building on a small street near Tran Hung Dao, a major Saigon thoroughfare. She hired workers to clean and remodel the cafe, transforming it into a beautiful, stylish nightclub.

Miraculously, in a week, the club was ready. We hired cooks, waiters and waitresses, and a band. Opening night was very exciting, and the club was crowded with people, most of whom were foreigners. I overheard people speaking English, as well as some French and Chinese.

I worked as the cashier, trying to keep receipts and bills organized, and helped Lynn supervise operations. She was busy running back and forth. Just watching her made me dizzy.

Within weeks, we had become well-organized and had developed a set routine. Each night, after the club closed and the cleaning crew went home, Lynn and I counted the receipts, took inventory, and prepared for the next day. Sometimes, we even worked until three or four in the morning. Then we were back at nine, giving us only a few hours to rest.

We ordered many kinds of meat and vegetables and a variety of drinks to serve at the nightclub. We also had to confirm arrangements with the band, the singers, or other entertainers, and had to make sure the cooks, waiters, and waitresses would be there. The work was long and hard, but I enjoyed it. Lynn gave me a lot of responsibility and authority, and I cherished her trust.

I adapted to my new status by wearing beautiful clothes and heavy makeup. In order to oversee the operation, I sat high on a bar stool in a corner of the nightclub. I was always busy with something and didn't have time to carry on a conversation with anybody, including the men.

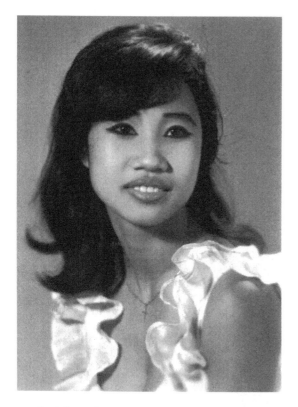

At eighteen, I was the club manager and cashier.

The girls working at the club were selected for their beauty, personality, and foreign language ability. Dressed in elegant and revealing clothes, their primary functions were to socialize with the patrons, provide conversation and a be dancing partner.

In return, the customers bought the girls drinks. These cocktails were many times more expensive than regular drinks, and the girls were given a fifty percent share for each drink they were bought.

Now and then, customers bought me drinks and sent them to my corner with a note attached. Some of the notes were funny and made me laugh out loud. If I had time, I wrote thank you notes and sent them back through the bartender. Most of the time, I could do no more than give the sender a thankful smile.

At the age of seventeen, I learned how to speak English, some French, and a little Chinese from the tutor Lynn hired to teach us. I also learned how to ballroom dance, thanks to Lynn and the instructor we hired. Besides being sent drinks to my corner, I was also asked to dance. If I wasn't busy, I danced with a customer or a friend. Most of the time, I waited for Lynn to take over my cashier duties before I left the corner, because I didn't trust just anybody with a drawer full of money. But somehow, we both managed to get in an occasional dance or two.

I began developing many friends through the club, both male and female. Some male friends wanted to be more than just friends, and when they did, I backed off.

It wasn't long before Lynn got pregnant and was often gone, leaving the club for me to manage. No one knew Lynn better than I, but even I did not know who the father of the baby was. I wondered if Lynn even knew.

Large numbers of American soldiers were arriving in Saigon during this period, most of them en route to different parts of the country. They knew little about Vietnamese culture and customs and were easy prey for the greedy. They were rich by comparison and never bargained when they bought something. They didn't realize they could purchase goods and services for much less, if they bartered.

Everyone loved to sell things to the Americans, and those who didn't have merchandise sold themselves or members of their families. Once, I saw a man sell his wife to an American soldier for twenty dollars. Another time, I saw a woman sell her daughter. Everyone was going into business.

During this time, bars began popping up everywhere. At first, only a few girls worked in the bars, and then word spread about how easy it was to make money from the gullible Americans, and that changed dramatically. College and high school students, discontented maids, officers' and soldiers' wives, and many others began exchanging conversation for cocktails. Some went beyond these innocent exchanges and went out with their customers to make more money.

The elfin peanut girl, the brassy shoeshine boy, and the beggar all competed to get their share. At first, I felt sorry for the GIs, because they were so innocent and naive. It wasn't long, however, before I too joined the competition.

The girls in the bars became adept at separating a GI from his money, and one evening, while writing tickets at the club, I heard a girl sobbing at a table near me. Over strains of music, I could hear her talking in broken English to the young American sitting with her.

"Last night, a rocket hit my house," she cried. "I'm the only survivor." She paused for effect and dried her tears. "All my dead relatives are still at the morgue," she continued, "and I don't have enough money to bury them. I really need help."

The GI couldn't contain himself and emptied his wallet on the table. He comforted her for a while, then left. A few minutes later, I heard sobbing again. The same girl was telling the same story to another victim. Before the night was over, she made a pocketful of money. She used this same story for the next several nights until she came up with a new line. I heard similar stories coming from different girls every night, and it was obvious they were just trying to make money from the softhearted GIs.

Before the Americans came in such numbers, we served full-strength cocktails to the girls, but they were not able to handle so much whiskey at once and asked the bartenders to add tea.

Even with the drinks at half strength, the girls still got drunk. We couldn't make money with drunken girls, so we started serving them plain tea. It looked like whiskey, cost the club little, and resulted in sober girls who could do their jobs. We learned later that other clubs were doing the same, and the term "Saigon tea" was born.

A half-dozen drunken American soldiers came to the club one night and demanded real whiskey be given to the six girls sitting with them. They smelled and tasted each glass to make sure it wasn't tea.

Later, all twelve of them were drunk, and their rowdy dancing and singing disturbed the other guests. Lynn and I asked the GIs to calm down, but they ignored us, and we told the girls to go into the back room.

After that, matters got worse. The GIs started throwing glasses and breaking bottles, and they demanded we bring the girls back. Before we could respond, several sober civilians and GIs who were sitting close by came to their table and asked them to quiet down. When the drunks resisted, a fight broke out. We finally had to call the military police, who came within minutes. The GIs calmed down when they saw the MPs and acted like nothing happened. "We were just having some fun," one of them said.

To prove it, they shook hands and hugged each other. The MPs just shook their heads and left. To patch things up, both the drunk and sober GIs started buying each other drinks. Soon they were all drunk.

A handsome young airman walked into the club one evening, and our eyes met. I was automatically attracted to him, and from the way he looked at me, I could tell the feeling was mutual. He sat at the bar near my corner, drank alone, and left after a few beers. For the next several nights, he visited the club, always sat at the same spot, and drank alone. He turned down the company of the other girls, and left without saying a word.

While he sat at his place at the bar, he often glanced over at me. When our eyes met, we smiled, but we said nothing. He ordered his usual drink, bought one for me, and sent me a note, along with the drink, through the bartender. I read it and sent him back a thank-you note. For a while, this was our only means of communication.

This went on for a few evenings, and then, instead of letting the bartender bring my drink, he brought it to me himself, and asked, "What's your name?"

I smiled and said, "My name is Mai Ly." I had changed my name again after the club opened.

"How old are you?" he asked.

"Seventeen," I replied.

"You look older than seventeen," he said with a smile.

"How about you?" I asked. "What is your name, and how old are you?"

"My name is Tony," he answered, "and I'm nineteen."

"You look older than nineteen," I said with a smile.

"May I sit closer to you?" he asked.

"I won't bite," I replied.

He moved closer, but he was still on the other side of the bar. Even though I was working, we managed to talk and laugh for the rest of the evening. Tony was friendly but very shy. He told me he was an E-2 in the air force and was stationed at Tan Son Nhut Air Base. He had been in Vietnam for two months. The longer we talked, the more we were attracted to each other.

We soon became friends, and he often brought me presents and flowers. One night, Tony came in with another young airman and introduced him to me. "This is Andy. He's my best friend." I smiled and shook Andy's hand.

They sat across from me at my corner, drinking "Ba Muoi Ba", meaning "33", a French beer, bottled in Vietnam. Some said the beer was called 33 because it contained thirty-three percent formaldehyde.

Andy was as handsome as Tony, but he looked older and was more outspoken. For the remainder of the evening, Andy didn't take his eyes off me. From then on, Andy always accompanied Tony to the club. He also came along when Tony and I went to a movie or to dinner. Sometimes, Andy came to the club by himself, and he brought me flowers and gifts. In time, he asked me to go out with him, and I told him I liked him very much, but I was in love with Tony. Andy was disappointed by my rejection, and he became jealous of Tony.

Andy began coming to the club early, so he could talk to me before Tony got there. One evening, he was by himself, sitting at the bar watching me. It was late, and Tony hadn't shown up yet, so I asked, "Where is Tony?"

Andy paused for a moment and said, "I hate to tell you this, but Tony has a new girlfriend in another club, and he said he didn't want to see you anymore."

I was stunned. It wasn't like Tony to disappear without a word. At first, I didn't believe Andy, but after two weeks passed, and Tony hadn't come back, I didn't know what else to think, and there was no way for me to get in touch with him. I was hurt and angry to think Tony could have been so callous.

Meanwhile, Andy came to see me every night to soothe me. He told me to forget about Tony because he was no good and liked to butterfly around. Deep inside, I did not believe Andy, because Tony seemed to be such a nice person, and he was just too shy to flirt around. When I cried, Andy was there to comfort me. His kind words and gestures were winning my heart, but for the longest time, I couldn't get over Tony's rejection. He was my first love.

Chapter 16

METAMORPHOSIS

AFTER TONY LEFT, I didn't feel the same. I had grown tired of being so proper, and I decided to transition from cashier to dancing girl. Lynn hired another cashier to take my place.

I liked to dance, and the more I danced, the more I drank. Instead of drinking tea, I asked for real whiskey, and sometimes, I drank too much. When I did, I couldn't go home, so I slept in the dressing room at the back of the club.

I woke up one morning, looked around, and realized I was at the back of the club again. I sat up and felt nauseous. I wanted to throw up, but I couldn't walk to the bathroom. In desperation, I knelt on my hands and knees and crawled there. After getting sick, I crawled back to the couch. My head was pounding, and the room was spinning. I looked across the room and saw myself in the full-length mirror on the wall. The apparition looking back at me was frightening and disgusting.

"What a mess," I thought. My heavy makeup from the night before looked

In my blue dress.

terrible now, the false eyelashes and black eye liner were smeared down on my face, and my hair was standing straight up, thanks to the teasing and overuse of hairspray. My beautiful, low-cut blue dress was crooked and wrinkled beyond recognition. I tried to stand up to change my clothes, but my head was heavier than my feet, and I fell back down on the couch.

I glanced around and noticed several pieces of folded paper scattered on the floor. With what little strength I had left, I gathered them together and brought them back to the couch. With my eyes half-open, I read each one. They had been written to me the night before by friends and customers and had either been thrown into the room or put in my pocket. I couldn't remember. The funny ones made me laugh, and when I laughed, the pain in my head just about killed me. I rolled the notes into a ball when I finished reading them, sat farther back on the couch, and did some thinking.

I looked so different than I had just a few months earlier. The fancy clothes and heavy makeup changed the way I looked on the outside, but inside I still felt the same. I was still a stubborn girl with a lot of self-respect, but I was also a sad and lonely girl with a very uncertain future. I stared at the closet full of clothes and thought of the girls who wore them. When they walked into the room, they were dressed in conservative clothes and wore very little or no makeup. Then the metamorphosis took place. They applied heavy makeup, combed and teased their hair, changed into sexy clothes, and put on high-heeled shoes. "What will happen to these girls a few years from now?" I thought. "What will happen to me?" I shook my head, realizing there was no way I could know the answer to these questions.

I lay on the couch until I felt better. Then, I got up and slowly changed clothes and went to visit Lan, a friend of mine. She was eighteen and lived with her mother and her half-American son. The boy's father didn't even know his son existed.

We decided we wanted to go see a movie, so Lan asked her mother to watch her son while she and I went to a show. It was an Indian love story with Vietnamese subtitles. We laughed and cried as we escaped into the make-believe screen. After the movie, we agreed to go to the Saigon Market to get something to eat. As we left the theater and walked down the street, a small group of about fifty demonstrators paraded down the sidewalk carrying some illegible signs and chanting.

"Get away from them!" Lan warned me.

"Don't worry," I replied, "they're just some small religious group. I'm sure they won't bother us."

Lan wasn't convinced and ran back into the theater. Out of curiosity, I lingered for just a moment. One young male demonstrator left the group and grabbed my arm. "What are you doing here?" he demanded. "Why are you standing in our way?"

"I just came out of the theater, and I'm not in your way," I replied.

"What is your religion?" he asked.

I had been through this before when two Buddhist demonstrators trounced me for admitting I was Catholic. Since most of the demonstrations were by Buddhist groups, I thought it would be safe for me to side with them.

"I'm a Buddhist," I said with pride.

It happened to be a Catholic demonstration. The young man twisted my arm behind my back as he shouted, "If you don't become a Catholic, you will die and go to hell!"

Like lightning, I said, "I am Catholic! I am Catholic!" He twisted my arm harder, as he yelled, "You're a liar! Catholics never deny their religion."

He let go of my arm, grabbed my shoulder, shook me violently, and said, "You are a liar! You are a liar!"

Then he kicked my behind, and I fell to the ground. I climbed to my feet, dusted off my clothes, wiped my tears, and watched him run to catch up with his group. When Lan saw me at work later that day, she apologized for running away. I laughed it off and told her what had happened to me, about how I was insulted and kicked to the ground. She was sympathetic and called them "stupid religious fanatics." Then she changed the subject by asking, "Do you want to come to my house and play cards tonight?"

"Sure. It sounds like fun," I replied.

We were still dressed in our fancy clothes when we left the club after midnight and caught a cyclo to Lan's house. Her mother was still awake and offered me some fruit and tea. Lan's baby was already asleep, and a few minutes later, two GIs and another girl came to the house. One of the GIs was Lan's boyfriend. We were all introduced, shook hands, and then got to know each other over fruit and tea. We began playing cards, using two decks, and often changed the game.

At around three in the morning, loud banging on the door startled us. The knocking was followed by a voice shouting, "Open the door, this is the police! We're here to check your family papers."

Lan hid the cards and told the GIs to crawl under the bed. If the police discovered them in the house, we would all be in serious trouble. The three of us jumped into bed, pretending we were asleep. Then, Lan told her mother to open the door.

Five or six armed policemen rushed into the house. With guns drawn, they checked everything, including the closet. One of them came to our bedroom, pointed his gun, and shouted, "Don't pretend you're sleeping! I know you're awake! Where are your family papers?"

Lan called her mother to bring her family papers to the room. "We don't have papers, because we don't live here," I told him. He ordered the two of us to get out of bed.

"You have broken the law by being in this house without family papers or proper permission." He glared at us for a few moments and waited. He was expecting payment for the broken law, and when we didn't respond, he handcuffed us and hurried us out. I managed to slip my feet into a pair of over-sized flip-flops. I didn't know who they belonged to. I was too scared and nervous to even think.

"Please let me go," I begged. "I didn't know I had to have a paper to spend a night with my friend. I promise I'll never do it again."

He ignored my pleas and pushed me through the open door and

into the darkness outside. He yelled at me to hurry up, but I wasn't fast enough for him, so he shoved me forward. I lost my balance and fell into a ditch containing raw sewage. I was handcuffed behind my back, and it was difficult for me to get up. He growled, grabbed my arm, and pulled me to my feet. I smelled horrible and could feel maggots crawling all over me. The other girl was also pushed, but, lucky for her, she didn't fall.

A few of the policemen took us to a jeep parked near the house, while others stayed behind to do more checking. They found the two GIs under the bed and ordered them out of the house. I heard the police asking for their names and ID cards, and, after checking their identification, they let the men go.

The police took us to the Tan Binh police station and removed our handcuffs. They pushed us into a cell and without a word, slammed the door and walked away. With my hands free, I was able to brush off the filth from my face and clothes. I looked around to see that we were all alone in the cell.

My companion and I talked until sunlight. When we finally exchanged names, I learned hers was "Ba." We had been calling each other "Chi." By tradition, when girls first meet, they show respect, by calling each other Chi, which means older sister.

I learned Ba was sixteen years old, and her name meant "three," even though she was the second born child in her family. South Vietnamese often call their children according to the order in which they were born, except the first child, who is called number two, and so on. Because of the superstitions of the cultures in the South, the children are also sometimes given nicknames. Their real names are almost never used, except for in legal documents. I'm from the North, and yes, I also find this confusing.

In the morning, a guard took us to an office for questioning. A fat man sat behind a cluttered desk, smoking a cigarette. "According to the police report," he said, "you were caught serving two GI customers." Ba and I looked at each other in astonishment. He continued, "You realize there is a heavy fine for your crimes."

Ba and I denied his accusations and said together, "We did nothing wrong. We just went there to play cards."

"It doesn't matter," he replied, "You got caught."

"Doing what?" I asked.

"We didn't even know them," Ba said.

"Of course, you don't have to know your customers in your business," he said.

"How much money did you two make last night?" he asked with a sneer.

"I'm innocent!" I protested. "I'm still a virgin."

He ignored me and asked, "Do you have money to pay your fines?"

We looked at each other in resignation and shook our heads no. When he realized we had no money, he immediately lost interest and walked out of the room. Minutes later, we were led back to the cell.

"My older sister works in a bar and makes lots of money," she said. "My mother told me to go to work with her. This is my first week." I discovered we had something in common; she was still a virgin, too.

While in jail, Lan brought us food and a change of clothes, and she told us she didn't have to go to jail, because her mother paid off the policemen who stayed behind. She was fortunate that her mother had enough money to pay the bribe.

Two days later, a policeman came to the cell, handcuffed us again, and drove us to a huge courthouse. Inside, the waiting room was crowded with people. We waited until afternoon before they removed the handcuffs and took us before one of the court's officials.

A tall, skinny man wearing reading glasses sat at a desk in the middle of the room, looking at a folder in front of him. "How much money did you make for sleeping with those two GIs?" he asked.

"We didn't sleep with those Americans," I declared. "We didn't even know them. We were invited to a friend's house to play cards, and we did nothing else. Besides, we're still virgins."

He laughed as he looked at me over his reading glasses. "All you hookers are virgins," he said. "You are lucky today, because I'm going to let you go. Both of you should go home and find a different job. You two are still very young and are decent-looking girls. I'm sure you can find something better to do, but if you decide to continue what you are doing now, you'd better not show your faces in this court again."

We bowed and thanked him for giving us our freedom. I didn't know who the man really was, and I wasn't about to wait around to find out. We were just happy to get out of there. They took us back to the police station, processed some more of our papers, and released us. I asked Ba if she wanted to go with me to Lynn's house, and she accepted my invitation.

I hailed a cab and I asked, "What do you think about coming to work with me as a dancer at Lynn's club?"

"I think it would be fun," she said, "but I can't dance."

"I'll teach you," I said. "How about changing your name?" I asked, "I think Ba is too conservative. Why don't you change your name to Mai Lan? Since the name I use is Mai Ly, we can pretend we are sisters."

She thought about it for a moment and said, "Sounds good to me. Mai Lan and Mai Ly; I like it."

In no time, Mai Lan learned to dance, and we became the best of friends. She lived with her mother and several sisters and brothers in one of the stilt shacks built over a river on the outskirts of Saigon. Some years before, her father had run away with another woman and had left her mother to raise a family of seven children by herself.

I loved visiting Mai Lan's family. Her mother was very sweet and generous, and she reminded me of my mother. I spent a great deal of time at Mai Lan's house, relaxing or swimming in the river. Her mother treated me like one of her own, and I felt right at home.

Mai Lan's older sister, Hai, brought her American boyfriend home one Sunday. He introduced himself as Bob. Mai Lan's seven-year-old brother stepped in front of him, shook his hand, and said, "Hello number one GI." Bob smiled and rubbed his head. He seemed like a nice person, but he was huge. He had to bend down to get through the door, and when he walked, the whole neighborhood shook.

Mai Lan and me.

After we were introduced and got to know each other, we asked Bob to play cards with us. The four of us sat at a small, low table, and poor Bob, with his big belly, had to maneuver for a while before he was able to lower himself to a small stool, which stood about a foot from the floor. We played cards until time for dinner.

"What do you want to eat?" Hai asked Bob.

"French fries and a hamburger will be just fine," he replied.

We looked at each other, and then at him. "What's a hamburger?" I asked. After he explained, Hai said, "Forget it. It would take too long to chop the meat and cut up the potatoes and fry them. What else do you want?"

"Spaghetti sounds good," he answered.

Again, we gave each other a puzzled look. No one knew what spaghetti was either. Mai Lan said, "Forget spaghetti," and asked, "How about steak?"

"Steak would be great," Bob said.

"Then steak it is," Hai said with finality.

Bob didn't know it, but we had to put our money together to have enough to buy a piece of meat for him at the market. The rest of us ate rice and vegetables with fish sauce.

When the meal was served, we didn't have a steak knife or a fork for Bob. Hai cut the meat into bite-size pieces with a butcher knife and gave Bob a pair of chopsticks to eat with. He poked at his steak with the chopsticks but had no luck. He had to eat the steak with his fingers. We all wanted to be polite, but it was difficult to keep from laughing at him.

Before long, Bob and Hai got engaged and were married. There was no party or celebration to commemorate the occasion, and after that, they moved to an apartment of their own. Mai Lan and I continued to work to help support her family. Mai Lan's family made me miss my own, as I had not gone home or been in contact with my family for almost two years, and I wondered how they were all doing.

It was about this time that Lynn gave birth to a beautiful baby boy, and while she was caring for her baby, I managed the club. Meanwhile, Andy kept pressuring me to be his girlfriend.

"I don't want to be anyone's girlfriend right now," I kept telling him. "I just want to be friends. Besides, what's the difference?" I asked, "We go out together, all the time anyway."

"Yes," he replied, "but to a movie, or to swim in the public swimming pool? Or to go out to eat, or to the park, or to the zoo? And we never go out alone, there is always someone else with us. I don't want to just be a friend," he persisted. "I love you and want to marry you." I fended him off by telling him I would think about it. There were many reasons for me not to love Andy.

I had two other male friends. One was Chinese, named Cong, and the other was an American soldier named Larry. I often went out with two, or sometimes all three of them at the same time. If I only went with one, I took Lan, Mai Lan, or another friend along wherever we went, because I didn't want to be alone with a man for fear of being taken advantage of. I wasn't interested in intimacy.

I just wanted to remain friends with all of them and nothing more. Cong was very personable, with a good sense of humor, but not good-looking. Andy was handsome, but he was devious, and he lied a lot. Larry was average looking and came from a wealthy family, but he was not very bright.

One evening, Larry came to the club and told me he didn't have to go back to the base and was free to go out all night. "Will you please go out with me when you get off tonight?" he asked. His intentions were obvious.

"I don't think I can," I said.

"If you really cared about me, you'd go with me," he said.

I didn't want to hurt his feelings or make him angry, but I had no intention of going anywhere with him.

"If it means so much to you, I'll go with you," I lied. "Go to the Saigon Market and wait for me. I'll meet you there when the club closes." He left with a silly grin on his face, and when the club closed, I went straight home.

The following day, when I arrived at work, Larry was standing at the entrance, waiting for me. "Where were you last night?" he demanded. "I waited hours for you."

"I waited for you, too, but you didn't show up," I replied, in mock disappointment. "Where did you wait?" he asked.

"I was at the back side of the market," I said.

"No wonder you didn't see me," he replied. "I was waiting for you in front."

I had made a lucky guess. Acting disappointed, I said, "I'm very sorry; we'll have to try it again another time," and we held hands as we walked into the club.

There were dramatic changes occurring in Saigon at this time. The city was taking on a new and sinister character as hordes of uniformed American servicemen roamed the streets and new bars and clubs opened all over the city. Many conservative and reserved Vietnamese women began to wear low-cut dresses, heavy makeup, and high-heeled shoes in public. You could see them on every street, every alley, and on every corner, especially on Le Loi, Nguyen Hue, and Thu Do streets.

Violence was also common in Saigon, with Viet Cong exploding bombs almost every day. The initial targets had been hotels, nightclubs, and restaurants where Americans gathered. Then the attacks became indiscriminate and soon spread to public markets and businesses that had no connections with the US forces. There was no logical reason for the spreading terrorism. During this time, Lynn's older maid, Nam, took some time off to visit her family. While there, she went to a movie and was killed when a bomb exploded inside the crowded theater. At her funeral, I realized no place was safe anymore. After Nam's death, Lynn and I took over her duties instead of hiring a new maid.

Le Loi Street was usually quiet in the early morning hours when I came home from work. I liked to step out on the balcony and enjoy the peaceful solitude. The stillness was broken one morning when three people were arguing and screaming in the middle of the street, illuminated by an overhead light. One of them was a very drunk American soldier. The other two were Vietnamese, a tattered pedicab driver, and a young girl, wearing almost nothing. Her dress looked as if it had been made from a mosquito net. The soldier accused the driver of stealing his money.

In broken English, the driver tried to make his point, "You give me money to find girl. I find you girl!" he shouted.

The GI yelled back, "The money was to pay for you and the girl, too!"

"No, no!" the driver retorted, as he shook his hat back and forth. "You give me money, I find girl. Now you pay girl."

"But that was my last dollar!" the American shouted. "I want my money back!"

The pedicab driver didn't understand the GI and screamed, "You number ten GI! You cheap Charlie!"

The girl didn't understand English and kept poking the American in the back. "Tien? Tien?" she repeated. (Tien means money.) The driver told the girl in Vietnamese that the American was too cheap to pay her.

The poor soldier was out of money, and no one understood him. They went round and round for a while, until the girl gave up and slipped away into the darkness. I heard the tapping of her high-heeled shoes as they faded into the night. When the GI realized she was gone, he tried chasing her, but she had disappeared.

The pedicab driver took advantage of the distraction, jumped on his bike, and tried to pedal away, but the GI didn't give up. He ran after the driver, grabbed the handlebars, and a tugging match followed. The drunk GI was no match for the strong pedicab driver, and he pulled loose and pedaled away as fast as he could. The poor GI staggered down the street, cursing and yelling at the top of his lungs. It was an amusing but disturbing scene, and I felt sorry for them all. It served to remind me of what was happening in my country; both the demoralization of my people and of the Americans. The Americans considered the Vietnamese small, uncivilized, and not too bright. The Vietnamese, on the other hand, thought Americans were huge, uncivilized, and not too bright. I sat in silence, wondering where it would all lead, but my mind and body were too tired to consider such oppressive thoughts, so I went to bed.

The following evening, while I was dancing at the club, Lynn ran onto the dance floor, crying hysterically. "Huong is dead!" she sobbed as she reached me. "My daughter is dead!" I stopped dancing to find out what had happened. I knew that Huong had been staying at her grandmother's for almost a week.

"What happened?" I asked.

"I'll tell you later," she wailed. "Right now, I want you to take care of the club and close it as soon as you can." Then she turned and left.

I was stunned by the news. I left the dance floor and ran sobbing to the dressing room. I loved Huong so much; she was sweet and beautiful and did not deserve to die. I was heartbroken. I looked up and saw Mai Lan, who had come to comfort me.

"I have to close the club," I told her.

Then, I wiped my tears and returned to the dance floor. I went to the microphone and asked the band to stop playing. "I'm sorry," I announced, "but we have to close the club early tonight. There has been a death in the family."

Most of the customers showed concern at the news and expressed their sympathy. A few drunks didn't want to leave and made some racket, but they eventually calmed down. I thanked everyone as they left and closed the door behind the last person.

Lynn changed completely after Huong died. She became withdrawn and seldom went out. She asked me, along with some of her other friends, to manage the club. A few weeks after the tragedy, while I was away, Lynn bought a razor, and told her maid to shave her head. I was shocked when I came home and saw her.

"Why did you do that?" I asked.

"I'm going to the pagoda to become a Buddhist monk," she replied.

"What about the club?" I asked.

"I don't care what happens to it now," she said. "You can sell it, rent it, or give it away. It doesn't really matter to me now." I felt terrible about Huong's death, but I felt sorrier for Lynn. Because she was in so much pain, I chose not to ask her about Huong's death. I had a feeling she was another war tragedy.

I helped Lynn sell the club weeks later. The club was so popular, it took no time to find a buyer. Although the club had a new owner, Mai Lan and I continued working there.

Lynn's daughter's death had been too much for her, and she lost touch with reality. All she did was cry all day, and there was no more fun and laughter. The atmosphere there was too depressing, and I decided I couldn't stay.

After making the necessary arrangements, I moved out of Lynn's apartment. Mai Lan and I rented an apartment together on Truong Tan Buu Street, and, out of necessity, we joined a local gang. We had to in order to survive in the neighborhood. The leader forced us to swear to be loyal to the gang and follow their rules. We could not lie, cheat, or steal from each other. Also, there could be no sexual relations between members, and we had to promise to come to the aid of our comrades if needed.

Larry, Cong, and Andy also joined the gang, just to be near me. We did no more than get together for parties and have fun. We sang, danced, and acted silly, and most of the time we were well-behaved, but when drunk, some members acted foolhardy. They sometimes fought with other gangs and got in trouble with the police. I never knew what they were fighting about, and I was never involved in the violence.

Eventually, Larry quit hanging around with us. Andy told me Larry had dropped out because he didn't want to see me anymore. Then, Cong joined the Vietnamese Army, but he still came back now and then to visit me. Andy was always there, at least whenever he was able to leave the base.

Mai Lan and I grew tired of the same old faces, quit the club, and started bar and club-hopping instead. We had fun collecting Saigon tea in exchange for conversation, a little dancing, some rigged card games, and many empty promises. The promises were no more than lies to make money. We never intended to fulfill any of these pledges. We were still virgins and did not want to sleep with anyone for drinks or money. We didn't stay at any one place for long, though, because the GIs got impatient and then suspicious when we continued to postpone delivery of our promises.

Soon, our gang started clashing with the law more often, and many members landed in jail for fighting, stealing, and curfew violation. Several boys were drafted into military service as a result, and two of them even joined the police force. Now and then, they visited our apartment.

As the group dispersed, Andy and I began a new relationship. We even went out alone, which we had never done before. The police often stopped our taxi, and they demanded money, because we didn't have proper prenuptial papers, and they threatened to take me to jail if we didn't pay. Depending on the greed of the policeman, the payoff was around five hundred piasters, or about twenty dollars. In the eyes of the police, as well as many Vietnamese people, any Vietnamese girl with an American was considered a prostitute and was an easy target for bribery.

One evening, Andy ran into the club where I was working and came immediately to my booth. He was out of breath and blurted out, "Larry is dead! He was killed yesterday in Pleiku, during a Viet Cong attack."

The shock of another death stunned me, and tears streamed down my face as I listened to Andy. Grief over Larry's death was not my only pain. I realized Andy had lied when he told me about Larry's reason for dropping out of our group. There had been no mention of a transfer to Pleiku.

Then my anguish turned to anger. "This is all your fault!" I screamed at Andy. "I wish I had been kinder to Larry while he was still alive."

Andy glared at me and replied, "No, it's really your fault. Because of you, he asked to be transferred."

We were striking out at each other blindly, trying to find some reason for Larry's death. After a short quarrel, we began drinking heavily. I remembered nothing about the night before when I woke up in the back of the bar's makeup room the next day.

About that time, Mai Lan fell in love with a gorgeous, young, blond-haired American. His name was Tom, and he was a staff sergeant in the air force. I often wished he were my boyfriend, but Mai Lan was my best friend, and I would never even think about taking him.

One day, she asked me what I thought about her moving into an apartment with Tom. I gave her my blessings and told her that if she didn't want to move in with him, I would. A few days later, she moved part of her belongings to an apartment they had rented, not far from where we lived. She stayed with Tom when he got a pass from Tan Son Nhut Base. The rest of the time, she stayed with me.

Tom came to the club to see Mai Lan one evening and brought a friend. Tom introduced him as Jim, who was about twenty-five, not very handsome but big and muscular. He looked like a bodybuilder and seemed like a nice man. The four of us found an empty table and sat down. Tom ordered a drink for Mai Lan, and Jim offered to buy me a drink, but insisted it be real whiskey. I was feeling sad and figured, "Why not?" For the rest of the evening, he bought me two drinks to his one, and the four of us drank and danced until way after midnight.

As the club was closing, Tom asked Jim and me to go to his apartment to play cards. It seemed like a good idea, and we both agreed. When we got there, we were all too drunk to play cards and decided to get some sleep. Mai Lan and Tom went to their bedroom, and Jim lay down on the couch.

I climbed the stairs to the loft, stumbling several times before I finally made it. The small loft was empty except for a bare mattress on the floor, and I collapsed on the mattress and fell into a sound sleep.

I woke suddenly to find someone on top of me. When I came to my senses, I realized it was Jim and tried to get up, but he forced me down and covered my mouth with his. He twisted my left arm behind my back and held both of my arms under me. With his free hand, he ripped off my clothes, then he forced his heavy body on top of mine. I fought and struggled, but he was too heavy and strong—two hundred and fifty pounds of muscle over an eighty-five pound girl. In the end, he got what he wanted.

He finished with me, let me go, and put on his clothes in a hurry. I lay there crying, as he climbed down from the loft and ran out of the apartment without a word. I was in so much pain, I wasn't able to move. My lips were swollen, and I tasted blood in my mouth. My arms and legs felt like they were broken, and the pain between my legs was unbearable. I had never experienced anything so painful and so disgusting in my life.

I tried to get up to find the stairs, but my tears blinded me. I tripped and almost fell from the loft. I climbed downstairs and took a quick look at myself in the dim light. My white dress was torn and covered with blood. More blood was running down my leg. I limped to Mai

Lan's bedroom door but decided not to knock. I turned back to the couch and lay there crying until daylight.

Mai Lan and Tom woke up, and I heard them talking and laughing. They opened the door and saw me lying on the couch with swollen, red eyes and lips, and they knew something was wrong.

Tom ran to me and asked, "What happened to you?"

I said nothing. Mai Lan looked around and asked, "Where is Jim?"

I just shook my head and cried. They looked at me and my clothes and realized what had happened.

"I'll kill the bastard!" Tom shouted. Mai Lan put her arm around me and tried to comfort me.

After a few minutes, I squeaked out a few words. "It was my fault," I said. "I shouldn't have been here in the same house with him. I allowed the situation to happen." I tried to smile and act nonchalant. "Besides," I said, "I'm almost eighteen, and I had to become a woman some day; it just happened to be today." I smiled again, but my tears were still dropping from my swollen lip. Tom changed his clothes and hurried back to the base to look for Jim. He said he was going to make him pay for what he had done to me. After he left, Mai Lan got dressed and took me home. Tom never told me if he found Jim, and I didn't ask. I wanted to erase the experience from my memory forever.

Mai Lan and Tom were engaged, and she spent most of her time with him. My apartment became very quiet with fewer people coming to see me. Cong seldom visited. I became lonely, and Andy continued to pester me about marrying him.

"I don't care if you love me or not," he sobbed, "I still love you and want to marry you," he told me while he was visiting my apartment.

I felt sorry for him, held him, and comforted him. He held me close to him, and in a very weak moment, I gave into his pressure. I agreed to marry him, and the following day, we went to the police station to obtain prenuptial papers, which allowed us to live legally under the same roof. Andy moved in with me early in January 1965.

Chapter 17

CICADA SHELL

IN JUNE OF 1965, I had to stop working, because I was five months pregnant. When Andy first found out, he wasn't very happy and pressured me to get an abortion. I refused, telling him I would take care of the baby by myself if he didn't want it. As my stomach grew larger, Andy avoided coming home.

At the time, we were living in a small apartment with a shared bathroom and kitchen. We decided to move to the upstairs apartment because the occupants had just moved out. It was larger and would give us more room when the baby came, but we still had to share the downstairs kitchen and bathroom with the new tenants who rented our old apartment.

The day we moved, Andy told me he couldn't leave the base and was unable to help me. It took me all day to drag the boxes and the bed, piece by piece, to the second floor. I made dinner and waited for Andy. By nine o'clock, I got tired of waiting and ate alone. After washing dishes, I went to bed.

A persistent knocking woke me. I looked at the clock and noticed it was after one in the morning. "It's about time Andy came home," I thought, as I opened the door. Instead of Andy, a policeman stood there glaring at me.

"Let me see your family paper," he demanded.

Half awake, I found the document in a pile of clothes and handed it to him. He opened the folded record and read it, from top to bottom. There were only two names on the paper, Andy's and mine, and it shouldn't have taken more than a few seconds to read it. This was not the case. When he finished, he rolled up the document and hit the palm of his hand with it as if he were thinking about something important.

He stood in quiet thought for a moment, acting very officious. "You're in the wrong apartment," he announced. "The number on your family paper is for the apartment downstairs."

"I just moved up here today," I explained, "and I haven't had a chance to report it yet. Besides, it's the same house, and we use the same bathroom and toilet." He paid little attention to my explanation.

"You have to pay a fine for not reporting your change of address," he said.

"I'm sorry, but I don't have any money," I responded.

He went downstairs with my family paper in his hand. I wished I had money to pay him, but I had just paid the rent with what little I had saved. A few minutes later, he returned with a younger policeman, and I apologized to both of them.

"Please forgive me," I pleaded. "I promise I will report the address change the first thing tomorrow morning."

The second policeman acted tougher than the first. "You must have enough to pay the fine," he insisted, after seeing Andy's name on our papers and looking at our picture on the wall. "You're living with an American, and I'm sure you have plenty of money."

"I don't have any money," I repeated. "You can search my apartment if you don't believe me."

"Well, I don't believe you," the older policeman said. "You'll have to come with us." They escorted me downstairs and handcuffed me.

I remembered I left the door open. "Would you please remove the handcuffs for a moment?" I asked. "I have to go upstairs and lock my door."

"If you don't have any money, why do you need to lock your door?" the young policeman commented, and they both laughed as one pushed me ahead. Suddenly, one of them ordered, "You stay where you are. We'll be back."

They left me standing there while they went to the apartment next door. The door was ajar, and I saw several girls wearing sexy nightgowns, smoking cigarettes, and playing cards with American GIs. When the policemen came to the door, the girls greeted them with happy smiles. A few moments later, they came out, and the door closed behind them. I could hear the raucous laughter behind the closed door as the police led me to their jeep.

I spent the night in jail, and they released me the following morning. I had no money for a taxi and had to walk nearly four kilometers back to the apartment.

I rested for a few minutes, and then cooked a bowl of noodle soup for breakfast. While eating, I glanced through a stack of newspapers. I enjoyed reading Ngon Luan, a very popular newspaper, because it always contained some tidbits of juicy gossip.

I read the section headed "Hot News," and I was surprised to see my name and address. The article read, "After many days and great effort by police investigators, a girl named Nguyen Thi Loan has been taken into custody. She works at the Tu Do Bar and was observed bringing American servicemen home with her each night after work, charging them five hundred piasters each. She was apprehended by the police, in the act, at her apartment on Truong Tan Buu Street. She is now in jail."

I was shocked! The vicious lies from one irresponsible reporter were sickening. He used my name, my address, my innocent arrest, and converted them into a loathsome, false story. I was outraged. I wanted to go to the newspaper publishers and confront them immediately, but I didn't have money for a taxi, and even if I did, it wouldn't have made any difference to them. They had the power to say whatever they wanted.

Angry tears streamed down my face as I reread the article. I had never been in the Tu Do Bar, much less worked there. The only person I knew of who did work there was the girl who rented an apartment next to mine, the same apartment the police had visited the night I was arrested.

During the later months of my pregnancy, Andy avoided me even more. He came home about once a week to give me money for rent and food, and sometimes didn't even spend the night. When I asked him why, he maintained there was a curfew, and he couldn't leave the air base.

Some of my friends told me they had seen him in various clubs and bars and had seen him going home with different girls. I didn't want to believe them, but deep inside, I knew they were telling the truth.

One night, a friend informed me that Andy was at one of the clubs, and I went to see for myself. There he was, sitting with a girl, their arms holding each other, with their heads bent toward one another. I walked up to him and said, "Hello Andy."

He looked up in shock. "Uh, hello, Honey," he replied, while loosening his grip on the girl. I was so upset that I didn't stay to see his reaction and ran out the door. I hailed a taxi and cried all the way home.

At three o'clock in the morning, I had finally fallen asleep when Andy came home, smashed. He slumped into a chair next to the bed, slamming into the table next to it. First, he apologized to me for being a bad person, then he began babbling incoherently. I tried to ignore him, but his incessant and drunken chatter kept me awake. When I heard him mention Tony, he caught my attention.

"There's one thing I want you to know," he slurred. "Tony never had another girlfriend. He loved you and was still carrying your picture in his wallet when he went back to the States." He stopped to catch his breath before he continued. "I told him you were in love with someone else and didn't want to see him again. That's why he quit coming to see you."

He stopped talking and started laughing. I had always known Andy was a liar, but this was too much. The more I prodded him, the more he told me.

"I told Larry the same thing," he said. "They were stupid enough to believe me." He started laughing again. The pillow was soaked with my tears as I pretended to sleep, letting him continue to mumble to himself. He left in the morning, and I didn't see him for days.

By the end of August 1965, I was seven and a half months pregnant. I couldn't go to work or do much of anything, except visit friends, clean house, cook, and read. I was in bed reading a Chinese Kung Fu story after dinner one night when I felt a sharp pain in my stomach. Suspecting food poisoning, I took medicine to calm my stomach and rubbed menthol ointment on my naval.

At midnight, the pain persisted, so I went to the bathroom downstairs, thinking a cold shower might help. When I removed my clothes, I saw blood running down my legs. I immediately put my clothes back on, went upstairs, grabbed my purse, locked the door, and walked to the midwife's clinic nearby. I knew I was not far enough into my pregnancy to have the baby yet, but I was scared and went for help.

A middle-aged woman in a white uniform met me at the door, and I explained what had happened. She helped me to a room upstairs.

After examining me, she said, "You are in labor."

"But I'm only in my seventh month," I replied.

"You better stay here. Your baby will be born soon," she said.

By then, my stomach cramps had grown more intense, and it took all my strength to keep from screaming. I could neither sit up nor lie down. Nothing diminished the pain, so I went to the window and pulled myself up on the steel bars. I pressed my stomach against the wall and slowly let myself down. The movements reduced the pain somewhat, so I continued the maneuver throughout the night.

The nurse called me to the delivery room to check me several times, but the baby wasn't ready to come. The pain was severe, and sometimes I had to crawl instead of walk. This continued for two days. My downstairs neighbor was a friend of the nurse who worked there, and she heard I was at the clinic and came to see me. "Would you go to my family and get my mother for me?" I begged. I'll pay for your expenses." At first, she refused, but I kept insisting; I believed I was going to die. I heard that it was common for women to die during childbirth. I pleaded with her to find my mother. When she agreed to help, I gave her the address, the money, directions to my home, and she left.

I hadn't seen Mother for more than two years. I didn't know if she still lived in the same place. I didn't even know if she would come to see me or not. I thought I was dying, and I wanted to see her before I died.

The pain continued, and I let out soft screams as I clenched my jaws together. I felt so alone. I wondered where everyone was when I needed them.

On August 20, I gave birth to a baby boy. He was very small, pale, and weak, weighing less than two kilograms, or about three and a half pounds, and was covered with hair. When the midwife told me he was too premature to survive, I closed my tear-filled eyes and prayed for him to live.

Then they rolled me from the delivery room, and to my great relief, Mother was there waiting for me in the hall. I reached out my hand to her and saw tears streaming down her face. "Mother, Oh, Mother!" I cried. "My baby is dying, and there is nothing I can do. Please help me and take him to a bigger hospital."

She wiped her tears, nodded her head, but said nothing as she walked into the delivery room where the midwife tended my baby. The nurse rolled me back to my room, told me to rest, and left. I dragged myself to the window and looked down to the street. I watched as Mother entered a taxi carrying my baby. A part of me went with them, and tears streamed down my face as I watched the taxi disappear in the traffic. I had no idea where Mother was taking my baby, and I wondered if she even knew herself. I returned to my bed and continued to cry.

For two days, I didn't hear anything about my mother or my baby. There were no phones and no one to relay messages. All I could do was pray. Late in the afternoon one day, Mother brought my baby back. He was still weak, but he was alive. We stayed at the clinic for two more days and then walked home, my baby in my arms and Mother carrying a bag of clothes and medicine. We arrived at the apartment, and Mother told me she couldn't stay any longer, because she had to get back to her home. I thanked her for helping me and handed her some money I had in my pocket for bus fare, but she wouldn't accept it and told me I needed the money to take care of my baby. With tears streaming down her face, she looked at me in silence. She took a long look at the baby cradled in my arms and then walked out.

It was good to see Mother, and I appreciated her help. She gave me such good advice while I was still in the clinic, telling me what to do and what not to do to take care of my baby and me. I loved my mother so much and treasured her advice.

The baby was over a week old when Andy showed up. He had been drinking, as usual and staggered toward the bed. He planned to lie down but was surprised to see the baby lying there. He frowned, pointed a finger at the baby, and asked, "Who is that?"

"He's your baby," I said.

He looked at me in shock for a moment and said, "I'm sorry for not being with you when the baby was born. I didn't think you were due for another month or two." I said nothing.

He sat next to me and started crying. I felt his remorse, smiled, and held his head to my chest to comfort him. I had forgiven him. We talked about the baby and decided to name him Edward. Andy said, "I promise I will take care of you from now on. I'll marry you and take you and the baby to America with me."

He sounded sincere, and I believed him. For the next two months, Andy came home more often and was somewhat nicer to me. He told me one afternoon that his tour of duty was over, and he was to return to the United States within a week. The day he left, I helped him pack.

He gave me a roll of money and said, "I promise I will come back for you and the baby as soon as I can. Meanwhile, I'll send money for you to live on. I want you to stay home and take care of our son until I come back."

For the moment, I loved him and believed everything he said. We both cried as we said goodbye. "Take care of yourself and hurry back," I told him.

"I will," he replied. "Take care of yourself and the baby, too." He kissed the baby and then me. "I love you," he said, as he walked out the door.

"I love you, too," I replied.

Not long after Andy left, I was running out of money and had to hire a babysitter while I went back to work. Months passed, and I didn't hear a word from Andy. I thought he must have been too busy to write. I worked hard, day and night, to support the baby and myself.

Mai Lan stopped by to see me now and then. We were still close, but seldom saw each other, since she and Tom were engaged. She spent most of her time catering to him, and I knew Mai Lan would be a very good and faithful housewife.

Cong came to see me whenever he was off-duty, and we often went to dinner or to a movie. I enjoyed being with Cong, but somehow, I couldn't think of him as more than a good friend, and we had never been intimate. At one visit, we went to a movie on Le Loi Street and watched "The Young Ones," with Cliff Richard. Suddenly, during the movie, Cong turned to me and asked, "Can I adopt your baby?"

"Why?" I asked in surprise.

"Because I want to marry you," he replied.

"I can't," I answered. "I have to wait for the baby's father." Cong showed his disappointment, but he never mentioned it again.

When Eddie was four months old, my parents paid me a surprise visit. They tried to persuade me to give the baby up for adoption and come home to live with them. My stepfather told me I was engaged to be married to one of his friend's sons, who was in medical school. The families were ready, and everyone was waiting for me.

Before then, I had not heard anything about an engagement. When I asked about my fiancé, Mother described him, and I vaguely recalled the young man. I was a good Vietnamese girl, and I knew I was supposed to obey my parents, but I also knew I could not accept their conditions.

"I'll marry whomever you want," I said to my stepfather, "but I can't give up my baby."

"If you want to come home again, you must give your baby away," my stepfather ordered.

I gave it a lot of thought and said, "I don't really want to marry any-body right now. I want to wait for the baby's father."

"It doesn't matter what you want," my stepfather growled. "The fact is, you are engaged, and it's time you were married. The boy's family is ready for you."

"Can't you break the engagement?" I asked.

My stepfather raised his voice, and said, "No, I cannot. I will lose face. From generation to generation, we have all been married by prear-rangement. If you don't obey me, you will be disowned."

He got up from his seat and prepared to leave. I asked them to stay for dinner, but my stepfather declined, claiming he was too busy.

"Come on," he told Mother. Before he walked out the door, he turned to me and gave me an ultimatum. "I will give you one month to give up the baby and move back home," he commanded, "and when you come home, you must never talk to anyone about the baby, not even your future husband."

Mother, who had been silent all this time, turned to me and added, "The secret about your baby will remain with you, and you will take it to your grave. Everyone who knows our family thinks you are in Saigon attending college." When Mother finished her words, they left.

I closed the door behind them, threw myself on the bed, and thought about my future. Though my parents were strict, they were far more liberal than most Vietnamese would have been under similar circum-stances. I recalled an unmarried girl in Tao Xa, North Vietnam, who got pregnant. Her father shaved her head and painted it white. He then dragged her around town while he beat on a bamboo gong and announced, "My daughter is pregnant out of wedlock." His purpose was to embarrass her and warn the father of the baby.

I gave the situation long and careful consideration. To pacify my par-ents, I decided to hide Eddie and let my parents think I had given him up. Through a friend, I found an older woman who agreed to take care of him in her house for a monthly fee.

I packed my clothes, bought gifts for my family, and caught the bus home to visit. When I approached the house, I thought I was at the wrong place. It had been remodeled and expanded and had a lot more furniture. It was obvious why my stepfather was so concerned about his reputation. If people knew the conservative Chinese Doctor Thuy had a daughter who had given birth to a child out of wedlock, and the father of the child was a foreigner, he and my mother would certainly lose face in the community.

It was good to be home and to see my brothers and sister—they had grown so much. At first they didn't even recognize me. Khai was three years old and had no idea who I was, but it didn't take long before he became friendly and warmed up to me. I gave each of them a gift that I brought from Saigon.

I asked about my fiancé and Mother said, "He's in medical school and will be on break soon. You will have a chance to see him then."

"What about my older stepbrother, Den?" I asked.

Mother said, "He joined the military and is an officer in the Rangers."

My step-grandmother still lived with my parents, and she was happy to see me as well. I stayed home and visited with everyone for a few days and then returned to Saigon.

When I returned, Mai Lan came to spend a day with me, because Tom was out of town on duty. We went to the market to shop for food and to visit Kim, another friend of mine. At eighteen, Kim was eight months pregnant and lived in a nice, furnished apartment. Her American boyfriend had just been killed in battle. She also couldn't work anymore and had to sell her furniture for food. We felt sorry for her and decided to stay longer to comfort her. We cooked, ate, and talked about our lives. In the afternoon, Mai Lan and I went to work, but we promised Kim we would come back after the club closed.

It was almost midnight when we returned from work. Kim had given us a key earlier, so I unlocked the door, and we walked in. We saw Kim crying in front of her boyfriend's picture. "Are you missing him again?" I asked. She gave us a weak smile and wiped her eyes.

"I'm so glad you two came back," she said.

I put my arm around her and patted her shoulder. Mai Lan and I decided to spend the night to keep Kim company, and we asked to borrow some pajamas. We changed into the more comfortable clothes, and Mai Lan asked, "Is anyone hungry?"

"I'm not hungry," Kim said, "but if you cook, I'll eat."

Mai Lan cooked scrambled eggs while I helped with the rice. We ate, talked, laughed, and cried together until two or three in the morning. I suggested we go to bed and get some rest, so we did.

A few minutes later, a persistent, violent knocking at the door woke us. A man's voice shouted, "This is the police. If you don't open the door, we will break it in."

We were all scared. Kim looked at me and said, "I have to open it." She started for the door, and I pulled her back and whispered, "Give us a chance to hide first."

Mai Lan and I ran out the back door and into a sugarcane field. We lay flat in a ditch, hoping to evade the police. They searched Kim's apartment for some time. They didn't believe Kim was alone, after seeing her American boyfriend's picture on the dresser. From the backyard, we heard the policeman questioning her.

"What took you so long to open the door?" one of them demanded. "There must be someone else hiding in the house." He meant an American.

"Where is your GI boyfriend?" another asked, after searching the house and finding no one. "Is he hiding in the backyard?"

Mai Lan and I heard them mention the backyard, and we whispered to each other. "We are going to die if they catch us, so lie low," I said.

We hugged the ground, as we heard two of them come outside and begin searching with a bright flashlight. They walked through the cane field from row to row and found us.

"Get up on your feet, but don't run!" one shouted. When they got within reach, they both slapped us hard on our heads with their guns. They questioned us as they dragged us inside by our hair and our ears.

"Who are you?" one questioned. "Why are you hiding?"

The other yelled, "You must be criminals or Viet Cong!"

"No," I cried, "We aren't criminals or Viet Cong. We hid, because we don't have family papers and were afraid of going to jail."

Inside, I saw another policeman questioning Kim. When he saw us he shouted, "All of you are going to jail!" Even though Kim had proper documents, they took her to the Quan Ba police station with us, where she was accused of harboring criminals. We were all in pajamas. They kept us in jail in a small, private cell away from the other prisoners without telling us what we were being charged with. Our only crime was being scared, but that meant nothing to them. Our fate depended on what they wrote in the police report, whether it was true or not. There was nothing to stop them from exaggerating or distorting the truth, especially if it made them look good. I just hoped they didn't accuse us of being Viet Cong terrorists.

Three days later, a policeman took us to a room for questioning. Then, a skinny, uniformed man limped in with a cane. He rested his cane against the wall, sat down, and lit a cigarette. He reminded me of the one-legged man I used to work for.

"What's your name?" he asked me.

"Loan, Nguyen Thi Loan," I answered. He asked Mai Lan and Kim the same question.

"Which one of you was trying to hide?" he demanded.

"We were," Mai Lan and I replied.

"Why were you hiding from the police in the middle of the night?" he snapped. Before I answered, he said, "You two must be Viet Cong sympathizers." Then he took a few more puffs from his cigarette and continued. "All of you have committed serious crimes and have to pay heavy fines."

"How much is the fine, sir?" I asked.

"A lot," he said. "A lot."

Because we didn't carry money with us, we took off all our jewelry and handed it to him.

"Are they genuine?" he asked.

"They are real," we assured him.

He got up, put the jewelry in his pocket, and said, "Wait here, I have to check with my superior to see if this jewelry will be enough to cover the fines." He never returned to the room, and we were released in the afternoon.

Upon release, we each went our separate ways, agreeing to get together soon. I was hungry, but there was nothing to eat at my house, and I had the urge to eat curried frog legs. So I went to the market and walked through several stands where frogs were sold. I watched the poor frogs trying to escape while bound together by the dozens, with strings around their waists. I felt sorry for the frogs, changed my mind, and came home with pork and vegetables instead.

While cooking, I heard a knock on my door. I stopped stirring and ran to open it. It was Ben, a close friend of Cong's. He used to come with Cong to visit me. I hadn't seen him for some time and was happy to see him. As we shook hands, I smiled, but he didn't. From the look on his face, I knew something was wrong.

I stopped smiling and told him to come inside. "What's wrong?" I asked. He took off his military hat and sat down without saying a word. "What's wrong?" I asked again while I poured tea for him and sat down next to him.

"Cong is dead!" he cried.

I sat in stunned silence with my hand over my mouth as he continued, "His body is at his mother's house. You should go to see him before he's buried."

I couldn't believe my ears. Cong and I had been together just the week before, and he had promised to take me to a movie when he got back from the battlefield. I had known Cong for a long time, longer than any of my friends, and he was one of my best friends.

"Cong died in my arms," Ben sobbed. "Before he took his last breath, he asked me to tell you he loved you."

The more he talked, the more I cried. I couldn't believe he was dead, and I wished then that I had married Cong.

Minutes later, Ben got up and said, "I have to go; there are many things I have to do before I return to my unit."

"I'll be at Cong's funeral," I told Ben through my tears. "Thank you for bringing me the message."

He left without drinking his tea. After he was gone, I ran to the kitchen and turned the stove off. Then, I rushed to Mai Lan's apartment to tell her the bad news. Cong was as much a friend to Mai Lan as he was to me.

The following day, we attended the funeral service at his family's home. Cong was Chinese and a Buddhist, and his customs and culture were quite different from mine. The funeral service was even more unfamiliar. When Mai Lan and I walked through the door, Cong's relatives handed each of us a square piece of white linen and some incense.

We didn't know what to do with either of them. I thought the white linen was for wiping tears from our eyes, and I rolled it into the palm of my hand. Although Mai Lan was Buddhist, she wasn't Chinese, so we were both confused. We stood in awkward silence for a few moments until we found two empty chairs.

A Chinese girl, about our age, recognizing our uneasiness, came to our rescue. She whispered to us and told us to put the white square of material over our heads while she lit our incense.

"You may pray for Cong now," she said, and moved away.

So, we got up from our chairs and walked to Cong's coffin. We knelt in front of it and prayed. I heard other mourners murmuring beside us and behind us, and in the corner of my eyes, I saw some of them staring at us through their white veils.

In the middle of prayers, Mai Lan and I looked at each other and started to giggle. It was hard for us to stop, because we had no idea what we were supposed to be doing. A few minutes later, we placed the lit incense in a jar in front of the coffin and returned to our seats.

More mourners arrived, and each was given the same two objects that we were given. They put the white linen on their heads, lit the incense, and prayed in front of the shrine, rather than in front of the coffin.

We realized then what we had done wrong. We looked at each other through our veils, and although our eyes were full of tears, we started giggling again.

I apologized to Cong for our terrible behavior. "Please forgive us for being so silly," I said under my breath, "but the differences in our customs and religions have us confused. If you were still alive you would be laughing with us, too."

Six men, wearing black uniforms with red trim, walked through the crowded room to the coffin and positioned themselves beside it. They picked up the coffin and carried it to a large, brightly colored hearse decorated with two huge dragons on each side. As we followed the hearse, the mournful tones from the funeral flutes wove their way through the air as the drums beat out their lamentable cadence. The flutes sounded sad, but as strange as it seemed, the beat of the drums made me feel like dancing. I was moving with the rhythm as I walked. The hearse moved slowly, followed by a long line of people. From a distance, the procession looked like a giant dragon with a colorful head.

A half hour later, we arrived at a cemetery in Cho Lon, a suburb of Saigon. The sky was cloudy, but the air was hot and humid. The black mourning clothes we wore were soaked with sweat and tears. Everyone tried to get closer to the coffin as it was laid on wood supports above the prepared grave. I listened to the sad chanting of a Buddhist monk as tears rolled from my swollen eyes. Then I watched as Cong's coffin was lowered deeper into the ground, and I felt dismal and empty. The pain and sadness were no less than what I had felt at my own father's funeral. I picked up a handful of dirt and threw it into his grave.

"Goodbye, Cong," I cried. "You were my good friend, and I can't believe you are leaving me. Although you are not here with me, I know you will forever be in my heart." When the grave was covered, Mai Lan and I walked back to the street to hail a taxi.

On the way home, Mai Lan said, "I just found out I'm pregnant. Tom and I plan to get married soon."

I was so excited and said, "I'm very happy for you."

"But," she said, "soon after the wedding, I have to go to America with him."

I had just buried Cong, and now I had to think about losing another close friend. I started crying again and wished I were dead and buried with Cong.

Chapter 18

INJUSTICE

IN 1966, the American troop strength in Vietnam grew to almost 400,000, and by the end of 1967, reached more than half a million. The Americans virtually took over the war. The bombing of North Vietnam, which President Johnson began in 1965, had little effect on communist military efforts, and if anything, strengthened their will to resist. The Viet Cong reacted to the American military initiatives by escalating the fighting in the South.

I tried to visit my family in Vung Tau as often as I could, but the bus rides there were very dangerous. Vung Tau is just a little over ninety kilometers (about 56 miles) from Saigon. With normal traffic, it took us about one and a half hours to get there, but sometimes it took us two to three hours to make the trip. The Viet Cong mined the road and blocked it with earthen mounds to hinder American and South Vietnamese troop movements.

The Viet Cong worked hard to plant mines and construct mounds at night, and during the day, American and South Vietnamese soldiers worked just as hard to destroy them. If it hadn't been so tragic, it would have been absurdly funny. Traffic was often caught in the middle of these efforts and was delayed for hours.

By parental arrangement, my stepbrother, Den, married a nice, sweet girl. They visited me often, and we became close friends. Uncle Ky and his family moved to Vung Tau, near my parents, and I stopped to visit him whenever I could. I led my parents to believe I had given Eddie up for adoption, and they seldom mentioned the matter.

I helped my parents buy a fruit farm on the river and build a large two-story house on the property. Though my stepfather made money from his medical practice, he lent what he made for interest and seldom spent any on the kids. I felt sorry for my brothers and my sister, and I tried to give them what they needed, from school supplies to bikes and watches. I gave Mother money to buy extra food for them. I loved my brothers and my sister, and I wanted to help care for them.

I visited my family often, but I still had not seen my so-called fiancé. I didn't want to stay home long enough to have the opportunity to see him, but one day my luck ran out. While I was in the living room, I looked through the open door and saw a young man open the gate by himself and enter our yard. Mother heard the gate open, and she ran out, greeted him, and invited him into the house. From the way Mother talked to him and the way she acted, I thought, "This must be the man." Then I heard Mother say, "She is inside." Like lightning, I ran out to the kitchen through the back door.

Mother walked into the kitchen, and I asked, "Isn't that my fiancé?" She smiled and nodded. "What's his name again?" I asked. "I forgot."

"His name is Hoa," Mother replied, "and he is a very good young man."

"Hoa is a girl's name," I said, "It's too feminine for a boy to be named flower."

She frowned at me and said, "What difference does it make? Just go inside and be polite. Pour some tea and talk to him." I didn't like the idea of seeing him, but the expression on my mother's face told me I had no choice.

I returned to the living room and saw him sitting on the couch. When he saw me enter the room, he stood up, nodded his head, and smiled. I smiled back and nodded my head as well. He wore a bright yellow necktie, which didn't match his light pink shirt and khaki pants. His coarse, short, greasy hair stood straight out from his head. I looked at him and smiled again; he smiled back. Then I poured tea for him, and asked him to sit down. For my parents' sake, I wanted to make a good impression, so I acted as timid as if I'd never seen a man in my life.

"I'm glad you're here today," he said with a big smile that showed a mouth full of uneven buckteeth. Slanted eyes were hidden inside of his wrinkled eyelids. Rubbing the palms of his hands together, he continued, "I've been waiting for this moment for a long time. You are even more beautiful than I could have imagined, and I can't wait for you to be my wife."

"I'm glad that you're glad to see me," I responded with the friendliest smile I could put on my face.

He must have liked me, because he giggled whenever our eyes met. It was difficult for me to keep a straight face because he looked so funny. Each time he laughed, his beady little eyes disappeared behind the folds of his eyelids. His face reminded me of a pig's.

"When will you move back home?" he asked between giggles.

"Why do you want to know?" I queried.

"Because I'm ready to marry you," he replied, and he began snickering again. He continuously rubbed the palms of his hands together as if he were trying hard to resist the urge to grab hold of me.

The mere thought of marrying him made me nauseous, but I remained calm and tried to maintain my composure. I didn't want to say anything to hurt his feelings, because he was the son of my stepfather's friend.

"I'll be coming home soon," I said, "but not too soon."

When I finished talking, he started giggling again. I couldn't take it anymore. "Excuse me," I said with a smile. "I have to help my mother in the kitchen." I stood up and walked away without giving him a chance to say another word.

"Mother, would you please keep him company and let me stay in the kitchen?" I begged. I think she knew how I felt about my fiancé and agreed to change places.

A few minutes later, he came to the kitchen to say goodbye. "Our marriage will be soon," he said, "I can hardly wait." I smiled and nodded my head. He grinned so big that his face was wrinkled, and I'm sure he could see nothing through his tiny squinted eyes. I just hoped he would stop smiling long enough so that he could see to leave the house.

The sound of his giggles made my hair stand on end. Mother walked him to the door, waited for him to leave, and returned to the kitchen. Before she had a chance to say anything to me, I said, "I think he is so ugly."

Mother replied, "He comes from a good family, has good manners, and to me that is more important than looks."

I could see her point, and, in my own way, I agreed with Mother, but I still thought to myself, "Beauty may only be skin deep, but in his case the rule of thumb does not apply." I couldn't sleep that night from thinking about having to marry that thing someday. So, I got out of bed, planning to take a walk in the garden, and I went down the steps into the backyard. I could hear explosions and gunshots in the distance. It sounded like a huge battle was taking place not far away.

A whole corner of the sky was lit by flares and exploding incendiary bombs, and airplanes and helicopters circled above the battlefield. I stood in silence with my back against a tree, staring at the senseless war. "How many lives are being sacrificed, and what are they giving their lives for?" I wondered.

My heart went out to the fighting men as tears streamed down my cheeks. I dropped to my knees, put my hands together, and looked up to the sky. I prayed for all those who were both above and below the bombs, regardless of which side they were on. The sounds of battle woke my parents, they joined me out in the yard, and we watched the horror together. When things calmed down, we went back to bed.

A sobbing voice woke me early the following morning. I jumped out of bed and ran downstairs to find my stepfather's sister-in-law sitting on the couch, crying hysterically.

My parents tried to calm her, as she cried, "My son is dead! He was killed in the fighting last night." She paused in a futile effort to gain some composure. "His friends brought his body home wrapped in a plastic bag," she sobbed. "When I opened the bag, it contained only parts of my boy."

I didn't know him well, but had attended his wedding party a few months earlier. His poor wife was pregnant. We were all in tears over his senseless death. "We will give you all the help and support you need," Mother said through her tears.

My parents recognized her helplessness and accompanied her home. I went to her house later the same day after I had collected myself, to pay my last respects. The remains of her son were lying in a bed covered with a bloodstained sheet. Friends and family, including my parents, prepared for his funeral, and as I looked around, I didn't see a dry eye in the house.

I excused myself, said goodbye to everyone, and returned to my parents' house. I grabbed my belongings and boarded a bus headed back to Saigon, but the bus didn't get very far before it was caught in a long line of traffic. Soldiers were cleaning up the mess and clearing the road from the previous night's battle—the same one I had watched from my parents' backyard.

The Viet Cong had mined the area and built numerous earth mounds across the road where my bus was trying to travel. South Vietnamese soldiers destroyed the mounds, but the road was still a big mess, with logs, mud, and dirt everywhere, and the bus had to detour through the wet rice fields. To prevent the vehicles from getting stuck from such a heavy load, all the passengers had to get off and walk in a line on the other side of the debris.

While waiting for my bus, I watched as the drivers maneuvered their vehicles, which were bouncing like frogs over the mud holes in the rice fields. My heart leaped to my throat whenever one of them teetered on the brink of overturning, and I felt sorry for the poor drivers, who risked their lives to get the buses back on the road and the passengers to their destinations. "What a job," I thought.

Finally, we were able to return to the bus. We resumed our journey, and the bus slowly crawled along. I looked through the window, and in the distance, saw a strange-looking mound on the roadside. As we drew closer, I realized it was a mountain of bloody, dead people. Many bodies were burned and mutilated beyond recognition. Some were naked, while others were partly clothed in black.

Someone on the bus said those dead were Viet Cong who were killed in the battle the night before. Another passenger said the South Vietnamese soldiers didn't seem to be in any hurry to bury the dead, because they wanted to show off their victory. It all sounded so absurd and pointless to me. All of the dead were human—they just had different points of view about war and politics. Only yesterday, they were someone's son, husband, father, or brother. How could anyone rejoice over that much death?

To my great relief, the bus sped up and moved away from the gruesome scene. I had just finished thanking God for getting us through the mess when the bus braked and slowed down again. "What now?" I thought.

I stuck my head out the window and saw several military trucks and tanks parked along the side of the road. Hundreds of American and Vietnamese soldiers carrying guns and grenades were running away from the road toward the battlefield, farther into the forest, while helicopters and airplanes swooped overhead, shooting and dropping bombs.

Just then, the bus rolled to a stop, and an American soldier motioned for us to get off. He pointed to a ditch and told us to take cover. I ran to the roadside with the others and quickly jumped into the ditch. We lay there, face down, as the battle raged around us. The sound of gunfire echoed through air, and explosions shook the earth. I crossed myself and resumed praying.

I don't remember how long I was in the ditch, but when the fighting calmed down, the road opened to traffic again. We got back on the bus and continued the trip. I sat next to a very friendly old lady, who began talking to me.

"We were lucky today," she said, with a sigh. "The last time I took this trip, my bus was the first on the road that day. When the driver saw a Viet Cong mound in the road, he detoured through the fields. Unfortunately, the field was also mined."

"The bus blew up and killed most of the passengers and wounded the rest, including me. It was early in the morning, and help didn't reach us until much later. The delay caused more deaths, and I almost died myself," she continued, as she showed me a scar under her blouse that went from the right side of her chest to her naval. "When the ambulance arrived, it took the wounded but left the dead scattered around the hole next to the damaged bus." We talked until the bus stopped in Saigon, then said goodbye and went our separate ways.

It was Friday, two days before Tom and Mai Lan were to be married, and I went shopping for the occasion. I bought a new dress and stopped at the beauty salon for a perm. At six in the evening, I got home and took a quick shower to cool off. I wrapped the towel around me and started making up for work. After applying a base makeup, I drew on eyeliner. I had just finished one eye, when someone knocked on the door. "Who's there?" I asked.

"It's me," Mai Lan answered.

"Come on in," I said. "The door's open."

Mai Lan bounced in looking happy and excited. Tom followed her carrying a magazine. He walked over to where I was sitting and handed it to me. I looked at the cover, read the title, and asked, "What is a Playboy?" I'd never seen the magazine before.

With a mischievous twinkle in his eye, Tom said, "Go ahead, open it."

I opened the pages as Mai Lan knelt next to my chair. We glanced at a few advertisements before we got to the exciting part. Mai Lan and I talked and laughed as we pointed to pictures of naked women. While I was laughing at the book, Tom and Mai Lan were laughing at me.

"You sure look funny, with just one eye made up," she said. Her remark reminded me that I'd better hurry up and get ready for work.

As I lay the magazine aside, there was another, more urgent knocking. Glancing at my friends, I walked toward the door. I reached for the doorknob, but it flew open, hitting me in the face. I staggered back as two armed policemen barged inside. They pointed their guns at us then handcuffed Mai Lan and me. Tom stood there in shock with his mouth wide open. Everything happened so fast, and we didn't know what to say or do.

One policeman asked Tom for his ID card, and after writing something on a pad, ordered him to leave the apartment. He refused to leave and demanded to know what was going on. The policeman pointed his gun at Tom, pushed him through the open door, and then shut it behind him.

The other one looked at me from head to toe and said, "It's a shame that someone as young and pretty as you two have to sell your bodies for a living."

"You're mistaken," I said. "I was just getting ready for work, and the American is my friend's fiancé. They are going to be married this Sunday."

The laughter from both of the policemen sent cold chills down my spine. "How can you deny it?" one asked. "We caught you here with an American soldier before you even had a chance to put your clothes on."

I tried in vain to explain, as they walked around the room looking at pictures on the wall. Tom started banging on the door, and one of them went outside to talk to him. The other one looked at us and said, "You have broken the law, and you must pay for it."

"I've broken no law!" I demanded.

"You'll be in jail for a long time," he threatened.

We both knew what he wanted. "I have some money at my apartment," Mai Lan said, "if you will let me go get it."

"You're not getting away that easy," he snarled. "What about you?" he asked me.

"Do you have any?"

"Yes, but not much," I replied. "I just returned from visiting my family in Vung Tau, and I spent most of my money on my hair and a dress to wear to my friend's wedding."

He said nothing more about the money as he removed my handcuffs and ordered me to get dressed. I cleaned off the eye makeup and put on my clothes. Then, he replaced my handcuffs and led us out to the alley. Tom followed behind, cursing and threatening the police as we walked.

"If you don't let them go, I'll blow up your police station with a bomb!" he shouted.

The police ignored him and laughed as they led us to their jeep. They shoved us into the back, and one of them climbed in beside us. The other one climbed into the driver's seat and started moving away. Tom tried to get on the jeep, but he was pushed off by one of the policemen. In desperation, he ran after us, yelling and cursing, until it sped off into the busy street, leaving him far behind.

Again, we were back in a jail cell. Mai Lan was very upset, because she knew there would be no Sunday wedding. No matter what I said to comfort her, she just sat in a corner and cried. Three days later, they took us to court.

We stood in front of the same skinny man we had confronted a few years earlier. He looked at us over his glasses, shook his head in dismay, and read the police report. Without asking us a single question, he said, "I thought I told you not to show your face in my court again." Then he told a policeman to take us away. I didn't know what was going to happen to us, and I felt so sorry for Mai Lan. Her wedding day had already passed. I wondered how Tom was doing. I knew he must have been looking for Mai Lan, but I also knew it wouldn't be easy for him, since he was an American, there were too many police stations, and besides Mai Lan was not her real name.

The police truck took a dozen of us to the Thu Duc women's prison where we waited for the court to review our case. We drove through the heavy iron gate, and I saw two huge cellblocks that held hundreds of prisoners. The truck stopped, we got out, and a female guard escorted us to a small office behind the gates, where officials checked our papers. Then she took us to a huge open cell and told us to stay there until our court date.

Every morning, we lined up to salute the flag and sing the national anthem, then had breakfast of brown rice and dried fish or cooked vegetables. It didn't matter what we had, there was brown rice with every meal. Brown rice was considered a cheap grain, and it was very abundant. People outside of prison fed brown rice to pigs and other livestock.

After breakfast, they gave us garden tools that we carried to the fields where we planted and harvested vegetables. Those who weren't in the field stayed behind to cook, clean, and do various other chores. Mai Lan was sick because of her pregnancy, and she was often unable to work in the fields. She couldn't do any heavy labor, so I tried to stay behind and help her whenever I could.

Tom hired a lawyer, who tracked us down. Finding us was complicated, because he didn't know either of our real names. Tom paid a large sum of cash to the officials to get Mai Lan out of jail, but he didn't have enough to pay for my release, and I didn't have enough money to pay the bribes demanded.

Mai Lan was freed, but, being a good friend, she came back to visit me often. She brought me clothes and gifts, and, during one of her visits, she told me why we were sent to jail. "The woman who owns the house next to yours had a grudge against you," Mai Lan said, "because you wouldn't rent her house, or kiss her feet, like everyone else who lives near her. If you did, you'd be protected, because she paid off the police that served her and protected the prostitutes who rented her house."

"She had been waiting for an American to come to your place," she continued, "and took the opportunity to get back at you. When Tom and I stopped by, she called the police and paid them to arrest you."

Mai Lan's revelation infuriated me. "I'll get even with her when I get out of here," I said, but deep inside, I knew there was little I could do. She was rich and had too many friends in high places. She also had an adopted daughter who was just as bad as she was, even though she was only about thirteen. She lied, cheated, and stole from me. She also came to my house to visit and spy on me for her mother and often made more trouble for me.

After Mai Lan's release, I made several new friends. One of them was a nineteen-year-old, half-Vietnamese, half-black French girl named

Jackie. She was big, strong, and had kinky hair. I liked her, because she was simple and honest.

On the way back to our cell from working in the field one day, Jackie confided in me, "This is not my first time in jail, and it won't be my last. I've been in and out of this prison often, and I'm beginning to like it here. I don't have to buy food or pay rent." She smiled as she kicked up a cloud of dirt.

"What are you in for this time?" I asked.

"I stole a GI's wallet," she said with a broad grin. "When I got caught, I beat up the policeman who arrested me and put him in the hospital. I wanted to get arrested, so I could come back in here."

I looked at her in disbelief and said, "Are you crazy, who wants to be in jail?"

"I do," she said.

We talked and laughed all the way back to our cell. It was hot that day, and we looked forward to taking a cold shower. We picked up our clean clothes and carried them to the shower room that was partly divided for privacy and had a water pipe above our heads.

Jackie looked up, pointed to the water pipe, and said, "A few months before you got here a girl hung herself with a rope from that pipe." I gazed to where she was pointing and could feel cold chills running up and down my back. "She left behind a long suicide note," Jackie continued. "She was from far away and came to Saigon to shop for her wedding dress. She missed the last bus home and had to spend the night at the bus station."

"She was arrested for vagrancy," Jackie added. "They made a mistake at the police station and charged her with prostitution. When she found out about the charge, she was afraid to go home and face her fiancé. She cried for days and then hung herself."

Jackie looked at me and added, "Now the shower room is haunted by her virgin ghost." I continued to look at the pipe, terrified.

I spent a month in prison before I went for my first court hearing, but the judge was too busy to hear my case. After the third attempt, and waiting almost half a day, I was led to a huge courtroom full of people. I was told to stand before several distinguished-looking judges, all dressed in black robes and sitting behind a massive desk. From the way they were dressed, they looked more like priests than judges. I stood in silence in front of them, while one of them reviewed my record.

"What are you in here for?" he asked.

"I don't know, sir," I replied.

"I'm not your *sir*, I'm Your Honor," he growled. "Now, how long have you been in jail?"

I couldn't speak for a moment and was shaking like a leaf, but I managed to sputter, "Several weeks, sir, I mean, Your Honor, sir."

I could tell he was getting angry as he threw my record to the side and glared at me. I thought I was going to wet my pants.

"All of you just wasted my time!" he yelled, meaning both the police and me. He looked at me and said, "I'm giving you one month's probation. Now get out of my court and stay out of trouble!"

His pronouncement shocked me. I was expecting no less than a summary execution—surely not a release. Happy tears flowed down my face. I bowed to the judge and thanked him for giving me my freedom.

Then, a policeman escorted me back to jail, where I waited for my release to be processed. I found Jackie and told her my good news, but she wasn't too happy for me.

"I feel sorry for you," she said. "You have to go out to face the world. I hope I can stay in here forever." I just smiled at her and said nothing. That was definitely not what I wanted.

Two days later, my name was announced over the loudspeaker, telling me to get my belongings and go to the office for release documents. I grabbed my bag of clothes and ran to the office where I received a legal paper. I waited there, with other released prisoners, for the truck to take us to a Saigon police station for final processing. I spent many hours at the police station before I was handed the piece of paper that said I was free.

Chapter 19

CONFINED FREEDOM

CARRYING ONLY MY bag, I hurried through the prison gate. Outside, I walked down the street, tasting and feeling the free air. A large group of about a dozen people came up from behind and rushed by me. Out of curiosity, I ran after them.

Not far away, we came to a crowd of people standing around a mound of burning flesh. After asking around, I learned that a disabled veteran had set himself on fire in protest of the war. The incident reminded me of the burning of a Buddhist monk I witnessed a few years earlier. I walked away, shaking my head in sadness and dismay.

The first thing I wanted to do after my newfound freedom was to see my baby. I hailed a cyclo, haggled with the driver over the price, and he took me to my babysitter's house. She was just getting home, and I met her at her front door. She told me that Eddie was sick, and they had just returned from the doctor. I held my hands out to him, but he was shy and turned away, hiding his face behind the sitter's head. I was heartbroken when my own baby didn't respond to me. The babysitter invited me into her one-room home, and after a few more futile attempts to hold my baby, I stopped trying. I told the babysitter what had happened, and why I was in jail, and I asked her if she could wait until the following month to be paid. She smiled and told me not to worry, so I thanked her and went back to my apartment.

When I got to there, I tidied up, took a shower, and got dressed to go job hunting. But first, I stopped by my landlady's apartment and apologized for being late with the rent. She was very nice and understanding and told me not to worry about the rent. I thanked her and asked her if I could borrow some money. She put her hand into her pocket, pulled

Eddie was one year old, and I was nineteen.

out a stack of bills, licked her fingers, counted out some money, and gave me what I had asked for. She said, "I know who caused you to go to jail."

"So do I," I responded. "Thanks for the money," I said, "I'll return it as soon as I can."

"I know you will," she replied with a smile.

I left her house and caught a taxi to a bar near Tan Son Nhut Air Base. I knew the bar owner. She was a friend of Lynn's, and she knew me well. When I asked for a job, she was happy to hire me. She was around fifty-five and was in love with a young American soldier who was about half her age. She spent all her time and money pampering him.

She paid me well to manage the bar. I also made extra money from drinking Saigon tea and exchanging black market money and foreign goods such as cigarettes, liquor, stereos, and canned food from the American commissary and PX. With the extra money I made, I rented and moved into a house on Truong Minh Giang, up the street from where I lived. I hired two sisters, named Ba and Tu, as live-in maids and brought my baby back to live with me.

Mai Lan got married while I was still in jail. Her stomach was getting bigger, and she stayed home from work. She didn't live far from me, but we seldom saw each other, because I was working and was busy with my little business. I envied her but was happy for her as well. She had found the man of her dreams, and he loved her and adored her. I hoped I would someday be as lucky as she was.

Whenever we were together, she always talked about her husband and her unborn child, and we reminisced about the crazy times we went through over the years.

"You should go home and marry that future doctor you're engaged to," she said one day.

"I wouldn't marry that ugly creature if he were the last man on Earth," I replied, and we both laughed.

One day, she came by the house while I was counting merchandise, and asked me to follow her back to her apartment. She was acting very mysteriously, and I thought to myself, "She must have cooked something good again." She always came to get me when she did. On the way to her place she didn't say much, and let me run my mouth about how much money I made from my merchandise.

When I walked into the apartment, I was shocked to see suitcases, boxes, and clothes scattered everywhere. "What's going on?" I asked with alarm.

"Tom has orders to leave Vietnam tomorrow morning," she said.

"Why so sudden?" I asked.

"I'm not sure," she replied. "Tom received his orders yesterday, but he couldn't tell me much. I just got the news late last night."

I started to cry. "I knew you would be leaving someday," I said, "but I didn't think it would be this soon. Now I won't have a chance to see your baby born." I threw myself on the couch and cried. She came over, held me, and we both cried. Minutes later, Mai Lan asked me to help her pack. I did, but my heart wasn't in it, and I often packed the wrong thing in the wrong place, and she had to repack it. We cooked, ate, laughed, and cried all day, until Tom came home. I gave him a big hug when he got there.

"I'm going to miss you and Mai Lan," I told him through my tears.

"We'll miss you, too," Tom said. "But don't worry; we'll write to you just as soon as we get to the United States."

"You can have Mai Lan tonight, but I'll be back to claim her tomorrow," I told Tom. I gave each of them a big hug and walked out. I cried all the way home.

I overslept the following morning. Jumping out of bed, I dressed as fast as I could and ran all the way to Mai Lan's house. It was deserted. "I'll have to catch them at the airport," I thought, and I ran back to the street and hailed a taxi.

I jumped in and told him to get me to the airport as quickly as he could. I hurried him all the way there, and as the taxi stopped, I jumped out, threw him some money, and ran into the waiting area.

I saw Tom and Mai Lan as they were just about ready to board the plane. I yelled at them, they saw me, dropped their suitcases, and ran to me. We hugged each other as we exchanged a few words and many tears.

Then the loudspeaker announced the last call, and they picked up their suitcases and walked away. Just before they entered the plane, they turned to wave at me, and I stood at the airport window, watching the airplane's door close behind them.

The plane slowly taxied away from the airport, and the jet motors whined louder and louder as it roared down the runway. I watched as it rose into the air, taking away my two dearest friends. I stood without moving, until the plane disappeared in my tears.

In the lonely months following Mai Lan's departure, I didn't receive a letter or even a postcard. I often wondered how they were doing. To cope, I started smoking and came home drunk almost every night. In the afternoon, when the bar was not busy, I sat at the window by myself, drinking and smoking cigarettes. My aimless thoughts wandered to my mother. I remembered when she started drinking and smoking after my father was killed. At the time, she was smoking tobacco far stronger than my cigarettes. I believe it contained a mild narcotic.

She had a smoking pot about the size of a grapefruit, which she filled halfway with water. It had a small open top and a small hole in the side, in which she inserted a long, hollow bamboo stick. Then she filled the top part with tobacco rolled into a ball. When she lit the tobacco and sucked smoke through the bamboo stick, it made a gurgling sound.

She inhaled the smoke until she was out of breath, and then she passed out. She lay on her back, and her eyes rolled back in their sockets. Each time this happened, I was so scared that she was going to die. I would cry and scream as I held her, until she came out of her stupor. When she saw me crying, she started laughing, and told me she wasn't going to die. I wiped my tears and she hugged me.

After my father died, my mother also drank rice whiskey, which affected her just like the smoking. Her reactions scared me, and sometimes I hid the smoking paraphernalia and whiskey from her. When she noticed her things were gone, she knew what I had done, and when she found them, she would hide them from me. One day, I found her rice whiskey hidden in a pile of rice straw, and out of curiosity, took a drink. At first, it tasted strong and hot. After a few sips, I got used to it, and drank the whole bottle. The last thing I remembered was getting dizzy, and then everything went black. I woke up in bed sick the following day.

Warning sirens from Ton San Nhut stirred me from my musings. GIs bolted from the bar and headed back to the base, and all the girls dashed out of the bar and hailed whatever transportation they could find to get home. All, that is, except me. I was indifferent to what was going on around me, so I sat like a statue, watching the war unfold in front of me, chain-smoking my cigarettes. It was unreal. Exploding rockets sent clouds of smoke and debris in every direction. It was like watching some grotesque movie, with sirens wailing in the background. I was numb in body and soul, except for my eyes. They followed each explosion, and I wondered how many innocent people were dying.

Just a few days before, I sat at the same window and watched military trucks speed toward the base. Through the openings in the back, I could see the bloody bodies bouncing up and down when the trucks hit potholes in the road, and I wondered, "Who are they, and where are they being taken?" Things quieted down, I put my cigarette out, emptied my glass, grabbed my purse, and headed home.

In late 1967, the Viet Cong fired rockets at the air base almost every night. When they missed their target, rockets fell on civilian homes instead. My house was near the base, and the rockets were always exploding nearby. I grew used to the bombing and often slept right through the attacks.

Urgent knocking at my door woke me early one morning. My maid opened it, and I heard someone scream at her, "Come home! Hurry! Come home! A rocket hit our home and everyone's dead, including your mother!"

Both of my maids started screaming and crying, as I jumped out of bed and ran to the door. One of them sobbed, "Our house was hit by a rocket last night, and many of my family are dead. Please let us go home now."

"I'm so sorry," I said. "Of course you can go, but wait for me. I'm coming with you." I changed my clothes, grabbed my house keys, and we hurried to their home, which was no more than two blocks away.

A crowd of curious people surrounded the house as we approached. The roof of their little shack was gone, and three bloody bodies were lying next to a big hole in the middle of the house. One of the dead was their mother. The injured had already been taken to the hospital. The maids ran to the body of their mother and cried hysterically.

I looked at the mess and realized my maids could have been killed, too, if they had stayed home that night. "There is no safe place from this crazy war, not even home," I thought. The maids' family was very poor, and they had to ask relatives and neighbors for help. I helped them as much as I could, but in the end, they still had to ask elsewhere for help to bury their dead and rebuild their home. I found someone to take care of my son temporarily, and I let the maids have a few weeks off, so they could take care of their family.

In the following months, I grew tired of watching the bombing and the dead bodies coming in and out of the air base. I moved from bar to bar and from club to club, until I ended up at the Victoria Bar and Club in downtown Saigon. The chubby owner harassed me to do more than just sell Saigon tea, but I always found an excuse to refuse her. She soon learned that I had standards, and she stopped trying to force me. She needed me more than I needed her, and it was a comfortable place to work.

At the time, I was twenty-one years old and had stopped drinking and smoking. But still, I was alone and had no dates. I was too busy being a mom and didn't have time for anybody else. Besides, I had lost interest in men—although some of them were very interested in me. I dealt with them only at the bars, strictly for Saigon tea and for exchanging money and American merchandise on the black market. Because of my English ability, I had an advantage over the other girls who had to sell themselves for less than what I got for selling American goods. I also had to keep what I did secret from the club owner, because she and I were in the same black market business.

I collected quite a few rings as testimony to the men who were interested in me. Those who claimed they were separated or divorced often gave me their wedding bands to prove their sincerity. I counted the rings I had collected and was surprised there were more than a dozen. I examined them and saw that some even had initials and wedding dates engraved inside. A few had the words, "I love you," inscribed on them.

Some were graduation rings, while others were just common rings with opal, sapphire, and even diamond chips.

I looked at the rings and wondered where all of their owners were now and where had they taken all of their promises. I smiled, put them in my pocket, and walked to the nearest jewelry store.

"Do you want to buy a bunch of old rings and wedding bands?" I asked the jeweler.

"Let me look at them," he replied.

I pulled a handful of rings from my pocket and laid them on the glass counter. He looked at them, at me, and jokingly asked, "Have you been married that often?"

"Yes," I said with a mischievous smile, "and they are all dead." After looking at the rings, he sighed and said, "I'm afraid these are worthless. They are just ten, twelve, or fourteen karat gold, and I don't deal with anything less than eighteen karat. I'm sorry."

"What about those with opal and sapphire settings?" I asked. "And some of them even have diamonds," I continued, trying to convince him to buy them.

He shook his head and said, "The opal is scratched, the sapphire is artificial, and the diamonds are only chips. No thanks."

I knew there was no way to talk him into buying the rings, so I put them back into my pocket. On my way home, I saw a man walking toward me, yelling at the top of his lungs, "Do you have any old watches, rings, silver, copper, or gold teeth for sale?"

Thinking this could be my opportunity to get rid of them, I ran to him and showed him my rings. He looked them over and said, "They aren't worth much."

"How much for all of them?" I asked.

He examined them again and gave me his price. After bartering back and forth, I got just enough to buy groceries for that day.

The Asian New Year fell on January 31, 1968, and as it approached, everyone was preparing for the Tet celebrations. The markets were selling candy and decorations from temporary stands, that went up everywhere. Many streets were full of flowers and lucky plants for sale, and there was a joyful mood of holiday in the air.

The armies had even agreed to a weeklong truce to celebrate the New Year. It was a time for the soldiers to lay down their guns and have some long overdue peace and happiness with their families.

I enjoyed shopping and preparing for the holiday with the maids and my son, who was almost three years old. The day before Tet started, my maids and I gave the house a thorough cleaning and decorated the living room with candy, fruit, plants, and flowers. With Eddie's help, I would put things up, and he would take them down. It took me longer to decorate, but we had a lot of laughter and fun, and he loved helping me. In the evening, we cooked traditional foods to be served to guests the following day. It was an exciting and happy time.

The government forbade the use of firecrackers, but I knew not many people would obey that law. Before midnight, I heard a few firecrackers start popping. The banging and popping grew louder and more frequent, so I went outside to watch and listen.

I was startled to see people running around in a panic. I stopped a young soldier running toward me and asked, "What's going on?"

In short, breathless bursts he said, "The Viet Cong are attacking Saigon, Miss, and you'd better get inside before you get hurt!" Without another word, he took off like lighting. He must have been one of the lucky soldiers who were home for a peaceful Tet.

I hurried back inside and locked the door, unable to believe what he had said. Both sides had declared a cease-fire. I couldn't understand how they could turn our most sacred holiday into a bloody battle. Ba and Tu were still awake and chatting with each other in the kitchen. When I told them what I just heard, they couldn't believe it either.

The fighting grew more intense as the night passed. Helicopters flew low over my apartment, and I heard gunfire mixed with firecrackers exploding everywhere. I couldn't tell one from the other. I turned on the radio, but no one seemed to know what was going on. It sounded like mass confusion. Eddie was sound asleep, but my maids and I stayed awake in fear all night.

It was near daybreak before the radio came back on. It said the Viet Cong had taken over the American embassy and had attacked Tan Son Nhut Air Base. The Viet Cong had staged bloody assaults throughout South Vietnam, and the city of Hue had been captured.

Since a truce had been announced before Tet, most of the South Vietnamese soldiers had gone home to visit their families, and no one was prepared for the surprise attack.

Soon, American and South Vietnamese forces reacted. The Viet Cong, who captured the American embassy, were dislodged, and were all killed. I'm sure they knew when they attacked the embassy they would never survive. I didn't like what they did to my Tet, but I had to give them credit for their courage. I suppose they were doing what they believed was right.

To me, there is no right, and there are no winners in war. All wars are insane, and there are only losers, even those who think they are the victors. What do they win? They win nothing but broken bodies, torn families, dead relatives, and mass destruction.

After the Tet offensive, Saigon seemed to undergo a dramatic change. There was a general feeling of fear and despair. Trust was destroyed and replaced by doubt. The enemy could not be distinguished from the friend. Viet Cong insurgents were imbedded among both the civilian and military populations. Unsuspecting maids, taxi drivers, barbers, government officials, and many others were revealed to be Viet Cong infiltrators. I discovered that some of my maids were among them.

The Viet Cong's efforts to terrorize the population were effective, and I sensed changes in the Americans, too. They seemed to give up hope, and all they wanted was to serve their year and get back home in one piece, and I didn't blame them. Soon, the rocket attacks increased, and the entire city became a target. I kept going to work and tried to forget about all the killing. I just tried to concentrate on my own survival. I learned later, that although the Tet invasion had been a military failure for the communists, in many other ways, it had been quite successful. By attacking cities, the scope of the war was broadened and was no longer confined to rural areas. All of South Vietnam became a battleground.

In America, the offensive had far-reaching effects. The bloody street fighting was presented every night on televised news programs, and Americans became more distressed by the price being paid in dead and wounded. Protests in the United States and in Vietnam soared to new heights.

After the offensive, a strict curfew was imposed in Saigon and throughout the country. Essential commodities such as food and gas were scarce, and unruly crowds emptied stores of their available goods. The government often changed currency, and everyone was trying to convert cash to tangible merchandise before the money became useless. Now and then, I, too, was left with a handful of worthless cash.

By nine in the evening, everything had to be closed, and no one was allowed on the streets. I went to work early and came home before nine to avoid breaking curfew. At around seven o'clock one evening, several policemen raided the club. That was a common event, and a way for them to collect a payoff. They pointed their guns around the room and ordered us not to move. Many girls chose to run away rather than face the police and took off in different directions. I didn't escape fast enough and was rounded up with a dozen other girls.

We were transported to the Quan Mot police station, where they took our names, addresses, and fingerprints. A policeman asked, "Why are you people not wearing uniforms?" Everyone looked at him, but no one answered. Instead, we acted timid and scared. The club owner paid our fine later that night, but when the police finished processing our papers, it was too late to go home, so we slept in the hallway of the police station.

Some of us lay on the floor, while others slept sitting up with their backs against the wall. The thirteen of us filled a long and narrow hallway. While we were asleep, a policeman entered the hall. I was still awake but feigned sleep. He woke a girl named Phuc and told her to go with him. She didn't refuse and followed him. I discovered later that Hung, the Chief of Police, liked her and invited her to spend the night with him. The rest of us were released the following morning.

A week later, the whole group was invited back to attend a party at the police station. I knew it would be more than just a party—it would be a girl for every policeman to toy with, and I refused to go.

"You must go," the bar owner insisted. "We have to cooperate with the police if we want them to quit harassing us."

I wasn't about to get involved in what she had in mind. "It's the wrong time of the month," I lied in a whisper.

She was disappointed but found someone else to take my place. Later, I was curious and asked Phuc about the party. "It was fun," she said. "Vice President Ky was there and took an interest in me," she continued. "He liked me and said he would be willing to give me anything I wanted or needed if I became his girlfriend. It's too bad, though. I've already fallen in love with his friend, Hung, the Chief of Police," she said with a mischievous smile.

"Did you go further than just conversation with the vice president?" I asked. She didn't answer. "You must have really given him something special for him to say that," I joked. She smiled but didn't respond.

Phuc chose Hung, and although he was married at the time, they became lovers. Because Phuc and I were close friends, I rented them one room of my house as their love nest. I was happy to accommodate Phuc, because with the Quan Mot District Chief of Police as a tenant, the police didn't bother me, and they quit raiding the club. Hung and Phuc were not the only two who rented from me. Two more of my girlfriends also shared my house. With the extra money, I hired a third maid to cook, clean, and do chores for my friends.

Chapter 20

GARDEN OF LOVE

MY SON, EDDIE, turned three on August 20, 1968. I invited friends over for his birthday party, and he was happy to get a lot of attention and toys from my mixed group of friends. The guests were Vietnamese, American, gay, straight, married, and single. All together, there were about thirty of us, and we had a good time eating, dancing, singing, and acting like a bunch of three-year-olds ourselves. Several hours passed, and as the party thinned out, I helped the maids clean up and put things away. They waited for the last guests to leave before starting to mop the floor, and I washed up and got ready for work. I was so tired that I thought about just showing up and then making an excuse to the club owner to go home early.

The club was quiet that afternoon. Only a few GIs sat around, drinking by themselves. The girls called them cheap Charlies, and no one sat with them. Either they didn't want to buy the girls drinks, or they didn't have the money. Either way, they were by themselves. There were a dozen or more girls, sitting in various places around the bar. Some were by themselves, while others sat in groups of three or more, talking and laughing. I walked through the door, smiled at some, and waved to others. I looked for a place to hide my purse. Then I walked back to the corner of the bar near the window, and sat by myself. I sat up high with my back against the wall, and I could see the whole place from there—it was my favorite corner.

As I sat there, I watched and listened to a group of girls sitting nearby. They whispered to each other, and now and then, they looked up at me and laughed. I had no idea what they were talking about and didn't care. I just smiled at them when our eyes met. They were near the window at a lower table, but they could still see outside, and we were all able to watch the activity out in the street from where we were.

Just then, a young, handsome American lieutenant walked by. He slowed down, stopped, and looked inside as I was looking out. Our eyes locked for a moment, and then he walked away. I thought to myself, "Too bad he didn't like me enough to come inside." A group of girls sitting by the window also saw him. Some ran to the door and opened it to take a closer look, while others looked at him through the window. After he was gone, they regrouped, acted disappointed, made fun of each other, and laughed aloud. I sat at my corner and smiled at their antics.

A few minutes later, the lieutenant returned. The girls saw him through the window, jumped from their seats, and ran to the door. This time, he opened the door and walked in. Most of the girls were still standing near the door. They looked at him, at each other, and were rather embarrassed, as if they had been caught doing something naughty, and they moved aside to give him room to enter.

He smiled at them and walked straight to the bar corner, where I was sitting. "May I join you?" he asked. I felt honored and replied, "Of course." He sat down and I looked at the other girls while his head was turned. I stuck my tongue out, telling them in my own mischievous way that he was mine.

The bartender came over and asked, "Hello, how are you, and what do you want to drink?" The lieutenant answered, "I'm fine, thanks, and I want a Ba Muoi Ba beer and a Saigon tea for her." He pointed to me and smiled. I smiled back. He impressed me with his looks, his rank, and his manners. I already liked him.

"You must have been in Vietnam for a long time to know about Saigon tea and Ba Muoi Bar beer," I commented.

"Not really," he said with a smile. "I just learned it from a lot of bar-hopping." We both laughed. I glanced at his blue eyes, found him staring at mine, and looked away.

"You are very beautiful," he said, "and I have never seen such pretty eyes."

"Thank you," I replied.

"You don't look like you are full Vietnamese," he commented. "Are you part French or Spanish?"

"I don't know," I said. "I will have to go home and ask my mother. She's the only one who knows."

We both laughed again. The bartender had already brought the beer and tea, poured the beer into a glass, and set them between us, but the lieutenant had not seen him do it. He didn't know the drinks were there, and when he laughed, he knocked the beer over. It spilled everywhere, but most of it on me. We both jumped up, and he immediately apologized. As I tried to brush the beer from my dress, I smiled and said, "Don't worry. In my job, I get spilled on all the time." I looked at the girls whom I stuck my tongue out at earlier, and they were laughing and sticking their tongues out at me now. I smiled and told them I would kill them later.

The bartender came over with a towel, asked us to move, and cleaned up. The lieutenant apologized to him for making such a big mess and asked him to bring us another beer and another tea, even though I had not drunk my first one yet. The table was cleaned, and we moved back to our seats, where we continued our conversation.

"What is your name?" he asked.

"My name is Linda," I answered, giving him the name I had recently chosen for myself.

"Is that your real name? It doesn't sound Vietnamese."

"No, it's not my real name."

"What is your name?" I asked him.

"Keith, my name is Keith, and I'm stationed at Tan Son Nhut Air Base." Keith asked, "Where do you live?"

"I live about a mile or two from the air base." I said. "I can walk there to see you." I joked, "It's not very far." We both laughed at my comment.

He looked at me and said, "There is something about your eyes; they are so enchanting."

"Thanks." I replied.

"When you laugh, your eyes laugh, too," he said. "Are you sure you are not half French?"

"No," I said. "I am Vietnamese and part Chinese; I just don't know which part," and we laughed again. "A lot of people ask me if I'm part of another race, but I think it's because I use a lot of makeup and false eyelashes, which might make me look different."

I stopped talking for a second and reached for my tea. But instead, I knocked it over, and this time, it spilled on him. We both jumped up and tried to get out of the way. Fortunately, the glass of tea was not as large as the glass of beer, so the spill was not so bad. The bartender came over and cleaned up again, and Keith ordered me another tea.

"I hope I get the chance to drink this one," I said with a smile.

Before long, we had been engrossed in conversation for hours. We drank, we talked, and we laughed, and we didn't pay attention to what was happening around us at all. My mind was on Keith and his was on me.

Suddenly, loud music and rowdy GIs jolted us from our deep involvement. We turned around and realized the place was filling up with more girls and more GIs of all races and ages, but most of them were white. Some sat at tables, while others stood around. More GIs were at the door, scrambling to get in. They talked, laughed, sang, and carried half-empty beer bottles in their hands. I heard them humming, "Hymn, hymn, F... hymn." They were already drunk. They were very loud, and the music had to be turned louder to be heard. Some of them began dancing. The quiet place had turned chaotic, and poor Keith and I had to shout at each other.

A little peanut girl, about ten or eleven, carried a big plastic bag filled with smaller individual bags of homemade roasted peanuts. She came to the bar daily and sometimes more than once a day, to sell peanuts to feed her family. She weaved her way through the big, tall, noisy GIs to find someone who would be interested in buying her peanuts. To avoid the rowdy GIs, she dashed behind the bar and walked up to us.

She asked Keith, "Do you want to buy peanuts for your girlfriend?"

He smiled, held out two fingers, and said, "Yes, I'll take two bags."

He reached for his wallet and pulled out the money to pay the girl. She threw two bags of peanuts on the bar and knocked over Keith's beer. We jumped up to avoid the spill, but it was too late. We were soaked! The peanut girl was scared and began apologizing to us. She reached into her large bag, pulled out another small bag, and threw it on the counter.

"This one's free," she said and ran away as fast as she could.

We just stood there, watching her run out the door. When she disappeared, we looked at each other, at our soaking wet clothes, and broke into uncontrollable laughter. We were drenched in beer and tea.

Keith looked at his watch and said, "It's late, and I have to get back to the base. And I do need to change clothes. But I will be back." He smiled and winked at me.

"I will be waiting right here," I said, as I winked back.

We walked to the door, shook hands, and said goodbye. I returned to the corner but had to wait for the bartender to mop up the spill. Minutes later, I was back in my seat. I stuck my feet in the bar's footrest to stretch my weary back. As I arched backward, trying to reach the floor, I stretched too far, the bar stool flipped, and I fell. My head hit the corner of a short table behind me, and it cut into my lower eyelid. Blood gushed out. Everyone in the club quieted down, and someone turned off the music. The atmosphere became serious. A couple of GIs rushed over and helped me up, while others left the club. No one knew what was going on, but some thought I had been shot when they saw blood. The bartender rushed over and gave me a beer-soaked rag. I took it from him and pressed it over my eye. I could smell the stench of alcohol in the wet rag.

The commotion caught the owner's attention. She came over to check on me and called for a taxi to take me to a nearby medical clinic. At the clinic, we took a number and waited with dozens of others until my number was called. The beer-soaked rag turned red from the cut, and more blood was running down my dress. Eventually, a doctor called my number, and we went to his office.

He examined my eye, smelled the alcohol on me, and shook his head. He said, "I think you've been drinking too much," and left the room.

I waited a long time before he came back. "The cut is too deep and too close to your eye to stitch," he said. "I'll put a bandage on it, and it should heal by itself."

The gauze and the bandage covered the left side of my face. I thanked him for helping me and left the clinic with the club owner. We hailed a taxi, and I asked the owner if she could take me home, because it was not far from the clinic. She agreed, and we spoke very little on the way. I thought she probably blamed me for ruining her night of business, and before I got out of the taxi, I apologized for being such a nuisance and told her I would be home until my cut heals.

She was very understanding and said, "That will be fine. Just take care of yourself and come back as soon as you can. I really need you, and the club won't be the same without you, even though you are a trouble-maker." She winked and continued, "I like you."

That was the first time I knew that she liked me. From the day I was hired, we never talked. I came to work, she paid me for the Saigon tea I sold, and that was it. I guess I was not her "buttercup," and I didn't kiss up to her like the other girls did. I think money only goes so far and only buys so much. It cannot buy everything and everybody. In that sense, I was stubborn and had self-respect. I knew she and I didn't get along, but I knew deep inside that she respected me. Before getting out of the taxi, I smiled and thanked her for the help she had given me.

As the days passed, I became more and more anxious to see the handsome lieutenant I'd just met. I couldn't stop thinking of him—of his smile, his laugh, and the way he looked at me. I checked my wound in the mirror several times a day to see if it had healed enough for me to return to work, but each time I checked, it was still red, swollen, and half of my eye was still black. "It doesn't look too good," I kept saying to myself, but then I couldn't take it anymore. I took off the bandage, against the doctor's advice, and covered the cut with a ton of makeup and a smaller bandage. I was determined to go back to work, hoping to see him, the lieutenant named Keith, before he saw someone else. I chose a nice red dress that was cute but not too sexy. I didn't want him to think I was too wild. My intent was to dress nicely to impress him, because I liked him. With my makeup finished and my hair teased up in the "bee hive" style, I put on my dress. "I look nice," I said to myself in the mirror. "Except for my swollen, black and blue eye and the bandage." Even heavy makeup could not cover all of the discoloration. The more I looked in the mirror, the more discouraged I became. I sat on the bed, wondering whether I should or shouldn't go back to work. I didn't want him to see me in that condition. Dejected, I unzipped my dress halfway down and prepared to stay home, but I changed my mind again and decided I could not wait any longer. I had to get back to work to see him.

I decided I didn't care what my condition was. I zipped my dress up and put my red shoes on. I grabbed a purse, said goodbye to Eddie, and told him to be a good boy and to go to bed on time. Then I left the house, covered my eye with one hand, walked to the street, and hailed a taxi. I arrived at the club thirty minutes later, and I paid the driver. Still covering my eye with one hand, I walked into the club.

The little peanut girl ran up to me as soon as I entered. She looked at my face and frowned for a few seconds, as if she wanted to know what happened to me. But before she asked me about my bandage, she got so excited and said, "I have something important to tell you. I saw your lieutenant boyfriend here every day, and he sat with another girl."

She looked at me, waiting for my reaction. She didn't have to wait long as my disappointment was obvious. In an instant, I went from excitement to disbelief. I felt like someone had just let all the air out of my balloon.

I thanked the peanut girl and walked toward the back of the club. She followed me and told me there was more. "The girl he was sitting with is your best friend."

"What?" I replied in anger. When I gave her the reaction she was looking for, she bolted for the door. She came to the club often and knew me and the other girls well.

At twenty-one, in my red dress, at work, waiting to see Don.

I felt like turning around and going home, but I looked for my "friend" instead. I saw her sitting with another girl in the back room; the room was quieter and near a bathroom.

"Hey, Von," I said, "Have you seen that lieutenant named Keith?"

"No" she replied.

"Well, the peanut girl said she saw you sitting with him every day. Is that true?"

"Oh," she said. "Are you talking about the good-looking guy?" she admitted.

"Yes, that's the one," I said, letting her know I had caught her in a lie. "You know him, because I talked to you about him. Why did you do that to me?"

I was so upset. It was not just about a man I liked, but to have my best friend betray me was even more painful.

"He was here," she said, "but he didn't ask about you. We just talked, and he bought me some Saigon teas. That's it." And then she walked away.

"I went to all that trouble to see him," I thought, "only to find out he was not here to see me—he came to see someone else."

I was so upset and disappointed that I considered going home, but instead, I decided to linger a bit longer. I hoped he might come in, and I could ask him for an explanation. Although we hadn't known each other long, I felt we had a strong connection. I just wanted to know if he felt the same way as I did. I put my purse away and went to my favorite corner of the bar where he and I first met.

I didn't have to wait long. The door opened, and the lieutenant walked in. He looked around for a second, and when he saw me sitting in my corner, his face lit up, he smiled at me, walked straight to where I was sitting, and sat down beside me. I smiled and was very happy to see him. For a moment I thought, "Is he here to see me or to see Von?" My expression turned from happy to confused. He stopped smiling when he looked closer at my face and, with concern, asked, "What happened to your eye?"

"I fell off this chair." I pointed to the stool I was sitting on. "I fell right after you left here that day." I told him the whole story about the accident and why I didn't come back to work.

The bartender came up to him and asked what he wanted to drink. "A beer for me and a Saigon tea for her," he said, pointing at me. I smiled and thanked him for the tea. Before long, Von saw him and came up to him with a big smile. He smiled back, and she put her arm around his waist, as if to claim him. I watched him push her arm away and ask her if she wanted a drink.

"Yes," she said, and he signaled to the bartender with one finger up and one on her, which meant to bring her one Saigon tea. The bartender understood and brought her drink. I stopped telling Keith about my misfortune and watched how he and Von interacted. The bartender sat the tea in front of her, she picked it up, turned to Keith, and said "chin, chin." In response, he picked up his beer glass and said "chin, chin," to her. They touched their glasses, and she drank her tea, but before he drank his, he turned to me and said, "chin, chin." I picked up my glass, said, "chin, chin," touched his glass with mine, and we emptied our glasses.

Keith turned to Von and said, "Thank you for keeping me company for the past few times I was here, but I came here to see Linda." He pointed at me and said, "She is here now, and I would like to talk to her alone."

Von showed disappointment and looked embarrassed. She said, "OK," and walked away.

Keith turned to me and asked, "Did she tell you I asked about you each time I was here?"

"No, but I did ask her about you," I said. "Now you are here, so let's just continue where we left off." I took off part of my bandage and showed him my eyelid. "This is the reason I couldn't come to work to see you."

He held up his hand and motioned for me to stop pulling off the bandage. "Don't touch it!" he said. "Let it heal, or you could make it worse. I'm so sorry you had an accident. If I had known about it, I would have found out where you lived and come to see you."

"Thank you," I said. "Thank you so much for worrying about me. Now that you are here, I am feeling better, much better. I'm very happy to see you and even happier to know you have been here and have been looking for me the whole time."

He ordered another beer and another tea and said, "I hope we won't bathe in our drinks today."

We laughed, and I said, "I hope we don't either."

We talked until dark, and it became time for him to go.

"I have to get back to the base. I have to go to work early in the morning, so I can take off early in the afternoon and come to see you," he said.

"I don't want you to go," I said. I could tell from the way he looked at me that he didn't want to leave either. So we left each other that night begrudgingly.

My lieutenant friend came to see me as often as he could, just about every day, and I learned he was married and had one son.

"We were married too young," he said, "and we grew apart as we grew older. We were infatuated, but not in love, and we don't even get along anymore. That's why I volunteered to come to Vietnam, to force a separation. And I hope the divorce will soon follow."

He seemed sincere, but I trusted him no more than the other GIs who told me similar stories before. Two weeks later, he gave me the wedding band from his finger, and when he did, I smiled and said nothing. I looked at the ring and asked myself, "And how long will this love last? Maybe until he finishes his tour of duty in Vietnam?"

He took a big gulp of beer and put it down. He turned the glass around and around with his thumb and finger and watched the bubbles in his glass. He said in a quiet but serious voice, "I'm so tired, so tired of living on Tan Son Nhut Air Base. Rockets and mortars pound us each night, killing someone almost every night, and sleep is almost impossible. I was wondering if you could help me find a place to live off base."

I smiled at him and replied, "You are in luck! My landlord is adding a room to my house.

It's not ready yet, but when it is, I'll let you know. Or, if you want to see where it is, I'd be happy to take you there tomorrow, if you are interested and have time."

Without blinking an eye, he said, "I'll take it!"

"It isn't ready yet," I repeated, laughing, "and you have no idea where it is or what it's going to look like."

"I don't care," he said. "If it's close to you, I want it." He opened his wallet, handed me a stack of money, and told me to give it to the landlord as a deposit. His quick decision surprised me and made me laugh again.

"I don't know how much the owner will want for rent," I said, with raised eyebrows.

"I don't care how much it costs," he said, "and I don't mind waiting until it's finished. I just don't want to miss this chance."

I took the stack of piasters, rolled them up, and held them in my hand all night. I didn't want to put the money in my purse for fear of losing it. Time passed, and again, he had to say good night, and he left. The next day, I took the money, gave it to the landlord, and told him to hurry up with the building. I was as anxious for the lieutenant to move in next door as he was. A few days later, I invited him to my house for lunch and to see the apartment he had rented.

Nam, helping me dress.

On the morning of his visit, one of my maids and I went to the market. We worked hard preparing special Vietnamese dishes all morning. We made egg rolls, spring rolls, and pho, a special beef soup. At one o'clock, I heard a knock on the door. I was still rolling spring rolls, so I sent Nam, the maid, to answer it. From the kitchen, I heard the lieutenant asking for Linda. Nam spoke to him in Vietnamese, asking him to come in, but he didn't understand a single word. I was afraid he might think he was at the wrong house, so I stopped what I was doing and ran to the door.

He looked quite impressive in his khaki air force uniform. We both smiled as we greeted each other. "Please come in and have a seat," I invited and pointed to a couch. When he entered, I noticed he carried a small bottle of soy sauce. "I'm going back to the kitchen to wash my hands, but I'll be right back." I told him.

I ran back to the kitchen to show the maids how to roll the rest of the spring rolls, washed my hands, and rejoined him in the living room. Instead of sitting, he wandered around the room admiring my decor and my music collection.

"This is a beautiful place, and I like your music collection," he said. He finished his remarks and handed me the bottle of soy sauce.

"Thank you," I said with a smile, but I didn't know if I was thanking him for his comments or for the bottle of soy sauce.

"Who opened the door for me?" he asked. "That's Nam, my maid," I answered.

"You have a maid, too?" he asked with surprise.

"I have three maids," I said. "One cooks, one cleans, and the other takes care of my baby."

"Speaking of your baby, where is he? I'd like to meet him," he asked.

"Oh, he's in preschool now, but he might be home before you leave," I said.

"How can you afford a nice apartment and three maids?" he asked.

"I lie, cheat, and drink a lot of Saigon tea," I joked. "The maids here are not very expensive," I explained, "and they work for food and a little money."

I had known him for weeks, but I still couldn't pronounce his name. It was Keith, but when I tried it, it came out Ky. We don't have the "th" sound at the end of any Vietnamese words, and I just couldn't get it right. I asked him if there was another name I could call him, and he suggested Don, short for Donald, his middle name. I told him I could handle that one easier, so he became "Don."

When lunch was ready, I asked him to come to the table. "I hope you won't mind if I use soy sauce instead of nuoc mam," he said. "I've heard about the fish sauce, and it has a bad reputation. I'm afraid it might make me sick."

I was a little disappointed by his request. It felt like he was saying that my food might make him ill. What he didn't know was that I had used nuoc mam, or "fish sauce," on every dish I prepared, and I wasn't about to tell him. I gave him an understanding smile and asked the maid to bring back the bottle of soy sauce he gave me earlier, and an extra bowl. I poured some into his bowl, and read the label, "Made in Japan." I smiled inside but said nothing. I let him think he was using his "American" soy sauce. He wasn't aware that Vietnamese use nuoc mam in almost everything we cook and seldom use soy sauce. Some Vietnamese have never seen or even heard of soy sauce, much less used it.

While eating, he asked, "Where do you get your food from?"

"At the market, an open-market." I answered. "Have you been to the market yet?"

"Not yet," he replied.

"I'll take you there one day," I told him. "I think you will like it. But you will have to get up early, because the market is only open in the morning and closes by noon. After that the food won't be fresh."

"Why?" he asked.

"Everything we are eating right now was running, crawling, flying, or swimming a few hours ago, and the vegetables were in the garden or in the field only a day or less before I bought them."

"That is wild," he said.

"That's why we have to go to the market at least once or twice daily," I explained.

"Don't you have canned or frozen food?" he asked.

"We don't have canned food, and we can't afford frozen food," I continued.

"Most of us don't have an icebox or a refrigerator, and the processed food costs more to make. Fresh food is all we have, and that's why we have to take a lot of time to prepare and cook each meal."

Don was surprised at our differences. "Where I come from, people don't have to cook unless they want to," he said, "All we have to do is open the can, box, or bag and eat. Sometimes we eat a 'TV dinner,' for our meal; they are cheaper, faster, and easier to prepare."

I listened to him and wondered what all of the food he talked about tasted like.

"I hope I will have the chance to come to your country, where I can eat out of cans, boxes, or bags without having to cook or kill for my meal," I told him.

We ate and talked, and then we talked and ate, and luckily, Don did not show any signs of being sick from the nuoc mam.

After lunch, I took him to see the messy, unfinished apartment next door. It was one big room, and it shared a common wall with my house. The owner tried to squeeze an apartment into a very small space to make extra money.

I pointed to an open window and said, "Look, my window opens right into the middle of your room. The owner intends to block it after the building is done."

"I don't mind," he said, with a devilish smile. "I love it."

"After you move in," I remarked, "and you have a girl over for a visit, I can always throw you a towel or two through the window, if you want it."

"I just might need it," he replied, and we both laughed.

I walked him to the back of the apartment and pointed out, "We will have to share the kitchen and the bathroom, too."

"That will be no problem," he assured me.

The kitchen and bathroom were both situated outside, so either one of us could use them.

The maids had cleaned off the dinner table and set out desserts of various kinds of fresh fruits, including hairy lychees, guavas, longans, and bananas.

"Please come back to the table and have dessert with me, Don."

"OK, what kind of dessert do you have?" he questioned, before he saw the fruit. "I love deserts, like pie and cake."

"I'm sorry, but I don't have either. All I have is fresh fruit; most of us eat fruit for dessert," I explained.

"I'll try it," he said. "I didn't know fruits were your dessert."

"Yes, we don't have many sweets like cake, cookies, and candy. We save them for special occasions." I explained. "In our country we have more fruit than we have money, and we can't afford the dentist to fix our teeth."

"We eat a lot of sweets in our country, and we have too many cavities," he joked. "We have to wear dentures or have no teeth at all." We both laughed at the thought.

Don and I sat and talked for a long time. We made each other laugh, and somehow it seemed we never ran out of something to say to each other. When Eddie came home from preschool, he ran to me, but his eyes were on Don. I told Eddie to shake hands and say hello to Don, and he did, like a little gentleman. To my surprise, instead of just shaking hands, Don reached over and gave Eddie a big hug. Eddie was shy, so he ran back to me and hid his face. I smiled at Don and called the maid to take Eddie and feed him his lunch.

Then I asked, "Don, do you have to go back to work?"

"Yes," he said, "and I'm late, but that's OK. I'll work late tonight to make up for it." He smiled, winked at me, and added, "The time here is worth the extra work."

Before leaving, Don thanked me and said, "I appreciate your hospitality; the food was excellent, but most of all, your company was so interesting, and I hate to leave. Oh, and thanks for finding me a place to live. I love it! I can't wait to move in."

I walked him to the door, and we waved goodbye. I thought to myself, "He's a nice guy, with a positive attitude. I have a feeling he will be a good neighbor."

Don continued to see me at the club after he finished with work each day, and before he left, he always said, "I can't wait to move to my new apartment and to be your neighbor. I can come home to see you every day, instead of coming here."

That next Monday was Don's day off, and he decided to move all of his belongings from the base to his new apartment, even though it wasn't finished yet. The window in the wall separating us hadn't been closed in, and there was no furniture, not even a bed. Tools, wood, bricks, and cement buckets lay everywhere. It was just one big, messy, unfinished room.

I helped Don put up some of his clothes, shoes, and small boxes and bags on the built-in counter and shelves, and we discussed where and how he would have to put his furniture when he got it.

"Right now, you're welcome to sleep on my couch until you get a bed," I told him.

His face lit up. "That's very nice of you," he said, with a bright grin. And then he sounded serious, "I don't like to sleep at the base, with all the noise from rockets and mortars exploding all the time. It's getting on my nerves."

I nodded, smiled, and let him know I understood. I decided not to go to work that afternoon and stayed home instead. I cooked and invited Don for dinner. That night, we stayed in the kitchen, talking, laughing, and eating all different kinds of food. I prepared blood clams, snails, rock crabs, and several different types of fruits. We had so much fun together that we forgot about the time until the sun rose. We looked at each other and realized that we had stayed up all night.

"The sun is up!" I exclaimed in surprise.

"So it is," he said. "What on earth did we do all night long?"

He was just as surprised as I was—the night had passed without us even knowing it.

"I think you have to get ready to go to work," I reminded him, "and I have to wake the maid up and go to the market for more food, just in case we decide to do this again tonight."

"I would love to do it again," he said.

We both smiled as we got up from our seats. We washed our faces, brushed our teeth, and I went back to the kitchen to make coffee and soup for us. After we had breakfast together, Don went back to the base, and I took a nap before starting my routine.

My daily routine was going to the market to buy food, helping with cooking, and running around organizing my black-market activities with friends and dealers. I contacted my friends who had American husbands or boyfriends and bought goods from them that had been purchased in the military commissary or Post Exchange. These goods were stereos, cigarettes, beer, whiskey, and even gold or diamonds. I also bought canned foods, such as tomato sauce, peanut butter, and jelly. I then sold these goods to a dealer, whom I knew well, for a profit. It was an easy and fast way to make money. In fact, most of the time I spent in the bars or clubs was to make contacts with Americans and other foreigners, in order to buy and sell their goods. Between dealings, I drank Saigon tea for extra money to complete my day.

After meeting Don, I had to add our late nights together in the kitchen to my routine. I told all of my friends who lived with me, and the maids, that the kitchen was mine to play in after dark. My friends who lived with me liked Don, and did not mind sharing our home with him. Don and I spent night after night in the kitchen and seldom went to bed. Those nights set the pace for our unfolding relationship, as we discovered we had a great deal in common, and our differences only magnified our interests. Our talk, our laughter, and our cooking disturbed our neighbors, however, who didn't react well to our late-night forays. At first, they asked us to be quiet, but when that didn't work, they yelled. "Be quiet!" and threw rocks and pebbles on the corrugated steel roof that covered our kitchen. "Be quiet!" they yelled, "Let us sleep. We have to get up early in the morning to go to work. Go to sleep, so we can sleep!" Of course, one of my neighbors making loud noise woke my other neighbors, and they all yelled at us at the same time. That created the sound of grumpy neighbors in the still of the night. We laughed at their antics, but we also did quiet down.

When the construction of Don's apartment was finally finished, he still hadn't found any suitable furniture or a bed yet. I don't think he looked very hard, and that's why he still slept on my couch. One evening, after stuffing ourselves with food and talking for hours in the kitchen, I suggested we must get some sleep, and Don agreed. I brushed my teeth, took a shower, and went to bed. Don took a shower after me, but instead of going to the couch, he climbed into my bed and lay next to me. I was surprised and a little bit disappointed by his rather bold move, but I did nothing to stop him. A few moments later, he had not attempted to make a pass at me, and I was pleased. We lay there, side-by-side, with our feet touching. We were close, but still separated by a foot or two. His obvious display of respect brought us even closer. He was on his side and I was on mine, and we talked until we both fell asleep. We had so much to talk about, so much to share, and we both needed companionship and love.

The next night, we lay together after our kitchen foray, and when our feet touched, we also held hands. At that moment, I thought to myself, "We are going too far," so I let go of his hand, moved away, and said "goodnight."

"Goodnight," he replied, and went to sleep.

On the third night, after an exhausting conversation, we lay resting in bed for a few moments. He reached over and squeezed my hand, and I responded by squeezing back. He put his foot on top of mine, and I didn't move. He moved closer, put his arm around me, and found no resistance. I returned his embrace, and for the first time, we kissed. When our lips touched, my heart beat faster, and my body grew weak. I could tell Don was nervous by the trembling of his body. We held each other so tight, and I felt true love. For the first time, I allowed myself to both give and receive love at the same time. Tears of joy streamed from my eyes as I gave myself to Don.

There were no words to explain how I felt about Don and our relationship. I had never felt that way before. If love was real, then I believed I had fallen in love. From then on, we spent every available moment together, day and night. We hugged, we kissed, we held hands, and it didn't matter what we were doing. Whenever our eyes met, we smiled at each other.

Chapter 21

DANCING RAINBOW

FROM THAT MOMENT on, we started living together as a family. Eddie and the maids liked Don, and they treated him like part of the family. The maids often talked to Don, but he couldn't understand Vietnamese, and the maids couldn't speak English. So I had to be their interpreter.

Don and I still spent a lot of time together in the kitchen cooking, eating, and talking—sometimes throughout the night, without a wink of sleep. Now and then, the neighbors still reminded us to be quiet, but they also got used to us. We never saw our neighbors anyway, even though only a wall separated us, because they entered their home from a different street. It was normal, crowded city living.

Don and I realized it was illegal for us to live together, and if the police raided our home to check our family papers, as they often did, we could go to jail or pay heavy fines. We got by with it for a few weeks, but knew it was just a matter of time before the police banged on our door. We decided to make our relationship legal, and on December 11, 1968, went to a local police station. There, we had prenuptial papers prepared, which legalized us as a temporary married couple. We were issued a family paper authorized by Hung, the District One Police Chief, and a friend of ours. He listed Don as an American Ambassador. Hung said, "That will discourage the police from questioning us any further." I loved it and loved seeing the policemen's face when they raided our home, read Don's title, and had to salute him.

For me, that was it. I was married to Don, and I didn't want to be apart from him for the rest of my life, even though there were shadows hanging over us. We had no way of knowing what might happen to us or to our future because of the war. Death and separation were always seconds away, and uncertainty haunted both of us every minute. Somehow, we still made it through each day without regret.

The more we were together, the deeper we fell in love, even though we had not yet exchanged the word "love." I was afraid it might jinx us. If feelings count, then I loved him, but I was afraid to put my feeling into words. I decided to wait for him to say it first. Then, one day, before Don left for work, he hugged me, said goodbye, and whispered in my ear, "I love you."

"I love you, too," I whispered back. Then we hugged each other for the longest time since we met.

He loosened his arm, looked me in the eye, and said, "Minh Oi, it doesn't matter what happens in the future. I will love you until I die, and if possible, after that."

I looked him in the eye and made my vows, "I'll love you for all eternity." Then we gave each other a kiss to seal our vows before he went to work.

Never in my life had I felt such love, not even from my own mother. I knew she loved me, and I always loved her, but no love compared to that shared by Don and me. It was so complete. He called me "Minh Oi," which in Vietnam is an intimate term for my darling, my baby, or honey. Don often bought me flowers and gifts and wrote poems and notes for me as well.

His poetry was beautiful and sensitive and sometimes brought tears to my eyes, but his notes were always cute and funny. They made me laugh and cry at the same time. Don just wanted to remind me of how much he loved me. I didn't write much to him, but I think he knew our feelings were mutual.

Our love and devotion left us both tired from staying up all night cooking, eating, talking, and sharing our life together. We were exhausted, and we both lost a lot of weight. I went from 105 to 88 pounds, and Don went from 170 to 148 pounds. I guess you could say our love wore us out.

I often tried to stay home from work, but the club owner didn't let me go that easily. If I stayed home for more than a couple of days, she told my friends who worked and lived with me to remind me to get back to work. Sometimes, she even came to my house to get me.

"The place is just not the same without you," she said, "even though you're a troublemaker and have a bad temper. You are fun and cheerful, I like you, and want to see you back at work."

"I'll come back. I promise," I told her, and I did, although I preferred to stay home with Don. I needed money to pay the rent, the maids, and buy food. Don helped, but his funds were limited. Whether I worked at the club or not, I continued with my black-market activities, and the money I made we spent together.

One day, Don asked me to quit working at the club. At first, I declined, because I didn't want to be dependent on him, but he insisted. He told me it hurt him to think of me going to work every day, being nice to other men to get Saigon tea. He was more than just a little jealous, I thought. He said our money would go further if I let one of the maids go instead. I gave his suggestion a lot of thought, and after more discussion, I gave in. I loved him enough to stay home to make him happy. I told him I would stop working at the club, but I wouldn't stop my black-market business, because we needed the money. He agreed with this arrangement, and our combined income provided us with just enough money to get by.

Money, however, was not always the biggest issue. Being able to buy the food and cooking fuel was another matter. Because of the continued escalation of the fighting, there was a shortage of everything. At times, I would have to stand in lines for hours, just to buy staples such as rice, sugar, kerosene, and the charcoal that we needed for cooking. To make matters worse, the curfew in Saigon became very strict; sometimes we couldn't leave the house after dark.

Don was often restricted to the base and, because of his work, was unable to come home for lunch. Sometimes, we didn't see each other at night. And sometimes it was days before we saw each other. That was hard on us, and on those nights, I often lost sleep from worry, but there was nothing I could do and no way for us to communicate. We had no phones. The rockets and mortars exploded around us every night, but most landed on the base where Don worked. I often thought, "Where is he now? Is he still alive? Is he dead? Has he already gone back to the States?" There was no way for me to find out, and I began praying for him and for his safety. I also prayed for every single human who was involved in the horrible war. I prayed for the animals, the trees, the flowers, and all living things.

I missed Don when he was not with me, and I believed he missed me as well. The conditions in Saigon, or should I say, in my country, were getting worse. The curfews increased everywhere, and shortages of food spread throughout the country. The fighting became more violent, and the death of American and South Vietnamese soldiers increased to staggering numbers. Death among civilians and North Vietnamese soldiers rose to the thousands every week.

"I don't know who will win or who will lose. What is gained if one wins? And what is lost if one loses?" I thought, "Most people I know don't care who wins or who loses; they just want the war to be over."

Finally, Don came home from the base on his day off, and we were so happy to see each other. It had been over a week since I last saw him, and there were a lot of hugs and kisses to make up for lost time. That afternoon, we sat down and talked, making plans for our future in what little time we had. We didn't plan far ahead, because we didn't know where our lives would be headed in the long run. We just knew we needed some plans for the next few days or weeks for our finances, our food, our rent, and the necessities needed for survival.

Don decided to give up his apartment next door, which he had rented but never occupied. I also agreed to cook for my girlfriends who lived with us in order to make extra money. I dismissed all but one of the maids, keeping only one to help me cook and clean. I wasn't too crazy about doing so much housework. I missed having all the maids and missed my work at the club, but I was happy to stay home for Don's sake.

Don's eating habits changed tremendously after a couple of months, and he no longer needed his "American" soy sauce. He mastered the use of chopsticks and savored every dish I put on the table.

Don wanted to come home for lunch but didn't want to fight the slow and crowded public transportation system and couldn't afford a taxi every day. So he decided to buy a used, beat-up, cheap motorcycle—a 90 cc Honda. He looked funny, but cute, with his helmet and sunglasses on.

I told him one day when he drove home on the Honda, "I hope our babies will look exactly like you."

"For your sake, I hope they aren't born with sunglasses and a helmet," he responded, and we both laughed.

Don on his Honda, 1968, at Tan Son Nhut Air Force Base.

We spent a lot of time listening to our favorite songs. The music was beautiful, but it also filled us with sadness and anxiety, because our future was so uncertain. Don and Eddie took to each other like a real father and son. Don carried Eddie on his back or shoulder whenever we went out. Eddie loved Don; he was the only father Eddie had ever known.

Don and Eddie, 1969.

One day, my parents surprised me with a visit. My stepfather saw Eddie first and realized that I had not given him up as I was told to do. We didn't have a chance to say hello to each other before my stepfather began scolding me. He said, "You must go home!" He raised his voice and told me, "Your fiancé is waiting for you."

Before I had a chance to respond, I heard the Honda's engine at the front door. Don came home for lunch. "Oh my God!" I thought, "Now what?"

I was scared of my stepfather, and my whole body was shaking. Don opened the door, walked straight into the living room, and greeted everyone with a smile. He shook my stepfather's hand and said hello. Then he turned to Mother, shook her hand, and said, "Hi, how are you?" Next, Don walked to me and gave me a big hug and a kiss. In our Vietnamese tradition, hugs and kisses belonged in the bedroom behind closed doors. With my parents in shock and confusion, Don excused himself, and went to the bathroom to wash his hands. He didn't know they were my parents, nor did he expect my parents to show up without letting me know first.

I was still in a state of shock and couldn't say a word. I motioned for my parents to sit down. They sat down and looked at me in grim silence for a few minutes.

"Who is he?" my stepfather asked, pointing to Don with his raised eyebrow.

My mother frowned and then chimed in, "Yes, who is he?"

I was too shocked to think of a believable story and told them the truth. "He's my boyfriend." I thought I was going to die or get beat up after saying that. I had not expected, nor wanted, this meeting to take place.

A heavy silence was in the air as neither my parents nor I came up with anything to say to each other. When Don returned to the living room with a broad smile on his face, I introduced him to my parents, and they to him.

He smiled and said, "Hi, I'm glad to meet you," and my parents said nothing as they shook his hand again.

At first, I thought my parents would kill us, or at least get up and leave. I was so nervous that I didn't know what to say or even how to act. Don was very cheerful and polite and was happy to meet them. Acting as an interpreter, I engaged them in polite conversation. My stepfather was impressed when I told him Don was an officer, had a college education, and was a Catholic. He was also impressed with the obvious respect Don was showing them.

My stepfather and Don had an amiable and polite conversation through me, and they developed an almost instant liking for each other. For the first time, my stepfather agreed to stay for lunch. There had been a few times my stepfather stopped by my apartment on his trips to buy Chinese herbs, but he stayed only long enough to check on me and pressure me to come back to Vung Tau to get married.

My parents were surprised and taken by Don's ability to use chopsticks and eat the Vietnamese food I prepared. Mother joked when she saw Don using chopsticks so well and eating all the food, "Don must have been Vietnamese in his last life and has been reincarnated as an American." We all laughed, and I explained to Don what Mother said.

The unexpected and nerve-racking lunch turned out very nicely in the end. My parents were surprised and impressed by my English-speaking ability, and they began to loosen their grip and show respect for me, which I never had from them in the past. My stepfather even changed the way he talked to me. I felt like I was in a dream, and that when I woke up, everything would be different.

Before Don returned to the base, my stepfather invited him to visit our family in Vung Tau. Don accepted the invitation, agreeing to go there with me at our first opportunity. Don shook hands with my stepfather and bowed to my mother as he left.

My stepfather turned to me and said, "I like Don. He seems to be all right for an American, and I think he has the potential to become an important man. I'm looking forward to seeing him again." Mother smiled and nodded her head in agreement. All I could do was smile back, in stunned silence.

I was dumbfounded by this turn of events. I had never expected my stepfather to approve of any man I might have selected, especially not an American. Besides, I was still engaged to that "thing" in Vung Tau, even though I had only seen him twice, and each time I had experienced nausea.

After my parents met Don, I felt more at ease and didn't worry so much about my so-called "fiancé" anymore. I hoped my parents would call off the engagement, because I knew I would die if I had to marry that grotesque man. Don didn't know much about our culture and customs. He assumed that if he loved me, and I loved him, nothing else mattered, regardless of what my parents might think. He did not know how lucky he was to be accepted into the family and have my parents like him. That made everything easier for us to love each other even more. I hoped and prayed for my parents' continued approval of Don. I didn't want to disappoint my parents, but I didn't want to be apart from Don either.

Don was serious about visiting my family and suggested we go on his next day off, but I was hesitant about making the trip with Don. I was worried about taking an American officer on the long road to Vung Tau. It was dangerous for both of us, but Don insisted.

We hired a taxi to take us there, agreeing to pay a flat rate for the whole day. We left in the morning and arrived before noon. It was more than sixty miles, but because of the road conditions and traffic, it took us about two and a half hours to get there. My parents greeted us and immediately made us feel welcome. My brothers and sister, then between six and fifteen, ran to see this curious-looking stranger. Don held out his hand, and the kids shook it. They had seen Americans before but never very close. They examined this strange person, with blue eyes, hairy arms, and skin much lighter than theirs, and they asked me if Don was real. "Of course he is," I replied. "If you cut him, his blood will be red, just like yours." That seemed to satisfy their curiosity. Don had been promoted to captain and looked impressive in his military uniform.

My stepfather sat at the end of the dining table and invited Don to sit next to him, at his right side, in the seat reserved for the eldest son or a special guest. They sipped rice whiskey and ate the pork intestines and blood pudding that Mother had prepared. I helped Mother and the kids set out the rest of the food. Then we took our seats and waited for my stepfather to say a prayer, and we all had our lunch.

While eating, Don and my stepfather continued their conversation, using me as their interpreter. I think the reason my stepfather liked Don was because Don was an American officer, and he was interesting to him. I think, too, that he might have liked the sound of a foreign language. Other than that, I didn't know why he liked Don. Their discussion covered a multitude of subjects, from my stepfather's medical practice to life in the United States. Mother told me she thought Don was very nice and was happy he was Catholic and was getting along so well with my stepfather. I remained in a state of shock, expecting to wake up from this pleasant dream at any minute.

Then, my stepfather presented me with yet another astonishing surprise. He turned to me, and like a judge granting a pardon, announced, "I have decided I will call off your engagement." After a few seconds of silence, orchestrated for effect, he continued, "Everything has just gotten out of hand. First, it was your baby, and now an American boyfriend. I'm afraid all the plans I had for you have been ruined." He paused again as everyone at the table held their breath. "But maybe it's just as well; I hope everything will happen for the better."

The room was so quiet, you could hear a pin drop. My stepfather was making life-changing decisions, and we all had to pay close attention to what he said.

My mind was reeling, but I still was not prepared for the second shock. "We are no longer going to suggest that you give up your baby. You are welcome to bring him home whenever you want." I was near tears as I thanked him. After lunch, we spent a few more hours visiting before we returned home.

We went to see my family as often as we could, and during those visits, Don met other family members, like Uncle Ky, both of my stepbrothers, and many of my cousins. Don loved my family and my relatives. He said he felt like they were his own family. Don and my two stepbrothers, Hen and Den, became friends, and they visited us often when they could get away from their military duties. Instead of renting a taxi on one of our trips, Don borrowed an old, four-door sedan from a friend.

Don and my family having lunch. From left: Don, Uncle Ky,
my stepfather, and my stepbrother, Den.

Because we had the car, we decided to take Eddie, a maid, and my friend, Von, who rented Don's old apartment next door.

Our plans were to visit with my family, spend a few hours on the beach just a few miles from my parent's house, and then return to Saigon before sundown. Three of my younger brothers and my sister decided to go with us. I had to let the maid stay behind at Mother's house, and all eight of us packed like sardines into the little car, and we headed for the beach. I'm surprised the car made it without blowing a tire.

We had so much fun that we forgot the time, until Don looked at the sun setting and realized it was late. "We have to leave right away!" he exclaimed, in alarm. We gathered the kids and rushed to the car. We dropped my brothers and sister off and picked up the maid before leaving for Saigon. Mother was concerned because the road was unsafe to travel at night, more so with an American. She asked if we could stay until morning, but I told her we couldn't, because Don promised his friend he would return the car. Because Mother couldn't stop us from going, she decided to come along, saying she would be too nervous for us if she stayed home. I tried to reassure her we would be all right, but she wouldn't listen, and climbed in the car. Don couldn't waste any more time, because we were so late already. He smiled and nodded his head to my mother, indicating she was welcome to come. With Mother inside, Don sped down the darkening road, heading back to Saigon. Once we were on our way, Mother kept reminding us how dangerous the road was at night.

My brothers and sister at Vung Tau beach, 1968. From left: Kinh, Nho, Bay, and Khai.

"There are so many cars, trucks, and motorcycles stopped by the Viet Cong at night. Some are kidnapped, tortured, and even killed. If the Viet Cong capture a military person, they will be taken north to prison. Just a few days ago, the Viet Cong built a dirt mound on the road and mined it. It caused many problems for travelers. They planned to cut off the road and take over a nearby town to get supplies and food. No one dares to travel at night."

My mother, as she looked in 1973.

Thank God, Don did not understand Vietnamese, and I was not about to translate Mother's story and information to him. I knew Mother told the truth, because I watched the television, heard it from other people, and read similar stories in the newspaper.

I said, "Mother, we are going to be fine. We just have to pray, and God will protect us."

Don turned to me and asked, "What are you guys talking about?"

Von just about opened her mouth to translate, but I took over. "It's nothing," I said. "Just an old story," I didn't want Don to get nervous.

The sky turned dark, and the road turned darker. The car's headlights were not very bright, and the road was bad and bumpy. Don couldn't drive any faster than twenty-five or thirty miles an hour. Then suddenly, the right rear tire went flat. Don got out of the car and asked all of us to get out, so he could change the tire. I held a small flashlight to help Don see. It took him a long time to finish the job, because the flashlight was so dim it was hard to see anything.

When the tire was finally fixed, we were happy and thankful to get back in the car and be on our way. The road was deserted, and there were no other vehicles in sight. It was quiet, except for our old car's engine.

"It's too dangerous to keep going," I told Don. "We should turn around and go back to Vung Tau."

"No," Don said. "We are almost halfway there now, and I think to turn around would be just as dangerous."

I didn't respond to his comment, but I kept thinking, "We may not make it through." Everyone knew this stretch of road belonged to the Viet Cong at night. We were extremely nervous, but we had no choice but to keep going.

We approached the small village of Quan Chim, and several black-uniformed men stopped us at gunpoint. Lucky for us, they were South Vietnamese soldiers guarding the small bridge at the edge of town against Viet Cong infiltrators, who were determined to destroy as many bridges as they could.

One soldier came to the driver's side of the car with his gun in hand. Don rolled the window down just in time to hear him yell, "Who are you? And what are you doing on the road this time of night?"

With no response, another guard beamed his flashlight on us, and when he saw Don, he said, "Are you people crazy? I don't believe you are trying to go through here with an American at this time of night. Aren't you afraid?"

"I'm sorry," I said, "We had a flat tire, and we had to stop and change it."

"What are they saying?" Don asked.

I didn't want Don to worry and replied, "They're just concerned about our safety on the road this time of night."

"Please let us pass," I begged. By then, a dozen guards surrounded the car. "Our car had a flat tire," I explained, "and it would be too dangerous for us to turn back, because we are almost halfway home. I will pay all of you for your inconvenience, if you will remove the barbed wire and let us through."

Someone in the group said, "It's not just barbed wire. The bridge was mined and is dangerous."

His words scared me, but I already knew that. The soldiers moved away from the car to discuss the situation. In the end, they accepted my offer and agreed to let us through. A guard said, "Tell the American to back up his car. We have to clear the road, and we don't want to accidentally set off an explosion that might kill all of you."

I translated to Don, and he backed up the car. The soldiers started to work, and in the distance, I could hear them cursing. It took at least thirty minutes to clear a portion of the road large enough for our car to pass through, and when it was safe, a guard waved his flashlight to signal us to start moving.

"Slow down," I told Don, as we passed the guards. I handed out a handful of money to one of them and thanked them for all the trouble we caused them. Not one of them said a word, but just waved us on, signaling us to hurry up. As we passed, I looked back and saw them under their flashlights, dividing the money I had given them.

As we went through the village, we had to stop often, because many people were sleeping on the road. I told Don, "Perhaps the road was cooler than their homes and that's why they are out here. They don't expect traffic at this hour. Keep your head down. I don't want them to know you are in the car, just in case some of them are Viet Cong."

I knew this town's reputation and knew that many of them were Viet Cong or their sympathizers, but I didn't want Don to know this.

Don continued to blow the horn to get people to move out of the way. They stood up as we approached and moved their grass mats and pillows so we could drive through. I stuck my head out and apologized for disturbing them. They didn't like getting up, and curses echoed through the air. I told Don, "Be quiet, don't say a word, and keep your head in the car." After we drove through, they returned to the road and spread out their grass mats and pillows. Lucky for us, they didn't see Don in the car.

We experienced the same welcome as we passed through another village. I could tell Von was also nervous, but neither of us said anything. Meanwhile, Mother and the maid started expressing their fears. "I told you not to go home tonight," Mother said to me, but I didn't respond. "If I had known this was going to happen," the maid said, "I would never have come along." I just looked at Von, who was sharing the seat beside me, and we both smiled. Deep inside, we were both very worried.

We just passed through the larger town of Long Thanh, when we heard gunshots and saw bullet tracers coming straight at us from the bushes. We were scared earlier, but now we were terrified. Don ducked his head and sped up. "Those are AK-47s, and we're being shot at! We're all going to die!" he yelled.

Those words from Don frightened me, and I thought, "This is it; we're going to die."

Our maid was scared and started crying. My mother kept calling for "Jesus, Maria, and Joseph" as the bullets whizzed by. Eddie was asleep until all the noise woke him, and he started crying.

"Shut up!" I shouted. "We're all going to die, so just shut up!"

They quieted down, but the maid began chanting a Buddhist prayer, "Mo Phat, Mo Phat, Mo Phat."

Being a devout Catholic, Mother didn't want to hear Buddhist prayers and told the maid to quit praying out loud, but the maid ignored her and continued her chanting. Mother wasn't about to give up that easily, so she started reciting Catholic prayers even louder. Von and I were sitting in the front with Don, and even though we were scared to death, we had to giggle at Mother and the maid. Don asked me, "What are you guys laughing at?"

I told him, "My mother is praying to Jesus, the maid is praying to Buddha, and they are trying to out-pray each other."

Don just shook his head, trying to concentrate on keeping the car on the road, and moving as fast as the car could go.

I was scared for Don, because most of the gunfire seemed to be coming from his side of the road. I tried to protect him by covering his side window with a pillow. He was okay with it for a few minutes, but the pillow kept falling down, and I kept pushing Don's head to the side, so I could fit the pillow between his head and the window. He couldn't take it any longer and yelled, "Take the pillow down, so I can see the road. That pillow is not going to stop AK-47 bullets, anyhow!" I took back the pillow and sat back in my seat.

Suddenly, a headlight went out, or was shot out, and the spare tire we changed earlier began losing air. This time we had to keep going—we had already used the spare. The broken headlight and flat tire slowed us down to about ten miles an hour, at best. Even if we had a spare, we couldn't stop, with bullets flying in our direction. The rubber on the flat tire began disintegrating and started banging on the bottom of the car. It sounded like we were returning the fire.

I started thinking about my life. "I'm going to die!" I thought and began reciting some Catholic prayers myself. My friend Von was a Buddhist, and she began chanting some Buddhist prayers aloud. The din inside the crowded car was almost as bad as the bullets and the shredded tire banging beneath it.

Don couldn't take it anymore and yelled, "Please shut up! All of you! Why are you trying to out-pray each other? If there are two Gods, neither one can hear you!"

After Don's outburst, everyone calmed down, and Don went back to his driving, but the faster he went, the louder the tire beat on the bottom of the car. Mother, who had been quiet for some time, said, "I bet we can walk faster than the car can drive." No one replied, but I think we all agreed with her. The car, by then, had only three tires and one dim headlight. It slowed to a crawl as Don maneuvered through the ruts in the road, left there by Viet Cong explosives.

"Sitting on the back of a charging water buffalo would be smoother than sitting in this car," I thought.

As the gunfire faded into the background, Don was able to slow down a bit, and the banging from the torn tire calmed down somewhat. The lights from Long Binh Army Base came into view, and we all breathed a sigh of relief. We hoped and prayed the noise from our tire wouldn't cause the American soldiers there to react and start shooting at us.

We finally reached the Bien Hoa highway at about midnight. In daylight, the trip from Vung Tau to Bien Hoa takes about two hours depending on traffic, but that harrowing night's trip took us more than five hours. Bien Hoa highway was well lit, and we saw the first vehicles on the road since the first flat tire.

"We are safe!" I exclaimed. Mother broke into uncontrollable laughter and could hardly talk. What she was trying to say was that the torn tire, hitting the bottom of the road sounded like someone was cursing in four letter words, and that seemed funny to her. Her laughter was contagious, and we all started sharing what each of us thought was funny. Soon, we were all laughing, except Don, who didn't understand what we were saying, so he just smiled. Really, there was nothing funny about our situation—our laughter was just an expression of relief.

Once we were safe, Don pulled the car off the road, and we got out to stretch our weary legs, but Mother was still laughing so hard she couldn't get out of the car. Don smiled and helped her out. Poor Eddie didn't know what was going on and was so tired he was half laughing, half crying.

Mother stopped laughing long enough to explain her uncontrollable laughter. "Even though it was scary back there," she said, "looking back at our turmoil, it just seems so hilarious now."

Seeing our car was in trouble, a Vietnamese soldier in a jeep stopped in front of us. He walked back to our car, shook Don's hand, bowed to Mother, smiled, and nodded to the rest of us. He introduced himself as Thung. Because he spoke no English, he asked me if he could help us, and I translated our conversation for Don. I told Thung about our plight, and he offered to take Von and me to a nearby mechanic to get the tires fixed.

I was reluctant at first and whispered to Von, "What if he tries to rape or kill us? How do we know if we should trust him?" Von shrugged her shoulders, without answering. I didn't want to lose the chance to get help, so we accepted his offer. I told Don I was going with the man to get the tires fixed, and Don had no choice but to let me go. He helped Don load the tires into his jeep, then Von and I went with him.

He left the highway and drove onto a dirt road to a shack in the middle of nowhere, with no lights or a garage in sight. I whispered to Von again, "This is scary, we shouldn't have come." But it was too late to change our minds.

When the jeep stopped, Von and I remained frozen to our seats, holding hands. Thung walked to the shack's door and knocked. A young boy, holding a flashlight, half-asleep, asked what he wanted. Thung explained the situation and told him he would pay him triple if he would help. Thank God, the shack was a local tire repair shop. The boy frowned, but accepted his offer and repaired the tires. I paid the boy and we went back to our car.

Thung helped Don change the tires and said, "The shredded tires looked like something one would see hanging as 'abstract art' in a museum." We all agreed and laughed at his comments. Thung escorted us back to Saigon to make sure we got home safe. His "military" escort was more than welcome because of the strict curfew in Saigon. The police would have stopped us, or done worse, had he not been with us. He became our friend and visited us often, until he, too, was killed in that senseless war.

During the following months, I learned more about Don and about his work at Ton San Nhut Air Base. He was the Casualty Officer, and although he didn't like to discuss it, I discovered his work dealt with servicemen who were killed in Vietnam.

He was a very sensitive person, and I knew his work bothered him. That presented one of the few dark clouds on our horizon. On occasions, he drank too much and sometimes used drugs, in an attempt to forget his grim work.

In mid-December, he came home one evening and sat on the bed without saying a word. From the expression on his face, I knew something was wrong.

"What's the matter?" I asked.

He started sobbing and said, "A close friend of mine was killed yesterday. He had one week left, just one week." He paused for a moment, and I could see anger mixed with his sadness on his face. "He was going back to Indiana to get married," he continued. "He was on his last skirmish and was shot in the head."

He looked at me with despair in his eyes and asked, "How can I write a letter to his family, telling them about the noble sacrifice he made for his country? The kid wasn't even twenty years old, and he's dead because some fools decided we should be over here killing each other. It just doesn't make any sense."

I put my arms around him, cradling his head on my chest. I felt his body shake as he sobbed, and I tried to comfort him until he calmed down.

I knew Don had changed since we first met. He was not the same carefree type of guy anymore. He seemed to turn inward and was often hard to reach. Sometimes, he just wanted to be alone with a bottle of whiskey. He always apologized for drinking too much, but he couldn't help it—his job was killing him inside. The mental pictures of dead soldiers never seemed to leave him, and he began having nightmares every night, crying and screaming at some invisible threat. His dream woke me one night. He shook like a leaf and yelled, "They are after me! They are awful!"

"Who is after you?" I asked.

"Those dead soldiers!" he cried, "They are all after me, chasing me every night, from the time I close my eyes to the time I open them. I don't know how long I can take it!"

I didn't know what to say to him, so I held and comforted him. I couldn't begin to imagine what he was going through.

A week later, Don came home and was upset again. When he walked in the door, I could see he had been, and was still, crying. I went to him and asked, "What's wrong, Honey?"

He sobbed, "Three young airmen who worked for me on the casualty team were killed today," he said through his tears. "The plane they were in was shot down right after it took off. They were on their way to Thailand for rest and recuperation." Don paused, trying to regain some composure, but he couldn't. "I approved their leave; I told them they could go, and now they are dead. In a way, I killed them!"

I hugged him and tried my best to comfort him, but this time I couldn't reach him. His guilt and his grief were beyond consolation.

After that night, Don became even more depressed, more withdrawn, and his nightmares only worsened. He often woke me up by jumping out of bed and yelling, "No, no, stop, stop!" or "Take cover, incoming!" Then he'd crawl around, mumbling to himself in a language I did not understand. I kept trying to reassure him by talking to him until he calmed down.

While he was still on the floor, he said, "Do you remember me telling you about the three airmen who worked for me and were killed? They were here! They were chasing me, and I'm afraid they blame me for killing them!" he cried. "They were partly burned and covered with blood. One had no legs, one had no arms, and the other was headless. It seemed as though just parts of their bodies were after me."

I believed his nightmares resulted from what he saw at his work. But to listen to his story gave me cold chills, and it made me realize how deeply his work and these experiences were affecting him. His erratic behavior carried over into his job, and in early January 1969, he was sent to Cam Ranh Bay military hospital for two weeks of psychiatric observation.

When he returned from Cam Ranh Bay, our relationship deepened, in spite of, and perhaps because of, the immense pressure of Don's work. Still, our future was uncertain. Don came home one afternoon, with sadness covering his face. He looked at me with a combination of love and sorrow in his eyes.

"Oh, no," I thought, "Not another friend killed. Poor guy."

"Minh Oi, I have some bad news," he said. "I have to go back to Cam Ranh Bay in three days and will be evacuated to America within the week." Our fears were finally realized, as we both knew they would be. I was shocked into silence as he continued. "The doctors at Cam Ranh Bay reviewed my case and told my commander I couldn't stay in Vietnam any longer. They're afraid I'm having some kind of breakdown."

He held me tight, and we both cried. "I'm afraid it's over," I sobbed, "because once you're gone, I know I'll never see you again. Many soldiers came to Vietnam to fight, to work, and to love, but most of them spend one year, and then they leave. Most of them never come back."

He looked me straight in the eye with his wet, red eyes and said, "Minh Oi, I have to go, but believe me, I will be back, one way or another. I don't know how or when, but I will come back for you." I wanted to believe him, but I had been through this before. I felt like my life was over, and I wished it had ended while we were in the car coming back from Vung Tau. At least, we would have died together.

During the three days before Don had to leave, we seldom ate and often cried. All it took was one look from each other to know what was going on in our hearts. We couldn't stop the tears. We spent most of our days listening to soft music, our love songs—the songs we loved and that haunted us when we were not together. Some of our favorite songs were classics. Our love songs and singers included "Unchained Melody," "Five Hundred Miles," "Yellow Bird," "Green Fields," the Everly Brothers, the Bee Gees, the Ventures, the Beatles, the Brothers Four, Paul Anka, Elvis Presley, Cliff Richard, and many more.

On the evening before he left, I helped him pack his clothes. We tried to avoid looking at each other because when our eyes met, we broke down. "This is it," I thought. "He's going, and he might as well be dead." I was afraid he'd never come back. It seemed everyone I had ever loved or felt close to always left me, and he was no different. We finished packing and sat down on the couch, where we held each other, listened to the music, and cried all night.

The sun rose as Don prepared to leave. He carried his duffel bag to the door and set it down. He said goodbye to Eddie, our friends, and the maid. Then he turned to me. He gave me one last kiss and said, "I love you, and I always will, no matter what happens."

"I love you, too," I said through my tears. He picked up the bag and walked out of the house. I followed him for a few steps, then watched him walk down the narrow alley. As his shadow disappeared behind the barbed wire gate, I thought, "This is it," and I ran back inside, threw myself on the bed, and cried into my pillow.

For the next few days, I did nothing but listen to music and cry. I found many love notes Don wrote before he left and hid around the house. They were so sweet and loving. I found the first one on the stereo. He knew I would go there first.

It read, "I love you, Minh Oi. Please wait for me because I'll be back. Try not to be too sad. Think of our good times together. Think of our happiness when I return." My tears streamed as I read his tender words. They were so comforting but also made me miss him that much more.

Two weeks passed, and I thought about going back to the club to work. I hoped that going back to work would make me feel better sooner, and I had to make money to support my son and myself. But each time I dressed up to go to work, I heard Don's voice saying, "I don't want you to go to work at the club anymore." So I changed my clothes, stayed home, or went to deal with one of my black-market friends.

Three weeks dragged by, and there was still no word from Don. I wondered, "Where is he and what is he doing." It was Saturday, and

I was getting ready for work, because I couldn't stay home any longer. Someone knocked on the door, and I was surprised to see Jim, one of Don's friends I had met before. I invited him in, and he handed me a large envelope as he said, "Don asked me over the phone to bring these to you in person. He sent them to me through APO mail because he was afraid they might get intercepted through regular mail service." I thanked him and offered him a cup of tea. When Jim finished his tea, he went back to the base.

As soon as Jim left, I tore into the large envelope and pulled out a stack of letters from Don. I was tense and nervous as I looked them over. I discovered Don was in a military hospital in Texas and had written a letter every day since he'd been gone. I put them in order by date and began reading them. Each had a tidbit of news about the day's happenings, and each was a tender outpouring of his love.

In one letter he wrote, "I loved you from the moment I saw you through the club window, when I passed by the first time. That's why I came back to talk to you." He had never told me that before, and I smiled at his sweet confession.

His letter continued, "My life was empty until you came to me. You brought me more joy than I have ever experienced. You have given me hope and life itself. I hadn't lived until I met you." Tears streamed down my face as I read on, "I miss you more than you can know, and I can't wait to hold you in my arms again."

I read each of his letters with care, so as not to miss a single word. His sensitive poetry and loving words made me cry, and his jokes made me laugh. It took me almost all day to read them.

He sent money with the letters and asked me not to return to work. I didn't go back to work but went to school instead. I took classes in English and typing, and bought a used typewriter to practice.

I went back to church, for the first time in years, and prayed for Don's health and safety. I also thanked God for sending Don to me. Though Don wasn't with me in person, I felt he was very much with me in my heart and in spirit.

Eddie was almost four now and still attended preschool every day. He often asked for his "Ba Don." He wanted to know where his daddy was and why he wasn't here with us. I told him his dad was taking a long vacation, and he would be back soon.

I visited my parents more often after Don left. My stepfather was friendlier with me. Hen and Den were both still in the military. Hen was a supply sergeant, and Den had been promoted to captain in the Rangers.

After some time my stepfather mellowed, and after twelve years, he finally accepted Hen's wife, and she visited often. My stepfather was getting older, had second thoughts about his values, and changed his attitude. My entire family was getting along much better than ever before. It took some time, but Den and I overcame our rivalry and were as close as any real brother and sister could be. My step-grandmother even told me I had turned out to be her favorite grandchild. We were happy, and I loved them all.

The weeks and months passed, and I continued to get letters and small amounts of money from Don. I wrote to him every day as well. I couldn't send all of my letters but did manage to get a few mailed through Don's friend Jim. The rest I stacked up, praying Don would come back one day and read them in person.

Though surrounded by people, I still felt alone without Don. I missed him most when night fell and remembered when we were happy and spent time with each other in the kitchen, cooking, eating, and sharing our stories, or when I played one of our favorite songs on the stereo.

Meanwhile, the war raged on. Bombs and rockets continued tearing my country apart, and people continued to die. There were times when bullets pierced my roof. Once, one of the bullets hit Eddie's bed, reminding me of how fragile life was.

One afternoon, while Eddie was still in school, I came home from typing class and went straight to the typewriter to practice, as had become my routine. I sat there poking away, writing a letter to Don. "It's been three months, ten days, and seven hours since you left me. Where are you? What are you doing right now? Do you miss me as much as I miss you? I wish you were here, so I could hold you in my arms. I promise I will love you until I die, and if possible, for all eternity."

In the middle of the word "eternity," someone knocked on the door and caused me to hit the wrong key. I was irritated because of the mistake and because the urgent knocking had disturbed my concentration.

"Tu Oi," I yelled at the maid, "See who's at the door, and whoever it is, tell them to go away. I'm busy!" Then I set about correcting the typing mistake I had just made. The maid opened the door and screamed excitedly. I couldn't tell what she was saying. "Now what?" I thought. I stuck my head around the corner to see what was going on. What I saw shocked me so much that for a moment I could neither speak nor move.

Don was standing at the door with the biggest, happiest smile on his face I had ever seen. We ran like lightning into each other's arms. Don picked me up off my feet and twirled me around the living room. We were both yelling and laughing from the excitement. When he finally put me down, I told him, "I am so happy you are home at last."

"I am, too," he said. We looked into each other's eyes and let the tears of happiness flow. We bent our heads toward each other, embraced, and let our bodies tremble with love. Don whispered in my ear, "From now on, my Minh Oi, we will never have to be apart again." Together, we listened to our hearts beat in exactly the same rhythm.

Don and I together at last, May 1969.

THE END (OF THE BEGINNING)

DON RETURNED TO Vietnam in 1969, we married, and he adopted Eddie. In 1971, we moved to the United States. Teresa was born in 1972, in Tennessee, and Nicky was born in 1973, in Oklahoma. Five weeks later, we returned to Vietnam, and stayed there until the American embassy ordered us to evacuate on the morning of April 4, 1975. We missed the plane because of traffic, thank God. The plane we were scheduled to be on was the ill-fated C-5 that crashed and killed 155 people. The majority of the casualties were Vietnamese orphans.

Don and I at our wedding party, 1969.

Since then, we have traveled from place to place and country to country, including Iran. Even with all the moving, I was able to earn my high school GED in California. I attended college and took many courses, including interior design, nutrition, family counseling, and creative writing. In 1980, we moved to Charleston, South Carolina, where I attended school and earned my degree in Cosmetology. I now own and operate a successful beauty salon, called Elegance by Linda B., and have many sophisticated and loyal clients, whom I call friends.

All of my brothers and my sister are now living in America, with their grown children and grandchildren. My children are also grown and now have their own children and careers.

Eddie, me, Nicky, and Teresa—passport photo, 1974.

Me, Kinh, Nho, Bay, and Khai in Charleston, South Carolina, 1999.

Today, I spend most of my time with Don, our children, our grand-children, and friends. I enjoy writing, fishing, gardening with my own compost, and caring for my many varied pets, such as birds, dogs, cats, koi, and sometimes even insects (some things never change). I believe clean living will bring a satisfying journey and I will do my best to leave a good footprint.

Don and I just celebrated our 46th wedding anniversary. Our journey has not always been easy, but our love never faltered. If anything, it has grown more solid. We remain each other's most ardent mentors and best friends. I am now working on another book, titled *Journey on Edge*.

ABOUT THE AUTHOR

LINDA LOAN THI BAER was born Nguyen Thi Loan in 1947, in the small village where she was raised, Tao Xa, Thai Binh Province, North Vietnam. Her father was killed during a Viet Minh attack on her village in 1951. Her mother married again, to a wealthy practitioner of Chinese medicine, and a war widower himself. Their family relocated to South Vietnam during the mass exodus of 1954, where they were forced to move constantly due to economic, political, and military conditions. They eventually settled near Vung Tau, south of Saigon.

Loan left home at an early age, to seek work at various menial jobs in Saigon to help her family, and to escape the physical abuse of her stepfather. She met and married an American Air Force officer in 1968, and accompanied him to the United States in 1971.

She became a naturalized American citizen in 1973, and while becoming a mother and raising two sons and a daughter, obtained her high school GED and attended many college courses.

Linda graduated first in her class from her school of cosmetology and received her certification from the state of South Carolina. She is the owner/operator of the successful "Elegance by Linda B." Beauty Salon in Charleston, South Carolina.

She is the author of *Red Blood Yellow Skin* and its sequel, *Journey on Edge*, to be released soon.

Made in the USA
San Bernardino, CA
11 June 2019